I0008314

MACHINE LEARNING
A Comprehensive Guide for Beginners

AUTHORS

Dr. G. Deepika, M.Tech,Ph.D
Assistant Professor, Dept. Of ECE
Malla Reddy Engineering College for Women, Hyderabad

Mr. Chinni Krishnaiah G, M.Tech
Assistant Professor, Dept. Of AIML
Malla Reddy University, Hyderabad

ISBN:979-83-1008-899-3

FIRST EDITION
2025

Copyright © **G. Deepika, Chinni Krishnaiah.G 2025**
All rights reserved. No portion of this book may be copied, shared, or distributed in any format—whether by photocopying, recording, or any electronic or mechanical means—without prior written consent from the publisher, except for brief excerpts used in reviews or articles.
Any mention of historical events, real individuals, or locations is purely fictional. The names, characters, and places depicted are creations of the author's imagination.

ISBN:979-83-1008-899-3

PREFACE

Machine Learning: A Comprehensive Guide for Beginners

Introduction

In an era driven by data and technological advancements, machine learning has become a fundamental force reshaping industries and revolutionizing the way we interact with information. This book, *Machine Learning: A Comprehensive Guide for Beginners*, is designed to provide a thorough introduction to the essential concepts, techniques, and applications of this rapidly evolving field. Whether you are a student, a professional looking to upskill, or an enthusiast eager to explore machine learning, this book serves as a structured and accessible resource.

Purpose of the Book

The goal of this book is to simplify machine learning principles and make them understandable for a broad audience. Machine learning often appears complex due to its mathematical and technical nature, but our objective is to present the material in a clear and engaging manner. By combining theoretical foundations with hands-on examples, we aim to equip readers with the knowledge and confidence to navigate the world of machine learning effectively.

Structure of the Book

This book is structured to guide readers progressively from fundamental concepts to more advanced topics, ensuring a solid understanding at every step. The key sections include:

1. Introduction to Machine Learning – This section provides an overview of machine learning, its significance in today's world, and different types of learning paradigms such as supervised, unsupervised, and reinforcement learning. Real-world applications are also discussed to highlight its transformative impact.

2. Mathematical Foundations – A strong grasp of mathematical principles is essential for understanding machine learning algorithms. This section covers key concepts in linear algebra, calculus, probability, and statistics to help readers build a strong theoretical foundation.

3. Core Algorithms and Techniques – Here, we explore widely used machine learning algorithms, including decision trees, support vector machines, neural networks, clustering techniques, and more. Each algorithm is explained with its workings, strengths, limitations, and practical use cases.

4. Model Evaluation and Selection – Understanding how to assess and improve machine learning models is crucial. This section covers evaluation metrics such as accuracy, precision, recall, and F1 score, along with techniques like cross-validation and hyperparameter tuning.

5. Practical Applications – This book includes real-world case studies and examples from industries such as healthcare, finance, and marketing. These case studies demonstrate how machine learning can be applied to solve practical problems and enhance decision-making.
6. Future Trends in Machine Learning – As machine learning continues to evolve, we explore emerging trends such as deep learning, natural language processing, and ethical considerations in artificial intelligence. This section discusses the future of machine learning and its potential impact on society.

Target Audience

This book is designed for a diverse audience. Students in computer science, data science, and related fields will find it a valuable resource as they build their knowledge in machine learning. Professionals seeking to enhance their skills or transition into data science will benefit from the clear explanations and practical examples. Additionally, technology enthusiasts with an interest in data-driven insights will find the content engaging and informative.

Acknowledgments

I extend my deepest gratitude to everyone who contributed to the creation of this book. To my mentors, colleagues, and peers—your insights and support have been invaluable throughout this journey. I also acknowledge the pioneering researchers and practitioners in the field of machine learning, whose work continues to inspire and drive innovation.

Conclusion

Machine Learning: A Comprehensive Guide for Beginners is more than just a book; it is a gateway to understanding a field that is shaping the future. As you embark on this learning journey, I encourage you to approach the material with curiosity and an open mind. Machine learning has the potential to revolutionize industries and improve lives, and by mastering its fundamentals, you can be a part of this exciting transformation.

Thank you for choosing this book. I hope you find it both enlightening and enjoyable.

Table of Contents

Chapter 1: Statistics

1.1 Statistics

Statistics is a field of study that involves the collection, analysis, interpretation, presentation, and organization of data. It provides methods and techniques for summarizing and understanding data, making sense of uncertainty, and drawing meaningful conclusions from information. In other words, it is a mathematical discipline to collect and summarize data. Also, we can say that statistics is a branch of applied mathematics. Simply to say statistics is nothing but measuring and analyzing the data. For example, in a class measuring how many boys and how many girls and, in a class, analyzing highest marks, lowest marks, average marks, etc

Statistics is a versatile tool used across many fields to analyze and interpret data such as

1. **Business and Economics**:
   - *Market Research*: Analyzing consumer preferences, market trends, and sales data to make informed business decisions.
   - *Financial Analysis*: Assessing investment risks, predicting stock market trends, and evaluating financial performance.
   - *Operations Management*: Improving processes and efficiency through quality control and process optimization techniques.
2. **Healthcare and Medicine**:
   - *Epidemiology*: Studying the spread of diseases, identifying risk factors, and evaluating public health interventions.
   - *Clinical Trials*: Designing experiments to test the effectiveness of new treatments or drugs and analyzing the results.
   - *Medical Research*: Analyzing patient data to understand disease patterns, treatment outcomes, and healthcare needs.
3. **Social Sciences**:
   - *Sociology and Psychology*: Conducting surveys and experiments to understand human behavior, social interactions, and societal trends.
   - *Education*: Evaluating teaching methods, assessing student performance, and analyzing educational outcomes.
4. **Government and Public Policy**:
   - *Census Data*: Collecting and analyzing demographic information to inform policy decisions and resource allocation.
   - *Economic Planning*: Using statistical models to forecast economic growth, unemployment rates, and inflation.
5. **Environmental Science**:
   - *Climate Studies*: Analyzing weather patterns, climate change data, and environmental impacts to understand and address ecological issues.
   - *Conservation*: Monitoring wildlife populations and assessing the effectiveness of conservation strategies.
6. **Sports**:
   - *Performance Analysis*: Evaluating athletes' performance, strategies, and game statistics to improve outcomes and inform coaching decisions.
   - *Sports Analytics*: Using statistical models to predict game results, player performance, and team strategies.
7. **Engineering and Technology**:

- o **Quality Control**: Applying statistical methods to ensure products meet quality standards and to identify areas for improvement.
- o **Data Science**: Analyzing large datasets to extract meaningful insights, develop algorithms, and drive technological innovations.

8. **Insurance**:
- o **Risk Assessment**: Using statistical models to estimate risks and determine insurance premiums based on historical data and predictive analytics.

Each of these areas relies on statistical methods to make data-driven decisions, understand complex phenomena, and improve outcomes. Statistics provides the tools to summarize data, identify patterns, and make informed predictions, which is crucial across virtually all domains.

1.2 Categories of Data

A data type is a classification that specifies which type of value a variable can hold and what kind of operations can be performed on it. In programming and data analysis, different data types are used to represent different kinds of data. A variable is a characteristic or property that can be measured or observed in a population or sample. Variables are fundamental entities in datasets that are used to describe and quantify different aspects of the data being analyzed.

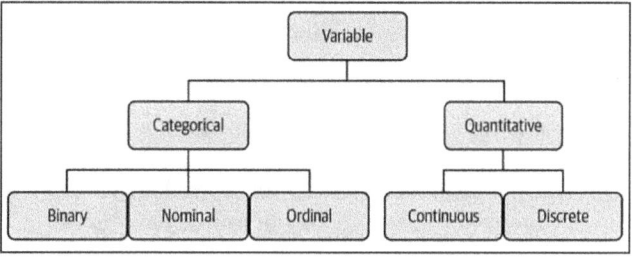

(a) Numerical or Quantitative Data

Continuous data: This type of data represents measurements that can take on any value within a certain range. It is typically represented as real numbers.
Example: Temperature (e.g., 25.5°C), Height (e.g., 176.2 cm), Weight (e.g., 68.9 kg).
Discrete data: The term discrete means distinct or separate. Discrete data is a count that involves integers — only a limited number of values is possible. The discrete data are countable and have finite values. For example: Number of siblings (e.g., 3), Number of pets (e.g., 2), Number of items purchased (e.g., 5).

(b) Categorical or Qualitative Data

Binary data: Binary variables are commonly used when measuring dichotomous outcomes and whether someone is classified as belonging to a particular group or not. Examples could include gender (male/female), current employment status (yes/no), etc.
Normal data: This type of data has categories with no inherent order or ranking. Example: Colors (e.g., Red, Blue, Green), Types of animals (e.g., Dog, Cat, Bird), Countries (e.g., USA, Canada, India).
Ordinal data: This type of data has categories with a meaningful order or ranking.
For example, Education level (e.g., High School, Bachelor's, Master's, Ph.D.) and rating scale (e.g., Low, Medium, High).
The below table represents the different types of data:

Dataset: Laptops Purchase Information

Laptop Name	City of Purchase	Color	No.of Items	Price	Size	Quality	Items Delivered
Dell	Hyderabad	Black	20	45066550.54	M	A	Yes
HP	Delhi	White	12	4685458.65	L	A	No
Dell	Mumbai	Silver	12	27945577.44	LL	B	Yes
Mi	Chennai	Red	15	34435457.534	S	B	No
Toshiba	Hyderabad	Pink	10	435465.4454	X	C	Yes

Nominal Data Discrete Data Continuous Data Ordinal Data Binary Data

1.3 Variables

In statistics, a **variable** is any characteristic, number, or quantity that can be measured or counted. It represents a data point that can change across individuals or over time. Variables are used in data collection and analysis to describe different aspects of a dataset. Machine learning works with two types of variables independent and dependent variables to understand patterns, relationships, and insights from the data they are working with. Independent and dependent variables are key concepts used in statistical modeling and analysis.

a) *Independent variables:* An **independent variable** is a variable that is manipulated or controlled in an experiment or study to observe its effect on a **dependent variable**. It is also called the **predictor variable** or **explanatory variable** because it helps explain changes in the dependent variable

b) *Dependent variable:* A **dependent variable** is the variable in an experiment or study that you **measure or observe** to see how it responds to changes. It's called "dependent" because its value **depends on** the changes made to other variables, typically the **independent variable**.

Let's consider a scenario of money spend for advertisement and sales of products of company, See Table. The relationship between advertisements and sales can be analyzed and modeled to understand how advertisements influence the sales of products. Company might collect data on advertising spend, ad reach, and sales over a period of time. Using this data, they can build a predictive model that takes

Advertisement (Rs) (X)	Sales (Rs) (Y)
10,000	20,000
20,000	40,000
30,000	60,000
40,000	80,000
50,000	1,00,000

advertising-related independent variables as inputs and predicts the sales as the output. By analyzing the model's results, they can identify which advertising strategies are most effective in driving sales and make data-driven decisions to optimize their advertising campaigns.

In the context of advertisement and sales, dependent variable is sales and independent variable is advertisement. The goal of analyzing the relationship between advertisement and sales is to determine how changes in advertising efforts affect sales outcomes. It represents the outcome or result that you are trying to predict or explain based on the independent variable(s) related to advertising. Sales are influenced by advertising campaigns.

1.4 Correlation

- Correlation refers to the statistical relationship or association between two or more variables.
- It measures the degree to which variables are related to each other and the direction and strength of that relationship.
- Correlation analysis is useful for understanding how changes in one variable are associated with changes in another variable

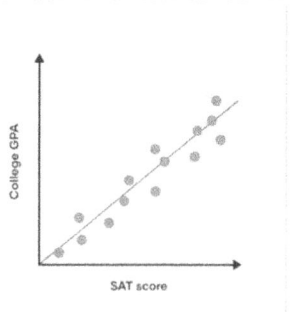

Let x(independent), y(dependent) are two variables, see above Figure. if and only if x increases/decrease then y increases/decreases then x, and y are said to be correlated, when there is no association established between them said to be uncorrelated

For examples

- *Investment-Profit are two variables:* When investment increase then profit also increase
- *Speed and Time are two variables:* When speed increase then time decrease
- *No of Persons and Workload are two variables:* When no of person's increase then workload on each person decrease.
- *No of Persons and work done are two variables:* when no of person's increase then work done by persons also increase.

1.4.1 Correlation Coefficient

The correlation coefficient is a statistical measure that determines how strongly the pair of variables are correlated or connected. It is denoted by "r" and it ranges for "-1" to "+1". See below Figure

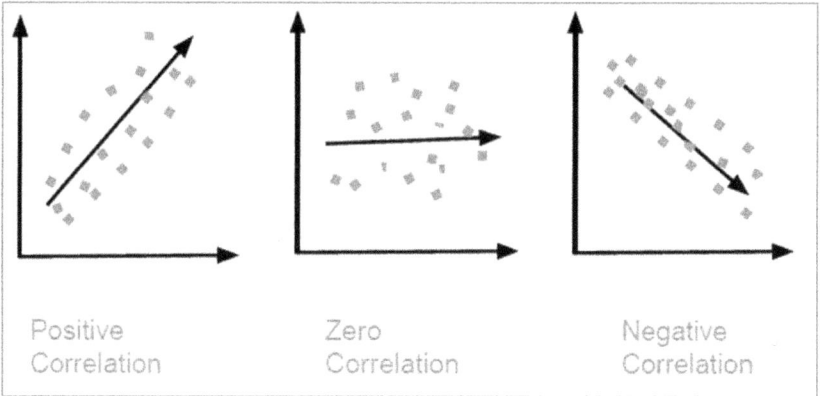

- A correlation coefficient of +1 indicates a perfect positive correlation, meaning that as one variable increase, the other variable also increases proportionally.
- A correlation coefficient of -1 indicates a perfect negative correlation, meaning that as one variable increase, the other variable decrease proportionally.
- A correlation coefficient of 0 indicates no linear relationship between the variables.

Examples of positive, negative, and no correlations

- *Positive correlation:* Height vs Weight, Investment vs Profit, Study time vs Marks obtained, No. of persons vs Work done.

- *Negative correlation:* Price vs Demand, Speed vs Time, No. of persons vs Workload
- *No correlation:* Qualifications vs Height, Investment vs Rank obtained

1.4.2 Correlation relationships

a) Strong Correlation

A strong correlation means that the variables have a strong linear relationship.

Strong Positive Correlation (r close to 1): As one variable increases, the other variable increases near-perfect linearly.

Example: The heights and weights of individuals might have a strong positive correlation. If the correlation coefficient is 0.9, it indicates a strong positive relationship.
  - Heights (cm): [150, 160, 170, 180, 190]
  - Weights (kg): [50, 60, 70, 80, 90]

Strong Negative Correlation (r close to -1): As one variable increases, the other variable decreases near-perfect linearly.

Example: The amount of exercise and body fat percentage might have a strong negative correlation. If the correlation coefficient is -0.8, it indicates a strong negative relationship.
  - Hours of exercise per week: [1, 2, 3, 4, 5]
  - Body fat percentage: [25, 22, 18, 15, 10]

b) Weak Correlation

A weak correlation means that the variables have a weak linear relationship.

- *Weak Positive Correlation* (r close to 0.1 or 0.2): There is a slight tendency for one variable to increase as the other variable increases.
- **Example**: The number of hours studied and exam scores might have a weak positive correlation. If the correlation coefficient is 0.2, it indicates a weak positive relationship.
  - Hours studied: [1, 2, 3, 4, 5]
  - Exam scores: [50, 55, 60, 62, 65]
- *Weak Negative Correlation* (r close to -0.1 or -0.2): There is a slight tendency for one variable to decrease as the other variable increases.
  Example: The number of hours spent on social media and academic performance might have a weak negative correlation. If the correlation coefficient is -0.2, it indicates a weak negative relationship.
  - Hours on social media: [1, 2, 3, 4, 5]
  - Academic performance scores: [90, 85, 80, 78, 75]

c) No Correlation

No correlation means that there is no linear relationship between the variables. The correlation coefficient is around 0.

- **Example**: The number of umbrellas sold and the number of cars produced in a year might have no correlation. If the correlation coefficient is 0, it indicates no relationship.
  - Umbrellas sold: [100, 200, 300, 400, 500]
  - Cars produced: [1500, 1500, 1500, 1500, 1500]

1.5 Population and Sample

Population refers to the entire group of individuals, objects, or events that you're interested in studying. It's the complete set that you want to draw conclusions about. For example, if you're studying the heights of all adult males in a country, then the population would be all adult males in that country.

Sample, on the other hand, is a subset of the population. It's a smaller group selected from the population, usually because it's impractical or impossible to study the entire population. Ideally, a sample should be representative of the population so that any conclusions drawn from the sample can be generalized to the population as a whole. The size of the sample is

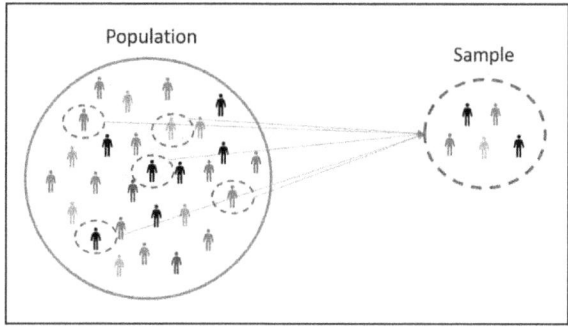

always less than the total size of the population. In research, a population doesn't always refer to people. A subset of a larger population that contains characteristics of that population. A sample is used in statistical testing when the population size is too large for all members or observations to be included in the test. The sample is an unbiased subset of the population that best represents the whole data.

There are different types of populations
- o Finite population
- o Infinite population
- o Existent population
- o Hypothetical population

Finite Population: The finite population is also known as a countable population in which the population can be counted and limited. In other words, it is defined as the population of all the individuals or objects that are finite. For statistical analysis, the finite population is more advantageous than the infinite population.

For Example, The students in a particular school, The cars produced by a specific manufacturer in a given year, and The employees working in a company.

Infinite population: The infinite population is also known as an uncountable population in which the counting of units in the population is not possible. For Examples The heights of all adult humans in the world and The daily temperatures recorded at a specific location over an extended period.

Existent population: The existing population is defined as the population of concrete individuals. In other words, the population whose unit is available in solid form is known as the existent population. Examples are books, students etc.

Hypothetical population: The population in which whose unit is not available in solid form is known as the hypothetical population. A population consists of sets of observations, objects, etc that are all something in common. In some situations, the populations are only hypothetical. Examples are the outcome of rolling the dice, the outcome of tossing a coin.

1.5.1 Sampling

The process of collecting data from a small subsection of the population and then using it to generalize over the entire set is called Sampling. The sample is part of the population. The sample includes one or two observations that are extracted from the population. The characteristic that can be measured, of the sample, is called a statistic. The process of selecting samples from the population is known as sampling. For example, some students in the class are the sample of the population. The sampling process is divided into two types they are, Probability sampling, and Nonprobability sampling.

1.5.2 Sampling Techniques

The method of selecting a sample is of fundamental importance and depends upon the nature of data and investigation. The techniques of selecting a sample are classified as

i) Probability Sampling
ii) Non-Probability Sampling

Probability sampling is based on the fact that every member of the population has an equal chance of being selected. In probability sampling, the population unit cannot be selected at the discretion of the researcher. This method is also known as random sampling.

In non-probability sampling, the population units can be selected at the discretion of the researcher. Those samples will use the human judgements for selecting units and has no theoretical basis for estimating the characteristics of the population. Nonprobability sampling involves selecting samples from a population using methods that do not rely on probability theory. In non-probability sampling, the sample is selected based on non-random criteria, and not every member of the population has a chance of being included.

The key difference between probability sampling and nonprobability sampling lies in whether every member of the population has a known chance of being selected (probability sampling) or not (nonprobability sampling).

Probability sampling methods allow for the calculation of sampling error and statistical inference, making them more suitable for generalizing findings to the population.

Nonprobability sampling methods are often quicker, cheaper, and more convenient but may introduce bias and limit the generalizability of findings. They are commonly used in exploratory research or when probability sampling is not feasible. Some of the differences between probability and nonprobability sampling are as shown in below:

Probability sampling	Nonprobability sampling
The sample is selected at random and everyone in the population has an equal chance of being selected	The sample is selected based on the subjective Judgement of the Researcher
The population is selected randomly	The population is selected arbitrarily
Results are unbiased	Results are highly biased
Inferences are statistical	Inferences are analytical
Researchers prefer to use probability sampling in quantitative research	Researchers prefer to use non-probability sampling in quantitative research
Hypothesis is tested	Hypothesis is generated
The method involved is objective	The method involved is subjective

1.5.2.1 Probability Sampling Techniques
(b) Simple random sampling

Simple Random Sampling is a basic sampling technique where **every individual or item** in the population has an **equal chance** of being selected. It's like drawing names from a hat—**completely random** with no bias.

Key Features:

1. **Equal Chance:** Everyone has the same probability of being chosen.
2. **Unbiased:** Since selection is random, it reduces selection bias.

3. **Independence:** The selection of one individual doesn't affect the selection of another.

Example:

Imagine a school with **100 students**, and you want to select **5 students** for a survey.

- **Method 1 (Lottery Style):** Write each student's name on a slip of paper, put them in a box, and randomly pick 5 slips.
- **Method 2 (Random Number Generator):** Assign numbers 1–100 to each student and use a random number generator to pick 5 numbers.

In both cases, **every student has an equal chance** of being selected.

Advantages:

- Simple to understand and use.
- Minimizes selection bias.
- Results are statistically reliable if the sample is large enough.

Disadvantages:

- Not practical for large, spread-out populations.
- Requires a **complete list** of the population.
- Random selection doesn't guarantee diversity in the sample.

(c) Systematic sampling

Systematic Sampling is a type of probability sampling where you select items from a population at **regular intervals**. Instead of choosing individuals completely at random, you start from a **random point** and then select every **k-th item** in the population list.

Advantages of Systematic Sampling:

- **Easy to Implement:** Simple process compared to random sampling.
- **Even Coverage:** Ensures the sample is spread out across the population.
- **Time-Saving: Faster than selecting each sample randomly.**

Disadvantages of Systematic Sampling:

- **Risk of Bias:** If the population has a hidden pattern that matches the sampling interval, it can distort the results.
- **Less Random:** Only the first selection is random; the rest follow a fixed pattern.

For example, All employees of the company are listed in alphabetical order. From the first 10 numbers, you randomly select a starting point: number 6. From number 6 onwards, every 10th person on the list is selected (6, 16, 26, 36, and so on), and you end up with a sample of 100 people.

(c) Stratified Sampling

Stratified Sampling is a probability sampling technique where the population is **divided into distinct subgroups** or **"strata"** based on specific characteristics (like age, gender, income level, etc.). Then, a **random sample** is taken from each stratum. This ensures that **all key groups** in the population are represented in the sample. To use this sampling method, you divide the population into subgroups (called strata) based on the relevant characteristics (e.g., gender identity, age range, income bracket, job role). Based on the overall proportions of the population, you calculate how many people should be sampled from each subgroup. Then you use random or systematic sampling to select a sample from each subgroup.

For example, The company has 800 female employees and 200 male employees. You want to ensure that the sample reflects the gender balance of the company, so you sort the population into two strata based on gender. Then you use random sampling on each group, selecting 80 women and 20 men, which gives you a representative sample of 100 people.

Advantages of Stratified Sampling:
- **Better Representation:** Ensures all important subgroups are included.
- **Increased Accuracy:** Reduces sampling bias and improves the precision of results.
- **Useful for Comparisons:** Makes it easier to compare specific groups.

Disadvantages of Stratified Sampling:
- **Complex Process:** Requires detailed population information to create strata.
- **Time-Consuming:** More effort is needed to divide the population and sample each group separately.
- **Risk of Misclassification:** If strata are not defined correctly, the results may be inaccurate.

(d) Cluster Sampling

Cluster sampling also involves dividing the population into subgroups, but each subgroup should have similar characteristics to the whole sample. Instead of sampling individuals from each subgroup, you randomly select entire subgroups.

This method involves dividing the population into groups or clusters and then randomly selecting some of those clusters. This technique is useful when the population is spread out over a large geographical area. But It is not possible or practical to survey everyone.

For example, The company has offices in 10 cities across the country (all with roughly the same number of employees in similar roles). You don't have the capacity to travel to every office to collect your data, so you use random sampling to select 3 offices – these are your clusters.

(e) Area Sampling

Area sampling is a method used in statistical analysis to collect data from a specific geographical area or region. It involves dividing the area of interest into smaller, manageable units called sampling units and then selecting a subset of these units for data collection. This method is particularly useful when the area of interest is large and it is not feasible to collect data from every part of it.

For example, Imagine you are conducting a study to determine the average household income in a city with several neighborhoods. Instead of trying to survey every household in the entire city, which could be impractical and time-consuming, you decide to use area sampling.

(f) Multistage Sampling

In multistage sampling, or multistage cluster sampling, you draw a sample from a population using smaller and smaller groups at each stage.

This method is often used to collect data from a large, geographically spread group of people in national surveys, for example. You take advantage of hierarchical groupings (e.g., from state to city to neighborhood) to create a sample that's less expensive and time-consuming to collect data from.

1.5.2.2 Non-probability Sampling Techniques
(a) Quota sampling

Quota sampling is a type of non-probability sampling method used in research where the researcher ensures that specific sub-groups within a population are represented in the sample. This method involves selecting participants based on predetermined quotas that reflect the proportions of these sub-groups in the broader population.

How Quota Sampling works
1. **Define Sub-Groups:** Identify key characteristics or demographic factors (such as age, gender, income level) that are important for the research.
2. **Determine Quotas:** Establish how many individuals from each sub-group (or quota) are needed to represent these characteristics accurately.
3. **Recruit Participants:** Select participants in a way that fills these quotas, often using convenience sampling or judgmental methods.
4. **Achieve Representation:** Continue recruiting until the specified number of participants for each sub-group is reached.

Example of Quota Sampling:
Suppose a researcher wants to study consumer preferences for a new product and needs a sample that reflects the age distribution of a city's population.
1. **Identify Key Characteristics:** The researcher decides that age groups are the key characteristics and wants to match the city's age distribution.
2. **Set Quotas:** The researcher determines the following quotas based on city demographics:
   o 20% aged 18-24
   o 30% aged 25-34
   o 25% aged 35-44
   o 15% aged 45-54
   o 10% aged 55+
3. **Select Participants:** The researcher then recruits people from various locations and sources (like malls, social media, etc.) to meet these quotas. For example, they might interview 20 people aged 18-24, 30 people aged 25-34, and so on, until each age group quota is filled.
4. **Ensure Representation:** By meeting the quotas, the researcher ensures that the sample reflects the age distribution of the city.

Advantages:
- **Representativeness:** Ensures that specific characteristics are represented in the sample.
- **Efficiency:** Can be quicker and less expensive than probability sampling methods.

Disadvantages:

- **Bias:** Because the selection of participants is not random, the sample may not fully represent the population, leading to potential biases.
- **Non-Random Selection:** Since participants are not chosen randomly, the results may not be generalizable.

(b) Convenience sampling

Convenience sampling is a non-probability sampling technique where researchers select participants based on their ease of access and availability. This method is often used when researchers need to gather data quickly and with minimal cost, but it does not aim to create a representative sample of the entire population.

How Convenience Sampling Works

1. Identify a Convenient Source: The researcher chooses a group of participants who are easiest to reach, such as individuals in a specific location, social network, or community.
2. Select Participants: Participants are selected from this group based on their availability and willingness to participate.
3. Collect Data: Data is gathered from these participants, and the results are analyzed.

Example of Convenience Sampling

Imagine a university researcher wants to study the study habits of college students.

1. Identify a Convenient Source: The researcher decides to use students from their own university because they are easily accessible.
2. Select Participants: The researcher posts a survey in the university's online portal and hands out paper surveys in popular campus areas like the library and student center. They ask students who are readily available and willing to participate.
3. Collect Data: The researcher collects responses from the students who respond to the survey, analyzes the data, and draws conclusions based on this sample.

Advantages of Convenience Sampling

- Ease of Use: It's simple to implement and doesn't require complex sampling procedures.
- Cost-Effective: It typically involves fewer resources, as researchers don't need to spend money on random sampling or extensive recruitment processes.
- Time-Saving: Data collection is quicker because participants are readily accessible.

(c) Judgement sampling

Judgment sampling, also known as purposive or selective sampling, is a non-probability sampling technique where the researcher selects participants based on their judgment or expertise. Instead of using random selection, the researcher chooses individuals who they believe are most relevant or knowledgeable about the topic being studied. This approach relies on the researcher's ability to identify and select the most appropriate participants.

How Judgment Sampling Works

1. **Define the Criteria:** The researcher determines specific criteria that participants must meet to be included in the sample. These criteria are often based on the researcher's expertise and the research objectives.
2. **Select Participants:** Using their judgment, the researcher selects participants who fit these criteria. This can involve choosing individuals who have particular experience, knowledge, or characteristics relevant to the study.
3. **Collect Data:** Data is gathered from the selected participants.

Example of Judgment Sampling

Suppose a researcher is studying the impact of advanced technologies on the education system and wants to gather insights from experts in the field.

1. **Define the Criteria:** The researcher decides that the sample should include:
   o Educational technology specialists
   o School administrators who have implemented advanced technologies
   o Teachers who actively use these technologies in their classrooms
2. **Select Participants:** The researcher uses their knowledge of the field to identify and invite specific individuals who meet these criteria. For instance, they might select:
   o Prominent researchers in educational technology
   o Technology coordinators from well-known schools
   o Innovative teachers recognized for their use of educational technology
3. **Collect Data:** The researcher conducts interviews or surveys with these selected experts to gather detailed insights.

Advantages of Judgment Sampling

- **Expert Knowledge:** Ensures that participants have relevant expertise or experience, which can provide valuable and in-depth information.
- **Targeted Insight:** Useful for studies where specific knowledge or opinions are crucial, such as expert panels or case studies.
- **Efficiency:** Can be quicker than other methods when dealing with specialized topics or hard-to-reach populations.

Disadvantages of Judgment Sampling

- **Bias:** The selection process is subjective and depends on the researcher's judgment, which can introduce bias. The sample may not be representative of the broader population.
- **Limited Generalizability:** Findings may not be generalizable to the larger population because the sample is not randomly selected.
- **Dependence on Researcher's Expertise:** The quality of the sample depends on the researcher's ability to identify and select suitable participants.

When to Use Judgment Sampling

Judgment sampling is particularly useful in exploratory research, qualitative studies, or when seeking in-depth insights from specific individuals with expertise. It's ideal when the research requires specialized knowledge that a random sample might not provide. However, researchers should be aware of the limitations and potential biases associated with this method.

(d) Snowball sampling

Snowball sampling is a non-probability sampling technique used primarily for hard-to-reach or hidden populations. It's often used in qualitative research when the researcher has difficulty accessing a study group or when there are no clear lists or records of the population. The technique leverages existing study participants to recruit additional participants, creating a "snowball" effect as the sample grows.

How Snowball Sampling Works

1. **Identify Initial Participants:** The researcher begins with a small group of initial participants who are relevant to the study. These individuals are often chosen based on their connection to the target population.
2. **Ask for Referrals:** The initial participants are asked to refer other individuals who also meet the study criteria. These new participants are then contacted and invited to join the study.
3. **Repeat the Process:** The new participants are similarly asked to refer others, and the process continues, allowing the sample size to grow through referrals.
4. **Collect Data:** Data is gathered from the participants as the sample expands.

Example of Snowball Sampling

Let's say a researcher wants to study the experiences of people who have recently undergone a rare medical treatment, but finding participants is challenging because they are not readily identifiable.

1. **Identify Initial Participants:** The researcher starts by contacting a few patients who have recently undergone the treatment, perhaps through a support group or medical facility.
2. **Ask for Referrals:** Each of these initial participants is asked if they know other individuals who have also undergone the treatment and are willing to participate.
3. **Expand the Sample:** The referrals provide contact details for additional participants, who are then invited to take part in the study. Each of these new participants may provide more referrals, further expanding the sample.
4. **Collect Data:** As the sample grows, the researcher collects data from all the participants who are reached through this referral process.

Advantages of Snowball Sampling

- **Access to Hard-to-Reach Populations:** Particularly useful for studying populations that are difficult to identify or access through traditional methods.
- **Efficiency in Recruitment:** Once initial contacts are established, the recruitment process can be relatively quick and efficient.
- **Network-Based Insights:** Can provide insights into social networks and relationships within the target population.

Disadvantages of Snowball Sampling

- **Bias:** The sample may be biased because participants are selected based on referrals, which can lead to a lack of diversity and overrepresentation of certain sub-groups within the population.
- **Limited Generalizability:** Findings may not be generalizable to the entire population since the sampling is not random.
- **Dependence on Initial Contacts:** The success of the sampling process depends heavily on the researcher's ability to find suitable initial participants and their willingness to refer others.

When to Use Snowball Sampling

Snowball sampling is ideal for research involving niche or hidden populations, such as:

- People with rare medical conditions
- Individuals involved in specific illicit activities
- Members of particular subcultures or social networks

It's particularly useful in exploratory research or when studying populations where traditional sampling methods are impractical. Researchers should carefully consider the potential biases and limitations when using this method and complement it with other techniques if possible.

1.6 Types of Statistics

Statistics is broadly divided into two main branches: **Descriptive Statistics** and **Inferential Statistics**. Each branch serves different purposes and uses different methods for analyzing and interpreting data. Here's a detailed explanation of each branch and its types:

1.6.1 Descriptive Statistics

Descriptive statistics is a branch of statistics that focuses on summarizing and describing the main features of a dataset. Its primary goal is to provide a clear and concise overview of the data, allowing you to understand its central tendencies, variability, and distribution without necessarily making inferences or drawing conclusions about a larger population. Descriptive statistics is a branch of statistics that involves the collection, analysis, interpretation, presentation, and organization of data. The primary goal of descriptive statistics is to summarize and describe the main features of a dataset. It provides a concise and meaningful representation of data, allowing researchers, analysts, and decision-makers to gain insights into the central tendency, variability, and distribution of the data.

1.6.1.1 Measures of Central Tendency

Measures of central tendency are statistical metrics used to describe the center or typical value of a dataset. They summarize a dataset with a single value that represents the "center" of the distribution, providing insight into the general trend of the data. The three most commonly used measures of central tendency are:

Mean: The average of all the data points. It's calculated by summing up all the values and dividing by the total number of values.
Mathematical formula for mean as given below:

$$\text{mean} = \frac{\text{Sum of all data points}}{\text{Total no.of all data points}}$$

$$\text{mean}(\overline{X}) = \frac{\sum Xi}{N}$$

Sum the values: Add up all the scores in the dataset.
Sum = 85 + 70 + 78 + 88 + 95 + 70 + 81 + 90 + 87 + 70 + 84 = 898

Count the values: Determine the total number of scores in the dataset.
Count = 12 (since there are 12 values in the dataset)

Calculate the mean: Divide the sum of the scores by the total number of scores.
Mean = Sum / Count
Mean = 898 / 11 = 81.63 (rounded to two decimal places)

Median: The middle value when the data is arranged in ascending or descending order. If there's an even number of data points, the median is the average of the two middle values.
To find the median, we first need to arrange the dataset in ascending order:
{70, 70, 70, 78, 81, 84, 85, 87, 88, 90, 95}

The median is the middle value in the ordered dataset. If there's an odd number of values, the median is the value at the exact center. If there's an even number of values, the median is the average of the two middle values.
In this case, there are 11 values in the dataset, which is an odd number, so we can directly find the middle value:
The middle value is the 6th value in the ordered dataset: 84.
Therefore, the median of the given dataset is 84
Mode: The value that appears most frequently in the dataset. There can be one mode, more than one mode (multimodal), or no mode at all.
First, let's count the occurrences of each value:
85 appears once
70 appears three times
78 appears once
88 appears once
95 appears once
81 appears once
90 appears once
87 appears once
84 appears once
The value that appears most frequently is 70, which occurs three times. Therefore, the mode of the given dataset is 70.

1.6.1.2 Measures of Spread

Measures of dispersion, also known as measures of variability/ dispersion, describe how spread out or dispersed the values in a dataset are. They provide insight into the variability or diversity of the data, indicating how much individual data points differ from the central value (mean or median). Here are the key measures of dispersion:
Range: The difference between the maximum and minimum values in the dataset.
Range=Maximum Value−Minimum Value
Example: For the dataset [2,4,6,8,10]:
Range=10−2=8
Variance: **ariance** measures how much the values in a dataset **spread out** from the **mean (average)**. It shows the degree of **dispersion** or **variability** in the data.

1. Population Variance (σ^2)

For a **population**, the variance is calculated as:

$$\sigma^2 = \frac{\sum(X_i - \mu)^2}{N}$$

Where:

- σ^2 = Population variance

- X_i = Each individual data point

- μ = Population mean

- N = Total number of data points

2. Sample Variance (s²)

For a **sample**, the variance is estimated using:

$$s^2 = \frac{\sum(X_i - \bar{X})^2}{n - 1}$$

Where:

- s^2 = Sample variance
- X_i = Each sample data point
- $\bar{X}$ = Sample mean
- n = Sample size
- $n - 1$ = **Degrees of freedom** (used to get an unbiased estimate of population variance)

Example: For the dataset $[2, 4, 6, 8, 10]$:

- Mean $(\bar{X})$ = 6
- Variance = $\frac{(2-6)^2+(4-6)^2+(6-6)^2+(8-6)^2+(10-6)^2}{5}$

$$\text{Variance} = \frac{16 + 4 + 0 + 4 + 16}{5} = \frac{40}{5} = 8$$

Standard Deviation: The square root of the variance. It indicates the average amount by which data points deviate from the mean.

1. Population Standard Deviation (σ)

For an entire **population**, the standard deviation is:

$$\sigma = \sqrt{\frac{\sum(X_i - \mu)^2}{N}}$$

Where:

- σ = Population standard deviation
- X_i = Each data point
- μ = Population mean
- N = Total number of data points

2. Sample Standard Deviation (s)

For a **sample**, the standard deviation is:

$$s = \sqrt{\frac{\sum(X_i - \bar{X})^2}{n - 1}}$$

Where:

- s = Sample standard deviation
- X_i = Each sample data point
- $\bar{X}$ = Sample mean
- n = Sample size
- $n - 1$ = **Degrees of freedom** (used for an unbiased estimate)

Example: For the dataset $[2, 4, 6, 8, 10]$:

$$\text{Standard Deviation} = \sqrt{8} \approx 2.83$$

1.6.1.3 Measures of Shape

Measures of shape, also known as measures of distribution shape, describe the characteristics of the distribution of data beyond central tendency and dispersion. They help in understanding the underlying pattern of the data distribution. The primary measures of shape are **skewness** and **kurtosis**.

Skewness: Skewness quantifies the asymmetry of a dataset's distribution around its mean. It indicates whether the data is skewed to the left (negative skew) or to the right (positive skew).It measures the degree of asymmetry of a distribution. Skewness is a statistical measure that quantifies the asymmetry of the probability distribution of a real-valued random variable about its mean

Types of skewness

    (a) Positive Skewness/Skewed Right
    (b) Negative Skewness/Skewed Left
    (c) Symmetric/No Skewed

(a) Positive Skewness
In positive skewness, the extreme data values are larger, which in turn increases the mean value of the data set. In simple terms, a positive skew distribution is the distribution with the tail on the right side.
Mean > Median > Mode

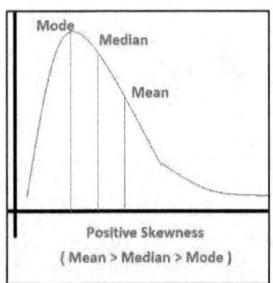

(b) Negative Skewness
In negative skewness, the extreme data values are smaller, which decreases the mean value of the dataset or the negative skew distribution is the distribution having the tail on the left side.
Mean < Median < Mode

(c) Symmetric/not skewed/Zero skewed

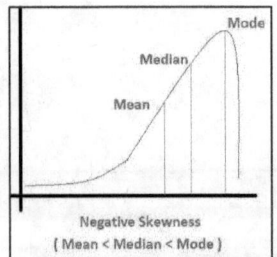

Zero skewness indicates that the data is perfectly symmetrical around the mean.
The mean, median, and mode are all equal in a dataset with zero skewness.
In a histogram, the distribution appears symmetrical, with the peak in the center and the tails extending equally in both directions.
Mean=Median=Mode

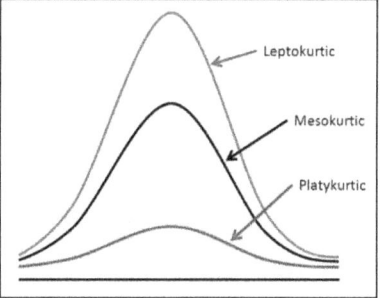

Kurtosis: The term "Kurtosis" comes from the Greek word "Kurtos", which means curved. Measures the "tailedness" of the distribution, indicating whether the data have heavy or light tails compared to a normal distribution.Kurtosis is a statistical measure that describes the degree of peakedness or flatness of a distribution. It measures the shape of the distribution, specifically the height and sharpness of the central peak, relative to that of normal distribution. It is the fourth moment of statistics.

Kurtosis is useful to identify the potential outliers in a dataset, as distributions with high kurtosis have more extreme values than normal distributions. Kurtosis describes the "fatness" of the tails found in probability distributions. Kurtosis is a statistical measure that describes the shape, or peakedness, of a probability distribution. It is used to understand the tails and the overall shape of a distribution compared to the normal distribution.

Types of Kurtosis
There are three kurtosis categories—
        (a) Platykurtic (Smallest/Flattest Peak)
        (b) Mesokurtic (Medium Peak)
        (c) Leptokurtic (Highest Peak)

  (a) *Mesokurtic:* A distribution with kurtosis equal to 3 is called mesokurtic. This means that its shape is similar to that of a normal distribution, with neither excessively heavy nor light tails.

  (b) Leptokurtic: A distribution with kurtosis greater than 3 is called leptokurtic. Leptokurtic distributions have heavier tails and a sharper peak than the normal distribution, indicating that they have more extreme values.

  (c) Platykurtic: A distribution with kurtosis less than 3 is called platykurtic. Platykurtic distributions have lighter tails and a flatter peak than the normal distribution, indicating that they have fewer extreme values.

1.6.1.4 Measures of Position
Measures of position in statistics refer to methods used to describe the relative standing or location of a particular data point within a dataset. These measures help in understanding how a specific value compares to other values in the dataset. The most commonly used measures of position include percentiles, quartiles, deciles, and z-scores.

Percentiles: Percentiles are a way of dividing a dataset into 100 equal parts, with each percentile representing a specific point below which a given percentage of the data falls. They are useful for understanding the distribution and relative standing of values within a dataset. For example, the 25th percentile (also known as the first quartile) is the value below which 25% of the data falls.

For examples,

P_{20}: The 20th percentile represents the value below which 20% of the data falls.

P_{50}: The 50th percentile (median) is the value below which 50% of the data falls.

P_{80}: The 80th percentile is the value below which 80% of the data falls.

Formula to Calculate Percentile Rank:

$$P_k = \frac{k}{100} \times (N + 1)$$

where:

- P_k is the position of the k-th percentile,

- k is the percentile rank (e.g., 25th, 50th, 75th),

- N is the number of observations.

Steps to Calculate Percentiles

1. **Sort the Data**: Arrange the data in ascending order.
2. **Calculate the Position**: Use the percentile formula to find the position in the sorted list.
3. **Interpolate if Necessary**: If the position is not an integer, interpolate between the closest ranks.

- **Example Calculation**

  a dataset has the following values:

  65,72,80,55,68,90,78,88,62,75,85,72,95,60,70,82,78,88,92,68,78,55,85,75,80,72, 68,92,62,70

  Arrange the values in Ascending order are below

  55,55,60,62,62,68,68,68,70,70,72,72,72,75,75,78,78,78,80,80,82,85,85,88,88,90, 92,92,95

    P_{20}: 20th percentile=66

    20th percentile=66 (The 20% mark is between the 6th and 7th values in the sorted dataset, so we interpolate.)

- **Another example**

  A data set has the monthly Income (1000's) of employees as shown below

  10,14,36,25,15,21,29,17

  Arranging in Ascending Order:

10	14	15	17	21	25	29	36
1	2	3	4	5	6	7	8

Where n=8 (no of data items)

Formula: $P_x = x(n+1)/100$ [th] Item

$P_{50} = 50(8+1)/100 = 9/2 = 4.5$[th] Item

= 4th+0.5(5th item-4th item)=17+0.5(21-17)=17+2=21

Quartiles: Quartiles are statistical measures that divide a dataset into four equal parts, with each quartile representing a specific segment of the distribution. They are useful for summarizing data and understanding its spread. The three quartiles are:

Q1: The value below which 25% of the data falls. It is also known as the 25th percentile.

Q2: The second quartile (median) is the value below which 50% of the data falls.

Q3: he value below which 75% of the data falls. It is also known as the 75th percentile.

- For example, data:
  65,80,55,68,90,78,62,75,85,72,95,60,70,82,78,92,68,78,55,85,75,80,68,92,62
  Ascending Order: 55,55,60,68,68,68,70,72,75,75,78,80,80,82,90,92,95

55	55	60	68	68	70	72	75	75	78	80	80	82	85	90	92	95
Q0			Q1					Q2				Q3				Q4

  Q1: First Quartile=68 (25% of the data is below 68)
  Q2: Median=75(50% of the data is below 75)
  Q3: Third Quartile=82 (75% of the data is below 82)

Z-scores: Z-scores (or standard scores) are a way of standardizing data points by converting them into a common scale. This is achieved by measuring how many standard deviations a data point is from the mean of the dataset. Z-scores help in comparing values from different distributions and understanding the relative position of a data point within a dataset.

The Z-score of a data point X is calculated using the formula:

$$Z = \frac{X - \bar{X}}{\sigma}$$

where:

- X is the individual data point.

- $\bar{X}$ is the mean of the dataset.

- σ is the standard deviation of the dataset.

Steps to calculate the Z-score value as follows:

1. Calculate the Mean ($\bar{X}$):

$$\bar{X} = \frac{1}{N}\sum_{i=1}^{N} X_i$$

where N is the number of observations, and X_i represents each data point.

2. Calculate the Standard Deviation (σ):

$$\sigma = \sqrt{\frac{1}{N}\sum_{i=1}^{N}(X_i - \bar{X})^2}$$

3. Compute the Z-Score:

$$Z = \frac{X - \bar{X}}{\sigma}$$

Example to calculate the Z-score for a sample data set as below:

Consider the dataset: $[10, 20, 30, 40, 50]$.

Step 1: Calculate the Mean $(\bar{X})$

$$\bar{X} = \frac{10 + 20 + 30 + 40 + 50}{5} = \frac{150}{5} = 30$$

Step 2: Calculate the Standard Deviation (σ)

1. Calculate the squared differences from the mean:

$$(10 - 30)^2 = 400$$

$$(20 - 30)^2 = 100$$
$$(30 - 30)^2 = 0$$

$$(40 - 30)^2 = 100$$

$$(50 - 30)^2 = 400$$

2. Calculate the variance:

$$\text{Variance} = \frac{400 + 100 + 0 + 100 + 400}{5} = \frac{1000}{5} = 200$$

3. Calculate the standard deviation:

$$\sigma = \sqrt{200} \approx 14.14$$

Step 3: Compute Z-Scores

To find the Z-score for $X = 20$:

$$Z = \frac{20 - 30}{14.14} \approx \frac{-10}{14.14} \approx -0.71$$

To find the Z-score for $X = 40$:

$$Z = \frac{40 - 30}{14.14} \approx \frac{10}{14.14} \approx 0.71$$

Interpreting above Z-score value as below:

- **Z = 0**: The data point is exactly at the mean.

- **Z > 0**: The data point is above the mean.

- **Z < 0**: The data point is below the mean.

- **|Z| > 1**: The data point is more than one standard deviation away from the mean.

Interquartile Range (IQR): Interquartile Range (IQR) is a measure of statistical dispersion that quantifies the range within which the middle 50% of a dataset falls. It is a useful metric for understanding the spread of the central portion of the data and is particularly effective in identifying outliers. IQR is the difference between the third quartile (Q3) and the first quartile (Q1) of a dataset. It provides a range where the central 50% of the data values lie, excluding the lower 25% and upper 25% of the data.

The formula for IQR as:

$$IQR = Q_3 - Q_1$$

where:

- **Q1** is the first quartile (25th percentile).

- **Q3** is the third quartile (75th percentile).

Example calculation of Q_1, Q_2, Q_3 and IQR as below:

Consider the dataset: $[12, 15, 18, 20, 22, 25, 30, 35, 40, 45]$.

1. **Sort the Data**: The data is already sorted: $[12, 15, 18, 20, 22, 25, 30, 35, 40, 45]$.

2. **Calculate Q1 (First Quartile)**:

   - There are 10 data points, so:

$$Q_1 = \frac{1}{4} \times (10 + 1) = \frac{11}{4} = 2.75$$

   - Interpolate between the 2nd and 3rd values:

     - The 2nd value is 15.

     - The 3rd value is 18.

     - Fraction = 0.75:

$$Q_1 = 15 + 0.75 \times (18 - 15) = 15 + 2.25 = 17.25$$

3. Calculate Q3 (Third Quartile):

- For the 10 data points:

$$Q_3 = \frac{3}{4} \times (10+1) = \frac{33}{4} = 8.25$$

- Interpolate between the 8th and 9th values:

  - The 8th value is 35.

  - The 9th value is 40.

  - Fraction = 0.25:

$$Q_3 = 35 + 0.25 \times (40 - 35) = 35 + 1.25 = 36.25$$

4. Compute the IQR:

$$IQR = Q_3 - Q_1 = 36.25 - 17.25 = 19$$

Interpreting the above IQR value

- IQR measures the spread of the central 50% of the data.

- A larger IQR indicates greater dispersion within the central portion of the data.

- A smaller IQR suggests that the central 50% of the data is more concentrated.

Outlier detection using IQR as shown below:

- Lower Bound: $Q_1 - 1.5 \times IQR$

- Upper Bound: $Q_3 + 1.5 \times IQR$

Values falling outside these bounds are considered outliers.

Example with Outlier Detection:

For our example, the bounds are:

- Lower Bound: $17.25 - 1.5 \times 19 = -10.5$

- Upper Bound: $36.25 + 1.5 \times 19 = 87.5$

Since all values in our dataset fall within these bounds, there are no outliers.

1.6.2 Inferential Statistics

Inferential statistics is a branch of statistics that focuses on making generalizations or predictions about a population based on a sample of data taken from that population. Essentially, it involves using data from a sample to make inferences or conclusions about a larger group. The goal of inferential statistics is to draw conclusions about the population based on the data obtained from the sample. This involves estimating population parameters, testing hypotheses, and making predictions.

Why Inferential Statistics

Inferential statistics is crucial because it allows researchers, analysts, and decision-makers to make conclusions about a large population based on a smaller sample. Here are several key reasons why inferential statistics is important:

1. **Practicality and Feasibility**:

- Cost and Time Efficiency: Collecting data from an entire population can be prohibitively expensive and time-consuming. A well-chosen sample can provide insights into the population at a fraction of the cost and time.
- Manageable Data: Working with a sample is often more manageable than dealing with data from an entire population, especially if the population is very large.

2. **Generalization**:
   - Population Inference: Inferential statistics allows us to generalize findings from a sample to the broader population. For example, if a survey of 1,000 people shows a certain trend, inferential statistics help us predict how that trend might apply to all individuals in the population.

3. **Decision-Making**:
   - Informed Choices: By analyzing sample data, organizations can make informed decisions about business strategies, policy changes, and other critical areas without needing complete data from everyone.
   - Risk Management: Inferential statistics helps in assessing risks and making predictions that can guide strategic planning and resource allocation.

4. **Hypothesis Testing**:
   - Scientific Method: It supports the scientific method by allowing researchers to test hypotheses and determine if observed effects or differences are statistically significant and not due to random chance.
   - Evidence-Based Research: Provides a framework for evaluating the validity of hypotheses and theories, thus contributing to scientific knowledge and evidence-based practice.

5. **Prediction and Forecasting**:
   - Modeling Relationships: Techniques such as regression analysis allow for the prediction of future trends and outcomes based on current data. For instance, predicting future sales based on historical data.
   - Scenario Analysis: Helps in forecasting various scenarios and assessing the potential impact of different factors on outcomes.

6. **Understanding Variability**:
   - Estimating Parameters: Inferential statistics helps estimate population parameters (like the mean or proportion) and understand the variability or uncertainty associated with those estimates.
   - Quantifying Uncertainty: Provides tools to quantify and express uncertainty through confidence intervals and p-values, giving a measure of how reliable the estimates are.

7. **Improving Methods**:
   - Sampling Techniques: Helps in designing effective sampling methods that reduce bias and improve the accuracy of conclusions drawn from the sample data.
   - Refining Approaches: Allows for the refinement of research approaches and methodologies based on insights gained from the sample analysis.

Inferential statistics is fundamental because it enables us to make educated guesses about a larger population, make data-driven decisions, and draw meaningful conclusions from sample data. This ability to infer, predict, and test hypotheses underpins much of scientific research, policy development, and business strategy.

Purpose of Inferential Statistics

The purpose of inferential statistics is to make informed conclusions, predictions, and decisions about a population based on data collected from a sample. This branch of statistics allows for generalization and hypothesis testing beyond the immediate data set. Here are the primary purposes of inferential statistics:

1. **Generalization**:
   - **Population Inference**: Inferential statistics enables you to make generalizations about a larger population based on observations from a smaller sample. For example, if you survey a sample of voters, inferential statistics can help you estimate the voting preferences of the entire population.

2. **Hypothesis Testing**:
   - **Evaluate Claims**: It provides methods to test hypotheses and evaluate whether observed effects or differences are statistically significant. This involves setting up null and alternative hypotheses and using sample data to assess the likelihood of the null hypothesis being true.
   - **Scientific Inquiry**: Allows researchers to test theoretical claims and research questions rigorously and determine if the results support or refute these claims.

3. **Estimation**:
   - **Point Estimation**: Offers estimates of population parameters (e.g., mean, proportion) based on sample data.
   - **Confidence Intervals**: Provides a range of values within which the true population parameter is likely to fall, with a specified level of confidence. This helps in understanding the precision and reliability of the estimates.

4. **Prediction**:
   - **Forecasting**: Uses sample data to predict future outcomes or trends. For instance, regression analysis can predict future sales based on past performance.
   - **Scenario Analysis**: Helps assess the impact of different variables on outcomes and predict how changes might affect future results.

5. **Decision-Making**:
   - **Informed Choices**: Facilitates making decisions based on statistical evidence rather than intuition or anecdotal evidence. This is crucial for policy-making, business strategies, and scientific research.
   - **Risk Assessment**: Helps in evaluating risks and making decisions with an understanding of potential uncertainties and their implications.

6. **Understanding Relationships**:
   - **Analyzing Associations**: Allows for the examination of relationships between variables and the determination of how one variable may influence another. For example, understanding how different factors contribute to a health outcome.
   - **Identifying Patterns**: Helps in identifying and quantifying patterns and trends within the data.

7. **Evaluating Variability**:
   - **Quantifying Uncertainty**: Provides tools to measure and express the uncertainty associated with sample estimates, helping to understand how much the sample might differ from the population.
   - **Assessing Variability**: Allows for the assessment of variability within and between samples, which is important for making accurate inferences.

8. **Improving Research Methods**:

- **Sampling Design**: Helps in designing and evaluating sampling methods to ensure they are representative and minimize bias.
- **Refinement of Models**: Assists in refining statistical models and methodologies based on findings from sample analysis.

In essence, inferential statistics is about using sample data to draw conclusions, make predictions, and guide decisions with a quantified level of confidence and understanding of uncertainty.

Where Inferential Statistics uses

Inferential statistics is used in a wide range of fields and applications to draw conclusions about a population based on sample data. Here are some common areas where inferential statistics is applied:

1. **Business and Economics**:
   - **Market Research**: To understand consumer behavior, preferences, and market trends by analyzing survey data and sales data.
   - **Financial Analysis**: For forecasting stock prices, assessing investment risks, and evaluating economic indicators.
   - **Quality Control**: To monitor and improve product quality by analyzing sample data from manufacturing processes.
2. **Healthcare and Medicine**:
   - **Clinical Trials**: To evaluate the effectiveness and safety of new drugs or treatments by analyzing data from clinical trials.
   - **Epidemiology**: For studying the prevalence, incidence, and risk factors of diseases in populations.
   - **Public Health**: To assess the impact of health interventions and policies on population health outcomes.
3. **Social Sciences**:
   - **Psychology**: To understand human behavior and mental processes through experimental and observational studies.
   - **Sociology**: For studying social phenomena, such as family dynamics, social attitudes, and demographic trends.
   - **Education**: To evaluate educational programs, assess student performance, and conduct educational research.
4. **Government and Public Policy**:
   - **Census Data Analysis**: To derive demographic information and inform policy decisions based on sample surveys.
   - **Policy Evaluation**: To assess the effectiveness of public policies and programs through statistical analysis of outcomes.
   - **Crime Statistics**: For understanding crime trends and evaluating the impact of crime prevention strategies.
5. **Environmental Science**:
   - **Climate Studies**: To analyze climate data and make predictions about climate change and its impacts.
   - **Conservation Efforts**: For assessing the effectiveness of conservation programs and understanding biodiversity.
6. **Sports**:
   - **Performance Analysis**: To evaluate athlete performance and develop strategies for improvement.
   - **Game Predictions**: To predict game outcomes and understand factors influencing team success.
7. **Marketing**:

- o **Customer Segmentation**: To identify different customer groups and tailor marketing strategies accordingly.
- o **Campaign Effectiveness**: To measure the impact of marketing campaigns and optimize advertising spend.

8. **Manufacturing and Engineering**:
   - o **Reliability Testing**: To assess the reliability and durability of products through sample testing.
   - o **Process Improvement**: For analyzing production processes and identifying areas for efficiency improvements.

9. **Finance and Insurance**:
   - o **Risk Assessment**: To evaluate financial risks and determine insurance premiums based on statistical analysis.
   - o **Portfolio Management**: For making investment decisions and managing risk through data analysis.

10. **Technology and Data Science**:
    - o **Machine Learning**: To build predictive models and algorithms using statistical techniques.
    - o **Data Analytics**: For analyzing large datasets to uncover patterns, trends, and insights.

In all these areas, inferential statistics provides the tools to make data-driven decisions, understand relationships and trends, and evaluate hypotheses with a level of confidence. It allows professionals to generalize findings from a sample to a larger population and make predictions or informed choices based on statistical evidence.

1.6.2.1 Inferential Statistics Techniques

Inferential statistics involves several key techniques that allow you to make conclusions or predictions about a population based on sample data.

Inferential statistics techniques allow us to make predictions, test hypotheses, and draw conclusions about a population based on a sample of data. Below are some of the key inferential statistics techniques, including their formulas and example calculations:

1. **Hypothesis Testing**:
   - o **Purpose**: To determine if there is enough evidence in the sample data to support a specific hypothesis about the population.
   - o **Example**:
     - ▪ **Null Hypothesis (H0)**: "The average test score of students in School A is equal to 75."
     - ▪ **Alternative Hypothesis (H1)**: "The average test score of students in School A is not equal to 75."
     - ▪ **Test**: Suppose you take a sample of 30 students and find a sample mean score of 78 with a standard deviation of 10. Using a t-test, you calculate a p-value. If the p-value is less than the significance level (e.g., 0.05), you reject the null hypothesis, concluding that the average score differs from 75.

a. t-Test (for comparing means)

- **Purpose**: To determine if there is a significant difference between the means of two groups.
- **Formula**:

$$t = \frac{\bar{X}_1 - \bar{X}_2}{\sqrt{\frac{s_1^2}{n_1} + \frac{s_2^2}{n_2}}}$$

Where:

- $\bar{X}_1$ and $\bar{X}_2$ are the sample means.
- s_1^2 and s_2^2 are the sample variances.
- n_1 and n_2 are the sample sizes.

Example:

- Group 1: Mean = 75, Standard Deviation = 10, Sample Size = 30
- Group 2: Mean = 70, Standard Deviation = 12, Sample Size = 35

Calculate the t-value:

$$t = \frac{75 - 70}{\sqrt{\frac{10^2}{30} + \frac{12^2}{35}}} = \frac{5}{\sqrt{\frac{100}{30} + \frac{144}{35}}} \approx \frac{5}{2.62} \approx 1.91$$

Compare this t-value to a critical value from the t-distribution table with appropriate degrees of freedom to determine statistical significance.

b. Chi-Square Test (for categorical data)

- **Purpose**: To determine if there is a significant association between categorical variables.
- **Formula**:

$$\chi^2 = \sum \frac{(O_i - E_i)^2}{E_i}$$

Where:

- O_i = Observed frequency
- E_i = Expected frequency

Example:

- Observed frequencies for two categories: (40, 60) and (50, 50)
- Expected frequencies: (45, 55) and (45, 55)

Calculate chi-square value:

$$\chi^2 = \frac{(40 - 45)^2}{45} + \frac{(60 - 55)^2}{55} + \frac{(50 - 45)^2}{45} + \frac{(50 - 55)^2}{55}$$

$$\chi^2 = \frac{25}{45} + \frac{25}{55} + \frac{25}{45} + \frac{25}{55} \approx 1.67 + 0.45 + 1.67 + 0.45 = 3.24$$

Compare this χ^2 value to the critical value from the chi-square distribution table.

2. **Confidence Intervals**:
   o **Purpose**: To estimate a range within which a population parameter is likely to fall, with a certain level of confidence.
   o **Example**:
     ▪ Suppose you sample 50 employees' salaries from a company and find a mean salary of $55,000 with a standard deviation of $5,000. A 95% confidence interval for the mean salary might be calculated as $55,000 ± $1,400, meaning you are 95% confident that the true average salary of all employees is between $53,600 and $56,400.

Formula:

$$CI = \bar{X} \pm Z \left(\frac{\sigma}{\sqrt{n}} \right)$$

Where:

- $\bar{X}$ = Sample mean

- Z = Z-value from the standard normal distribution (e.g., 1.96 for 95% confidence)

- σ = Population standard deviation (or sample standard deviation if population is unknown)

- n = Sample size

Example:

- Sample mean = $55,000

- Standard deviation = $5,000

- Sample size = 50

- For a 95% confidence level, $Z = 1.96$

Calculate the confidence interval:

$$CI = 55,000 \pm 1.96 \left(\frac{5,000}{\sqrt{50}} \right) = 55,000 \pm 1.96 \left(\frac{5,000}{7.07} \right) = 55,000 \pm 1,384$$

$$CI = [53,616, 56,384]$$

3. **Regression Analysis**:
   o **Purpose**: To examine the relationship between one dependent variable and one or more independent variables

Formula:

$$Y = \beta_0 + \beta_1 X + \epsilon$$

Where:

- Y = Dependent variable
- X = Independent variable
- β_0 = Intercept
- β_1 = Slope
- ϵ = Error term

o **Example**:
Predicting a student's final grade (dependent variable) based on hours studied (independent variable). If the regression equation is Final Grade = 50 + 5 * Hours Studied, and a student studies for 10 hours, you would predict a final grade of 50 + 5 * 10 = 100.
Example:

- Suppose you want to predict test scores based on hours studied. You collect data and find the regression equation:

$$\text{Test Score} = 50 + 5 \times \text{Hours Studied}$$

- For a student who studies for 10 hours:

$$\text{Test Score} = 50 + 5 \times 10 = 100$$

4. **ANOVA (Analysis of Variance)**:
   o **Purpose**: To test if there are significant differences between the means of three or more groups.
   o **Example**:
   - Suppose you want to compare the effectiveness of three different teaching methods on student performance. You collect test scores from students using each method. ANOVA will help you determine if there are significant differences in the mean test scores among the three groups. If the p-value is less than 0.05, you conclude that at least one teaching method leads to different scores.

5. **Chi-Square Tests**:
   o **Purpose**: To examine the relationship between categorical variables or test if the observed distribution of data differs from an expected distribution.
   o **Example**:
   - Suppose you want to test if there is an association between gender and preference for a new product. You survey 200 people and record the frequency of preferences among men and women. Using a chi-square test, you find a chi-square statistic of 10.2 with a p-value of 0.02. If this p-value is less than 0.05, you conclude that there is a significant association between gender and product preference.

6. **Correlation Analysis**:
   o **Purpose**: To measure the strength and direction of the relationship between two variables.
   o **Example**:
   - **Pearson Correlation Coefficient**: Suppose you measure the number of hours spent studying and exam scores for 50 students. If you find a Pearson

correlation coefficient of 0.85, it indicates a strong positive correlation, meaning that as study hours increase, exam scores tend to increase as well.

7. **Non-Parametric Tests**:
   o **Purpose**: To make inferences when data doesn't meet the assumptions required for parametric tests (e.g., normality).
   o **Example**:
     ▪ **Mann-Whitney U Test**: If you want to compare the median scores of two independent groups that are not normally distributed, such as customer satisfaction ratings from two different stores, the Mann-Whitney U test can be used. If the test shows a p-value less than 0.05, you conclude that the median satisfaction ratings differ between the two stores.

Each of these inferential statistics methods helps in making decisions or predictions about a population based on sample data, with various techniques suited to different types of data and research questions.

Chapter 2: Machine Learning Introduction

2.1 Machine Learning Introduction

Machine Learning (ML) is a branch of **Artificial Intelligence (AI)** that allows computers to **learn from data and make predictions or decisions without explicit programming**. Instead of being manually programmed with rules, ML algorithms identify patterns in data and improve their performance over time.

Key Features of Machine Learning

Learns from Data – ML models improve as they process more data.
Automates Decision-Making – Can make predictions without human intervention.
Handles Complex Patterns – Detects trends that are hard to program manually.
Improves Over Time – The more data it gets, the better it performs.

How Does Machine Learning Work

Data Collection – Gather relevant data.
Data Preprocessing – Clean and prepare data.
Choose an ML Model – Select the best algorithm.
Train the Model – Feed data to the algorithm.
Test & Evaluate – Measure accuracy with test data.
Deploy & Improve – Use it in real-world applications.

Why Machine learning

Machine Learning (ML) is transforming industries by enabling computers to learn from data and make intelligent decisions **without explicit programming**. It is used to **automate tasks, analyze massive datasets, and improve decision-making** across various domains.

Key Reasons to Use Machine Learning

1. Handles Large & Complex Data

ML can process massive amounts of data that traditional programming cannot handle efficiently.
 Example: Google analyzing trillions of web pages to improve search results.

2. Automates Decision-Making

ML models can make **fast, accurate decisions** without human intervention.
Example: Fraud detection systems analyzing millions of transactions in real-time.

3. Improves Over Time (Self-Learning)

ML models get better as they **learn from new data** and refine their predictions.
Example: Netflix improving movie recommendations based on user preferences.

4. Detects Hidden Patterns & Trends

ML identifies relationships in data that are difficult to spot with traditional analysis.
Example: Stock market prediction by analyzing price trends and news sentiment.

5. Personalization & Customer Experience

ML tailors services based on user behavior, making experiences **more relevant**.
Example: Amazon and Spotify recommending products and music.

6. Reduces Human Effort & Increases Efficiency

ML automates repetitive tasks, reducing manual labor and human errors. Example: Chatbots handling customer service inquiries 24/7.

Real-World Applications of Machine Learning
Healthcare – Disease prediction, medical imaging, personalized medicine
Finance – Credit scoring, fraud detection, stock market analysis
Retail & E-commerce – Recommendation systems, demand forecasting
Self-Driving Cars – Tesla, Waymo using ML for object detection and navigation
Natural Language Processing (NLP) – Chatbots, virtual assistants (Siri, Alexa)

Why Now? The Rise of Machine Learning
Big Data Availability – More data means better learning.
Faster Computing Power – Advanced GPUs and cloud computing accelerate ML training.
Better Algorithms – Improved ML techniques like Deep Learning enhance accuracy.

Machine Learning vs. Traditional Programming
Machine learning and traditional programming handle tasks differently. Traditional programming uses specific, human-made rules. A developer tells the program what to do step by step. Machine learning, though, learns from the data itself. For example, an ML model can predict loan risks by studying past loans1. This shift towards learning from data changes how we solve problems today.

The difference between machine learning (ML) and traditional programming lies in how they approach problem-solving and the nature of the tasks they are suited for. Here are the key distinctions:

Traditional Programming
1. **Approach**:
   o In traditional programming, a developer writes explicit instructions (code) to solve a problem or perform a task. The logic is predefined and based on the programmer's understanding of the problem.
2. **Data and Rules**:
   o The process involves defining a set of rules and conditions to handle input data. The output is determined strictly by these predefined rules.
3. **Flexibility**:
   o Traditional programs are rigid. Any change in requirements or data structure often necessitates rewriting or modifying the code.
4. **Examples**:
   o Calculators, web servers, operating systems, database management systems, etc.
5. **Predictability**:
   o Outputs are predictable as long as the inputs and rules remain the same. There's little to no adaptation based on new data unless explicitly programmed.

Machine Learning
1. **Approach**:
   o In machine learning, instead of writing explicit rules, a developer creates a model that learns patterns from data. The model makes predictions or decisions based on this learned knowledge.
2. **Data and Learning**:
   o The process involves feeding data into an algorithm that adjusts its internal parameters to learn from the data. The model improves its performance as it is exposed to more data.
3. **Flexibility**:

- o ML models are adaptive. They can adjust to new data without needing explicit reprogramming. This makes them suitable for dynamic environments.
  4. **Examples**:
    - o Image recognition, speech recognition, recommendation systems, autonomous vehicles, etc.
  5. **Predictability**:
    - o Outputs can vary based on the data the model has been trained on. ML models may adapt and change over time, making them less predictable but often more accurate as they learn from new data.

Key Differences
1. **Development Process**:
   - o **Traditional Programming**: Developer defines rules -> Input data processed by rules -> Output
   - o **Machine Learning**: Developer defines learning algorithm -> Input data used to train model -> Model makes predictions based on data
2. **Handling Complexity**:
   - o **Traditional Programming**: Suitable for problems with clear, well-defined rules.
   - o **Machine Learning**: Suitable for complex problems where rules are not explicitly known or are too complex to define manually.
3. **Adaptability**:
   - o **Traditional Programming**: Changes require manual updates to the code.
   - o **Machine Learning**: Models adapt automatically to new data.
4. **Efficiency**:
   - o **Traditional Programming**: Efficient for simple, rule-based tasks.
   - o **Machine Learning**: Efficient for tasks involving large amounts of data and pattern recognition.
5. **Use Cases**:
   - o **Traditional Programming**: Used for tasks where logic and rules are known and static.
   - o **Machine Learning**: Used for tasks requiring prediction, classification,

2.1.1 History of Machine Learning
The early days
Machine learning history started in 1943 with the first mathematical model of neural networks presented in the scientific paper "A logical calculus of the ideas immanent in nervous activity" by Walter Pitts and Warren McCulloch.

Then, in 1949, the book The Organization of Behavior by Donald Hebb was published. The book had theories on how behavior relates to neural networks and brain activity and would go on to become one of the monumental pillars of machine learning development.

In 1950 Alan Turing created the Turing Test to determine if a computer has real intelligence. To pass the test, a computer must be able to fool a human into believing it is also human. He presented the principle in his paper Computing Machinery and Intelligence while working at the University of Manchester. It opens with the words: "I propose to consider the question, 'Can machines think?'"

1940s–1950s: The Birth of AI & Early Concepts
1943 – First Neural Network Model
Warren McCulloch & Walter Pitts developed the first mathematical model of an artificial neuron, laying the foundation for neural networks.

1950 – The Turing Test
Alan Turing proposed the Turing Test to measure machine intelligence, inspiring future AI and ML research.
1952 – First Machine Learning Program
Arthur Samuel created a self-learning checkers program that improved by playing against itself. He coined the term "Machine Learning."
1957 – The Perceptron
Frank Rosenblatt invented the Perceptron, the first neural network model for pattern recognition.

1960s–1980s: Rule-Based AI & The ML Winter
1967 – Nearest Neighbor Algorithm
The k-Nearest Neighbors (k-NN) algorithm was introduced for pattern recognition.
1970s–1980s – AI "Winter"
ML research declined due to lack of computing power and funding. Early rule-based AI systems failed to scale.
1986 – Backpropagation Revolution
Geoffrey Hinton & others developed the backpropagation algorithm, which allowed neural networks to learn more effectively.

1990s: Machine Learning Rises Again
1997 – IBM's Deep Blue Beats Chess Champion
Deep Blue, an AI-powered chess computer, defeated world champion Garry Kasparov.
1999 – Support Vector Machines (SVM)
SVMs became popular for classification problems in ML.

2000s: The Era of Big Data & ML Expansion
2006 – The Deep Learning Boom
Geoffrey Hinton introduced Deep Belief Networks, marking the rebirth of Deep Learning.
2009 – Google's Self-Driving Car
Google started testing autonomous vehicles, showcasing ML's real-world potential.

2010s–Present: AI Breakthroughs & Industry Adoption
2012 – AlexNet Wins ImageNet Competition
AlexNet, a deep neural network, won the ImageNet challenge, proving that Deep Learning outperformed traditional ML techniques. 2014 – Generative Adversarial Networks (GANs)
Ian Goodfellow introduced GANs, enabling AI to generate realistic images and videos.
2016 – AlphaGo Defeats Human Champion
Google DeepMind's AlphaGo beat the world's best Go player, demonstrating reinforcement learning.
2020s – AI in Everyday Life
ML powers applications like ChatGPT, self-driving cars, medical AI, and fraud detection.

Why Do We Need Machine Learning?
Another important question that arises here is- why do we need machine learning?
    1. **Accurate Predictions**
Accurate predictions about customer preferences, the economy, the stock market, etc. are essential. Right implementation of ML algorithms makes it possible to identify patterns and trends, helping organizations and individuals.
    2. **Speech Recognition**
ML has helped speech recognition apps in enhancing the interpretation of voice-based inputs received from customers and other sources. This aids in decreasing the need to have humans do this task or recognition and interpretation. Consequently, the errors also go down.

3. **Autonomous Vehicles**

With ML, vehicles can learn safe navigation in the real world. As ML gets better with time, these autonomous vehicles will also become better. This will ensure safer roads with less disruptions and collisions.

4. **Detecting Frauds**

Many organizations and fields like banking, finance and education face fraud issues quite often. With ML algorithms, these frauds can be detected early through patterns and change in activities.

5. **Better Products**

Companies want to appease their customers but the data is too huge to work with. In fact, making changes after something is done is a hefty task. With ML, predictions about trends and wants can be made way in advance.

2.1.2 How does Machine Learning work

ML utilizes a systematic approach for predicting new values by following a set of steps. These steps are -

1. **Data Collection**- The data quality is imperative in determining the accuracy of the predictions. Data sets can be built-in or collected from websites, APIs, social media, etc.
2. **Data Preprocessing**- Missing and duplicate values are removed, format is standardized and outliers are dealt with.
3. **Model Training**- An algorithm is used to model the data set, which is divided into two parts namely training and testing sets. Different models and techniques are used here.
4. **Model Evaluation**- This step determines the accuracy of the model. It is tested via different techniques and metrics.
5. **Model Deployment**- Trained models are integrated into real-world issues with the aim of solving them. The models are practically used here.

2.2 Data collection for Machine Learning models

a) Manual Data Collection
- **Human-Generated Data**: Surveys, interviews, research studies.
- **Web Scraping**: Extracting data from websites using Python tools like BeautifulSoup or Scrapy.

b) Automated Data Collection
- **APIs (Application Programming Interfaces)**: Accessing live data from platforms like Twitter, Google Maps, and OpenWeather.
- **IoT Devices & Sensors**: Data from smart devices (temperature, humidity, motion sensors).
- **Logs & System Data**: Collected from apps, servers, and databases.

c) Public Datasets & Open Data
- **Government & Research Databases**: Kaggle, UCI Machine Learning Repository, Google Dataset Search.
- **Industry-Specific Datasets**: Financial reports, medical research datasets.

d) Synthetic Data
- **Generated Data**: Created using simulations or algorithms when real data is limited.
- **Example**: GANs (Generative Adversarial Networks) for image generation.

Websites for datasets

There are numerous websites where you can find datasets for various types of projects. Here are some popular ones:

Kaggle: Kaggle is one of the largest platforms for data science competitions and also hosts a vast collection of datasets across various domains.

UCI Machine Learning Repository: Run by the University of California, Irvine, this repository hosts datasets specifically curated for machine learning research.

Google Dataset Search: Google Dataset Search helps you find datasets stored across the web, making it easier to discover datasets relevant to your project.

GitHub: Many researchers and organizations share datasets on GitHub repositories. You can search for datasets using GitHub's search feature.

Data.gov: If you're looking for government-related datasets, Data.gov is a good place to start. It hosts a wide range of datasets from various government agencies in the United States.

AWS Public Datasets: Amazon Web Services (AWS) provides access to a variety of public datasets hosted on their platform.

Microsoft Research Open Data: Microsoft Research provides access to a collection of datasets across various domains, including computer vision, natural language processing, and more.

OpenML: OpenML is an open science platform that allows you to share datasets and machine learning experiments.

Reddit Datasets: The subreddit r/datasets is a community where users share and request datasets for various purposes.

DataHub: DataHub hosts a wide range of datasets across different domains and allows users to explore, share, and visualize data.

2.3 Structured data versus Unstructured data

In machine learning and data science, data can be broadly categorized into structured and unstructured types. Understanding the difference between these two types is crucial for choosing the appropriate techniques and algorithms for data analysis and machine learning tasks.

Structured Data

Structured data refers to highly organized data stored in a fixed format such as tables, databases, or spreadsheets. It is easy to search, process, and analyze because it follows a predefined schema

Characteristics of Structured Data

Organized in Rows & Columns – Data is stored in tables like in SQL databases.
Follows a Schema – Each column has a defined datatype (e.g., integers, text, dates).
Easily Searchable – Can be queried using SQL (e.g., SELECT * FROM customers).
Stored in Databases – Found in relational databases like MySQL, PostgreSQL, and Oracle.

Where is Structured Data Used?

Banking & Finance – Customer accounts, transactions, and credit history.
Healthcare – Patient records, appointments, and medical history.
Retail & E-commerce – Product inventory, orders, and customer details.
Education – Student enrollment, courses, and exam results.

How is Structured Data Stored?

Relational Databases (SQL Databases) – MySQL, PostgreSQL, Oracle, Microsoft SQL Server.

Spreadsheets – Excel, Google Sheets.
Data Warehouses – Amazon Redshift, Google BigQuery.

Unstructured Data

Definition: Unstructured data is not organized in a predefined manner or format. It is often textual or multimedia data that does not fit neatly into rows and columns and is more complex to analyze.

Characteristics:
- **Flexible Format:** Can be text, images, videos, audio, etc.
- **No Predefined Schema:** Does not have a consistent structure or format.
- **Complex to Analyze**: Requires more advanced techniques such as natural language processing (NLP) for text, or computer vision for images.

Examples:
1. Text Data:
   o Example: Customer reviews or social media posts.
   o Data Sample:
     ▪ "The service at the restaurant was excellent. I will definitely come back!"
     ▪ "I had a terrible experience with customer support. Very disappointed."
2. Images:
   o Example: Photographs, medical imaging.
   o Data Sample: A dataset of photographs containing different types of animals.
3. Audio Data:
   o Example: Voice recordings, music files.
   o Data Sample: Audio files of people speaking or various musical tracks.
4. Video Data:
   o Example: Surveillance footage, video clips.
   o Data Sample: Videos from security cameras or YouTube videos.

Difference Between Structured & Unstructured Data

Feature	Structured Data	Unstructured Data
Format	Organized (Tables, Rows, Columns)	Unorganized (Text, Images, Audio)
Storage	Databases (SQL)	NoSQL, Cloud Storage, Data Lakes
Querying	Easy (SQL, Queries)	Hard (NLP, AI Processing)
Examples	CRM Data, Sales Records	Emails, Videos, Social Media Posts

2.4 Labeled Data versus Unlabeled Data

In machine learning, labeled and unlabeled data refer to the presence or absence of annotations or target values associated with the data points. These concepts are crucial in different types of learning tasks and influence how algorithms are applied.

Labeled Data

Definition: Labeled data is a dataset where each data point is paired with a corresponding label or target value. The label represents the outcome or category the data point belongs to and is used for supervised learning tasks.

Characteristics:
- ***Annotated Data:*** Each sample in the dataset has a known output or classification.
- Used in Supervised Learning: Algorithms learn from this data by mapping inputs to outputs.
- ***Provides Ground Truth:*** The label acts as a "ground truth" for training and evaluating the model.

Examples:
1. Image Classification:
   - Dataset: A collection of images where each image is labeled with a category.
   - Example Data:
     - Image: Picture of a cat.
     - Label: "Cat"
     - Image: Picture of a dog.
     - Label: "Dog"
   - Use Case: Training a model to classify images into "cat" or "dog."
2. Email Spam Detection:
   - Dataset: A set of emails with each email labeled as "spam" or "not spam."
   - Example Data:
     - Email Content: "Congratulations! You've won a $1000 gift card!"
     - Label: "Spam"
     - Email Content: "Hi, let's schedule a meeting for next week."
     - Label: "Not Spam"
   - Use Case: Training a model to filter out spam emails.
3. Sentiment Analysis:
   - Dataset: A collection of text reviews where each review is labeled with sentiment.
   - Example Data:
     - Review: "The movie was fantastic and I loved it!"
     - Label: "Positive"
     - Review: "The movie was boring and a waste of time."
     - Label: "Negative"
   - Use Case: Training a model to classify reviews as positive or negative.

Unlabeled Data

Definition: Unlabeled data is a dataset where the data points do not have associated labels or target values. This type of data is used in unsupervised learning tasks where the goal is to uncover hidden patterns or structures within the data.

Characteristics:
- ***No Annotations:*** Data points are present without predefined outcomes.
- ***Used in Unsupervised Learning:*** Algorithms explore the data to identify patterns, clusters, or relationships without predefined targets.
- ***Exploratory:*** Useful for exploring the structure or distribution of data.

Examples:
1. Customer Segmentation:
   - Dataset: Customer data without any predefined segments or labels.
   - Example Data:
     - Customer Data: Age, income, purchase history.
     - Label: None

- o Use Case: Using clustering algorithms to segment customers into distinct groups based on similarities in their data.
2. Topic Modeling:
   - o Dataset: A collection of documents without topic labels.
   - o Example Data:
     - Document: "The stock market has been very volatile this year."
     - Document: "New advancements in AI are rapidly evolving."
   - o Label: None
   - o Use Case: Using topic modeling algorithms to identify underlying topics in a set of documents.
3. Anomaly Detection:
   - o Dataset: Data from normal system operations without explicit labels for anomalies.
   - o Example Data:
     - System Metrics: CPU usage, memory consumption.
     - Label: None
   - o Use Case: Identifying unusual patterns or outliers in system metrics that could indicate potential issues.

2.5 Categories of Machine Learning

Machine learning (ML) can be broadly categorized into several types based on the nature of the learning process and the type of data used.

2.5.1 Supervised Learning

Definition: Supervised learning involves training a model on a labeled dataset, where the input data (features) and the corresponding output (target) are both provided. The goal is for the model to learn the mapping from inputs to outputs so it can make predictions on new, unseen data.

Characteristics:
- Labeled Data: The training dataset includes input-output pairs.
- Training Process: The model learns from examples to predict the output or classify data.

Examples:
- Classification: Assigning labels to data points. For instance, classifying emails as "spam" or "not spam."
- Regression: Predicting a continuous output. For example, predicting house prices based on features like size and location.

Common Algorithms:
- Linear Regression
- Logistic Regression
- Decision Trees
- Support Vector Machines (SVM)
- Neural Networks

2.5.2 Unsupervised Learning

Definition: Unsupervised learning involves training a model on a dataset without labeled responses. The goal is to identify patterns, relationships, or structures in the data.

Characteristics:

- Unlabeled Data: The training dataset includes only input features without associated output labels.
- Exploratory: Used for discovering hidden patterns or intrinsic structures.

Examples:

- Clustering: Grouping similar data points together. For example, customer segmentation based on purchasing behavior.
- Dimensionality Reduction: Reducing the number of features while preserving essential information. For instance, using Principal Component Analysis (PCA) to visualize high-dimensional data in 2D.

Common Algorithms:

- K-Means Clustering
- Hierarchical Clustering
- Principal Component Analysis (PCA)
- Independent Component Analysis (ICA)

2.5.3 Reinforcement Learning

Definition: Reinforcement learning (RL) involves training an agent to make decisions by interacting with an environment. The agent learns to take actions that maximize cumulative rewards over time.

Characteristics:

- Trial and Error: The agent learns through trial and error by receiving feedback in the form of rewards or penalties.
- Sequential Decision Making: The learning process involves making a series of decisions to achieve a goal.

Examples:

- Game Playing: Training an agent to play games like chess or Go, where it learns strategies to win by playing numerous games.
- Robotics: Teaching robots to perform tasks like navigation or manipulation by interacting with their environment.

Common Algorithms:

- Q-Learning
- Deep Q-Networks (DQN)
- Policy Gradients
- Actor-Critic Methods

Chapter 3: Data Preprocessing

3.1 Data Preparation

It is also referred to as data preprocessing. Data pre-processing refers to the transformations applied to our data before feeding it to the algorithm. Data preprocessing is a technique that is used to convert the raw data into a clean data set. In the Data preprocessing, it has various techniques and steps taken to clean, transform, and prepare raw data for analysis or machine learning tasks. The goal of data preprocessing is to ensure that the data is in a suitable format and quality for accurate and effective analysis.

Why data preparation

Raw data that is collected in the data gathering stage is neither in the proper format nor in the cleanest form. A real-world data generally contains noises, missing values, and maybe in an unusable format which cannot be directly used for machine learning models. Data preprocessing is required tasks for cleaning the data and making it suitable for a machine learning model which also increases the accuracy and efficiency of a machine learning model. Data preprocessing is a required first step before any machine learning machinery can be applied, because the algorithms learn from the data and the learning outcome for problem solving heavily depends on the proper data needed to solve a particular problem – which are called features.

Improving Data Quality: Raw data can be messy, containing missing values, outliers, errors, and inconsistencies. Preprocessing helps identify and handle these issues, leading to better data quality and more reliable results.

Enabling Effective Analysis: Clean and well-organized data makes it easier to perform exploratory data analysis (EDA) and gain insights into the underlying patterns, trends, and relationships within the data.

Facilitating Machine Learning: Machine learning algorithms often require data to be in a specific format. Preprocessing prepares the data by converting categorical variables, handling missing values, and scaling features to ensure that it is suitable for training machine learning models.

Avoiding Garbage In, Garbage Out (GIGO) Problem: If the data fed into the analysis or models is of poor quality, the results and predictions will also be unreliable. Data preprocessing helps mitigate the GIGO problem by ensuring that the input data is clean and relevant.

Reducing Overfitting: Feature selection and dimensionality reduction techniques employed during preprocessing can help in reducing the complexity of the data and, in turn, reduce the risk of overfitting in machine learning models.

Saving Computational Resources: Large datasets can be computationally expensive and time-consuming to analyze. Data reduction techniques, such as dimensionality reduction, can help in reducing the data's size while retaining essential information, thus saving computational resources.

Enhancing Model Performance: Preprocessing can lead to improved model performance by removing noise, irrelevant features, and inconsistencies, allowing the models to focus on the most relevant patterns in the data.

Enabling Better Decision Making: High-quality data and accurate models lead to better-informed decision-making processes, which is essential for businesses and organizations to gain a competitive edge.

Overall, data preprocessing is a fundamental step in the data science workflow that lays the foundation for accurate analysis, meaningful insights, and successful machine learning models. It ensures that the data is in the best possible shape for the subsequent stages of the data science process.

The Major Steps of Data Preprocessing are included:

Data Cleaning: Raw data often contains errors, missing values, or inconsistencies. Data cleaning involves:

- **Handling missing data:** Impute missing values or remove incomplete records.
- **Dealing with outliers:** Identify and possibly remove data points that deviate significantly from the rest of the dataset.
- **Correcting errors:** Detect and correct any inaccuracies or inconsistencies in the data.

Data Transformation or Wrangling

- **Encoding:** Encoding is the process of converting categorical data into numerical values so that it can be used by machine learning algorithms. Most algorithms require numerical input, so encoding is necessary for categorical features.
- **Normalization/Scaling:** Scaling involves adjusting the range of numerical features to ensure they are on a comparable scale. This helps improve the performance and convergence of many machine-learning algorithms.
- **Transformation:** Transformation refers to applying mathematical operations to features to make them more suitable for modeling. This can include a variety of techniques to improve the distribution or the relationship between features and the target variable.
- **Discretization**: Discretization is the process of converting continuous variables into discrete intervals or categories. This can be useful for certain types of analyses or when working with algorithms that require categorical data.

Feature Selection:

- Identify the most relevant features that contribute the most to the predictive power of the model.
- Remove redundant or irrelevant features to reduce dimensionality and computational complexity.
- Feature selection can be performed using statistical methods, correlation analysis, or domain knowledge.

Data Splitting:

- Divide the dataset into training, validation, and test sets. The training set is used to train the model, the validation set is used to tune hyperparameters and evaluate model performance during training, and the test set is used to assess the final performance of the trained model.
- The typical split ratio is around 60-80% for training, 10-20% for validation, and 10-20% for testing, depending on the size of the dataset.

By performing data preprocessing effectively, we can ensure that the input data is of high quality, relevant, and properly formatted, leading to better-performing machine learning models.

3.2 Data Cleaning

Data Cleaning is particularly done as part of data preprocessing to clean the data by filling missing values, smoothing the noisy data, resolving the inconsistency, and removing outliers. The data cleaning process typically involves the two steps handling/remove missing values and handling/remove the outliers in the dataset.

3.2.1 Missing Values
What is a missing value?
Missing values refer to the absence of certain data points or entries in a dataset. When working with real-world data, it is common to encounter missing values, which can occur due to various reasons, such as data collection errors, data corruption, or simply because certain information was not recorded.

Missing values can present challenges in the data analysis and machine learning process because many machine learning algorithms cannot handle missing data directly. Therefore, it becomes necessary to address missing values before training the machine learning models.

Let's consider a simple example of a dataset with missing values. In this example, the columns contains missing values (NaN) for Survived, Age and Fare. These missing values indicate that the values for these columns were not provided or recorded.

	Survived	Age	Fare
0	1.0	22.0	7.250
1	NaN	NaN	NaN
2	NaN	26.0	7.925
3	NaN	NaN	53.100
4	0.0	35.0	8.050
...	...	...	...
886	0.0	27.0	13.000
887	1.0	19.0	30.000
888	0.0	NaN	23.450
889	1.0	26.0	30.000
890	0.0	32.0	7.750

891 rows × 3 columns

Approaches to detect missing values
In Python-Pandas, a DataFrame provides several functions and methods to identify missing values. These functions help you check for the presence of missing data and understand the distribution of missing values in your dataset. Here are some commonly used functions are isnull(),notnull(),isna(), notna() and sum().sum(). When use isnull() or isna(), the sum() function counts the number of missing values in each column. It returns a Series with the sum of missing values for each column. There are several approaches to identify and handle missing values, depending on the nature of the data and the extent of missingness. Here are some common approaches are Visual Inspection, Summary Statistics and Heatmap,..etc

Approaches to handling missing values
Once detected the missing values in our dataset, we need to handle these missing values i.e we need to make dataset without missing values. There are several approaches to handle missing values, explained below as
Deletion: Remove rows or columns with missing values. However, this approach is suitable only when the missing values are sparse and randomly distributed, and you can afford to lose some data. Deletion is not recommended if missing values are prevalent in critical features.
Mean, Median, or Mode Imputation: Replace missing values with the mean, median, or mode of the non-missing values in the same column. This method is simple and can work well for numerical data. However, it may not be the best choice if missingness is related to specific groups or categories. Mean or median values can replace the numerical(continuous) data, whereas mode is used for categorical or distinct data. The mode is the most frequent value in the dataset.
Constant Imputation: Replace missing values with a predefined constant. This method is useful when missing values have a specific meaning or when you need to preserve the distribution of the non-missing data.
The choice of the appropriate method depends on the nature of the missing data, the size of the dataset, the domain of the problem, and the specific machine learning algorithm you

plan to use. It's essential to evaluate the impact of different imputation methods on the performance of your model using cross-validation and other evaluation techniques.

Replacing missing values with mean, median or mode in a dataset can mainly achieved through two ways, one is with manual code of dataframe methods of pandas, other with methods/classes of sklearn and feature_engine libraries

Python libraries to replace missing values

(a) Replacing missing values using the "SimpleImputer" class of the sklearn library

SimpleImputer

SimpleImputer is a class in scikit-learn (sklearn) that provides a simple strategy to impute missing values in a dataset. Imputation is the process of filling in missing data with appropriate values, allowing the data to be used in machine learning models that cannot handle missing values. The SimpleImputer class allows you to replace missing values in a dataset with a constant value or statistics like the mean, median, or most frequent value of the respective feature. It works with both numerical and categorical features.

The synax of SimpleInputer class has below:

sklearn.impute.SimpleImputer(*, missing_values=nan, strategy='mean', fill_value=None, copy=True, add_indicator=False, keep_empty_features=False)

Where,

        sklearn is a library

        impute is a one of the module of sklearn library

        SimpleImputer is class

Parameters of SimpleImputer

missing_values: int, float, str, np.nan, None or pandas.NA, default=np.nan

The placeholder for the missing values. All occurrences of `missing_values` will be imputed. For pandas' dataframes with nullable integer dtypes with missing values, `missing_values` can be set to either `np.nan` or `pd.NA`.

strategy: str, default='mean'

It is the imputation strategy to apply for missing values

  a) If "mean", then replace missing values using the mean along each column. Can only be used with numeric data.

  b) If "median", then replace missing values using the median along each column. Can only be used with numeric data.

  c) If "most_frequent", then replace missing using the most frequent value along each column. Can be used with strings or numeric data. If there is more than one such value, only the smallest is returned.

  d) If "constant", then replace missing values with fill_value. Can be used with strings or numeric data.

fill_value: str or numerical value, default=None

When strategy == "constant", `fill_value` is used to replace all occurrences of missing_values. For string or object data types, `fill_value` must be a string. If None, `fill_value` will be 0 when imputing numerical data and "missing_value" for strings or object data types.

Methods of SimpleImputer

fit(X, y=None): Fit the SimpleImputer to the input data X. This method calculates the imputation values (e.g., mean, median, most frequent) based on the chosen strategy and missing values in the data. It returns the fitted SimpleImputer object.

transform(X): Replace missing values in the input data X with the imputed values based on the strategy learned during the fit() process. It returns the transformed data with missing values filled in.

fit_transform(X, y=None): A combination of fit() and transform(). It fits the SimpleImputer to the input data X and returns the transformed data with missing values filled in.

(b) Replacing missing values using classes of "feature_engine" library

One of the module "imputation" in feature_engine library has classes like SimpleImputer class in sklearn library to replace the replace missing data by parameters estimated from data or arbitrary values pre-defined by the user. Summary of Feature-engine's imputers main characteristics

Transformer	Numerical variables	Categorical variables	Description
MeanMedianImputer()	√	×	Replaces missing values by the mean or median
ArbitraryNumberImputer()	√	x	Replaces missing values by an arbitrary value
EndTailImputer()	√	×	Replaces missing values by a value at the end of the distribution
CategoricalImputer()	√	√	Replaces missing values by the most frequent category or by an arbitrary value
RandomSampleImputer()	√	√	Replaces missing values by random value extractions from the variable
AddMissingIndicator()	√	√	Adds a binary variable to flag missing observations
DropMissingData()	√	√	Removes observations with missing data from the dataset

Syntaxes of above classes are as below:

i. feature_engine.imputation.MeanMedianImputer(imputation_method='median', variables=None)

ii. feature_engine.imputation.ArbitraryNumberImputer(arbitrary_number=999, variables=None, imputer_dict=None)

iii. feature_engine.imputation.EndTailImputer(imputation_method='gaussian', tail='right', fold=3, variables=None)

iv. feature_engine.imputation.CategoricalImputer(imputation_method='missing', fill_value='Missing', variables=None, return_object=False, ignore_format=False)

v. feature_engine.imputation.RandomSampleImputer(variables=None, random_state=None, seed='general', seeding_method='add')

vi. feature_engine.imputation.AddMissingIndicator(missing_only=True, variables=None)

vii. feature_engine.imputation.DropMissingData(missing_only=True, threshold=None, variables=None)

3.2.2 Outliers

An outlier is a data point that lies far away from the majority of other data points in a dataset. Outliers are data points that deviate significantly from the expected or typical behavior of the data and can have a noticeable impact on statistical analyses and machine learning models.

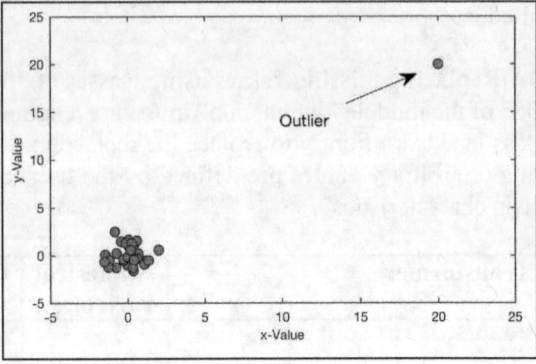

Why outliers in the dataset

Outliers can occur in datasets due to various reasons, some of the common reasons for outliers in datasets are as follows:

Data Entry Mistakes: Human errors during data entry can result in outliers. For example, enter the age of a candidate as 300 years, and enter the distance traveled by a candidate as -30 Kilometer.

Impact of the outliers in the dataset

Outliers can have a significant impact on the performance of machine learning models. They can affect the accuracy of the models and lead to incorrect predictions. For example, in a regression model, outliers can result in a significant deviation from the true line of best fit, leading to inaccurate predictions.

Outliers can also affect the training of machine learning models. When outliers are present in the training set, the model can become overly sensitive to these points, leading to overfitting. Overfitting occurs when the model becomes too complex and fits the training data too closely, leading to poor performance on new, unseen data.

For Example, A temperature data set has the outlier and we see how outlier impact on mean, median and mode and range as below calculations:

DATA SET

| 15.0 °C |
| 20.5 °C |
| 26.0 °C |
| 30.5 °C |
| 31.0 °C |
| -350.0 °C | ← Outlier |
| 31.0 °C |

STATISTICAL CALCULATION

MEASURE	WITH OUTLIER	WITHOUT OUTLIER
Mean	-28	25.667
Median	26	28.25
Mode	31	31
Range	381	16

Approaches to detect outliers in the dataset

Detecting outliers in datasets is an essential step in data analysis and is crucial for ensuring data quality and accurate model training. There are various methods to detect outliers, ranging from basic statistical techniques to advanced machine learning algorithms. Here are some common methods:

By visual inspection: Plotting the data and inspecting for extreme values. Box plots, scatter plots, and histograms are useful for visualizing the distribution of data and identifying potential outliers.

By statistical methods

a) Z-Score: Calculate the Z-score for each data point, which measures how many standard deviations a data point is away from the mean. Data points with Z-scores beyond a certain threshold (e.g., Z-score > 3 or < -3, Z-score > 2 or < -2) can be considered outliers.

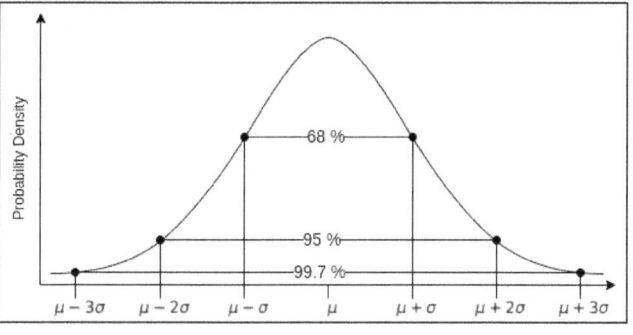

Z-score measures the variance of an observation from the mean in terms of standard deviation, assuming a normal distribution. To calculate z-score, we transform the data into a normally distributed bell curve, with mean and standard deviation. Then, we calculate the z-score of an observation x:

$$z = \frac{(x - \mu)}{\sigma}$$

Data point — x Mean — μ Standard deviation — σ

Mean (μ) – The mean, or average, value of the data set
SD (σ) – The Standard Deviation of the data set

We define a threshold range and mark the observations falling outside the range as outliers. Let's recall the empirical rule and coverage of standard deviation around the mean:

$\mu \pm \sigma$ covers 68.27%
$\mu \pm 2 \times \sigma$ covers 95.45%
$\mu \pm 3 \times \sigma$ covers 99.73%

b) Interquartile Range (IQR): The Interquartile Range (IQR) is a statistical measure that assesses the spread or variability of a dataset. It is calculated from the quartiles of the data and is used as an alternative to the standard deviation when data contains outliers or is not normally distributed. To compute the IQR, you first need to find the first quartile (Q1) and the third quartile (Q3) of the dataset. The first quartile (Q1) represents the 25th percentile of the data, and the third quartile (Q3) represents the 75th percentile. In other words, Q1 divides the lowest 25% of the data, and Q3 divides the upper 25% of the data.

Once you have Q1 and Q3, the IQR is calculated as the difference between Q3 and Q1:

$$IQR = Q3 - Q1$$

The IQR provides a measure of the spread of the central 50% of the data. Data points outside the range of Q1 - 1.5 * IQR and Q3 + 1.5 * IQR can be identified as outliers.

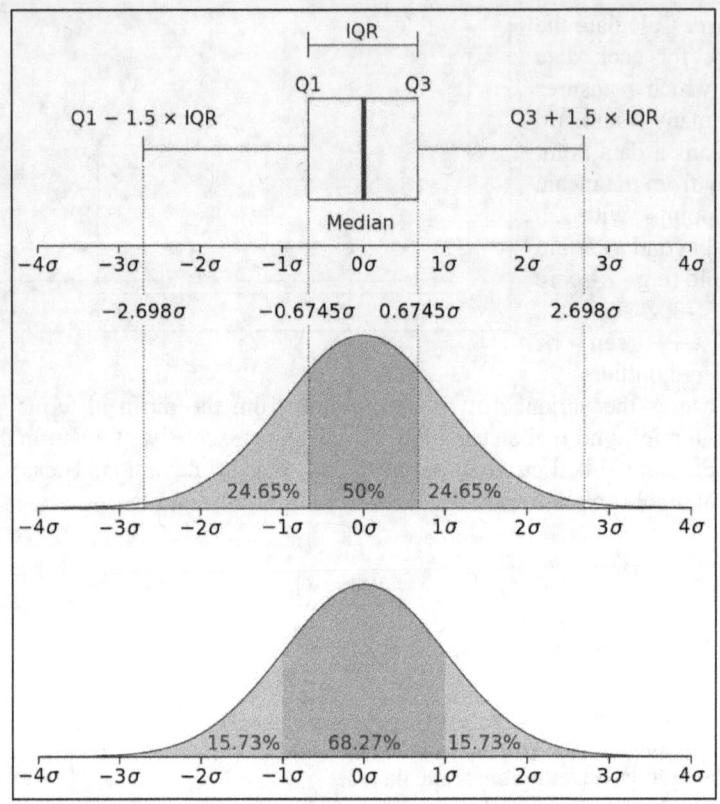

c) **Capping or Flooring:** In Capping method their values can be capped (set to a maximum value) or floored (set to a minimum value). This approach retains the information of outliers without excessively impacting the model.

d) **Arbitrary Capping**: It is possible that the term "arbitrary method" could be referring to a custom or ad-hoc technique used by some analysts to replace outliers with specific values.

Python Libraries to handle outliers
Classes to handle outliers
"Feature_engine" libray has some classes in the "outliers" module to replace the outliers by appling statics methods
Summary of Feature-engine's outlieres classes main characteristics

Transformer	Description
Winsorizer()	Caps variables at automatically determined extreme values
ArbitraryOutlierCapper()	Caps variables at values determined by the user
OutlierTrimmer()	Removes outliers from the dataframe

Winsorizer
Winsorization is a data preprocessing technique used to handle outliers in a dataset. Outliers are extreme values that deviate significantly from the majority of the data points and can have a substantial impact on the performance of certain machine-learning models. It is named after the statistician Charles P. Winsor.
The Winsorization process involves capping or limiting the extreme values to a predefined percentile. Instead of removing the outliers or replacing them with a fixed value,

Winsorization replaces the extreme values with the values at a specified quantile or percentile. This helps in preserving the overall distribution of the data while reducing the influence of outliers. Winsorization can be performed on either side of the distribution (lower and upper tails) based on the requirement.

Winsorizer is a class from the feature-engine library, which is a Python library designed for data preprocessing in machine learning and feature engineering tasks. The Winsorizer class provides a method to handle outliers by winsorizing the data. Syntax of Winsorizer class as show below:

feature_engine.outliers.Winsorizer(capping_method='gaussian', tail='right', fold=3, add_indicators=False, variables=None, missing_values='raise')

where feature_engine is a library, outlier is a module of the feature_engine library and Winsorizer is a one of the class of outliers module.

The Winsorizer() caps the maximum and/or minimum values of a variable automatically with determined values, and optionally adds indicators. The Winsorizer() works only with numerical variables. A list of variables can be indicated. Alternatively, the Winsorizer() will select and cap all numerical variables in the train set.

The extreme values beyond which an observation is considered an outlier are determined using:

    i.   Gaussian approximation
    ii.   inter-quantile range proximity rule (IQR)
    iii.   percentiles

Gaussian limits:
        right tail: mean + 3* std
        left tail: mean - 3* std

Usually, we round the numbers and call the coverages to be $68 - 95 - 99.7$:

IQR limits:
        right tail: 75th quantile + 3* IQR
        left tail: 25th quantile - 3* IQR
        where IQR is the inter-quartile range: 75th quantile - 25th quantile.

A quartile divides the observations into four parts. Q_1 is called the first quartile, and it represents the 25th percentile of the dataset. Similarly, **Q3** denotes the third quartile and marks the 75th percentile of the data.

Progressing further, we define the interquartile range as:

In the quartile analysis method, we define the values falling outside the k*IQR range to be outliers. A commonly used value for the multiplier k is 3. Hence, the values residing outside the 3*IQR range are outliers:

percentiles:
        right tail: 95th percentile
        left tail: 5th percentile

You can select how far out to cap the maximum or minimum values with the parameter `'fold'`.

If `capping_method='gaussian'` fold gives the value to multiply the std.

If `capping_method='iqr'` fold is the value to multiply the IQR.

If `capping_method='quantiles'`, fold is the percentile on each tail that should be censored. For example, if fold=0.05, the limits will be the 5th and 95th percentiles. If fold=0.1, the limits will be the 10th and 90th percentiles.

Parameters of Winsorizer

capping_method: str, default='gaussian'

Desired outlier detection method. Can take 'gaussian', 'iqr' or 'quantiles'. The transformer will find the maximum and/or minimum values beyond which a data point will be considered an outlier using: **'gaussian'**: the Gaussian approximation. **'iqr'**: the IQR proximity rule. **'quantiles'**: the percentiles.

tail: str, default='right'

Whether to look for outliers on the right, left or both tails of the distribution. Can take 'left', 'right' or 'both-'.

fold: int or float, default=3

The factor used to multiply the std or IQR to calculate the maximum or minimum allowed values. Recommended values are 2 or 3 for the gaussian approximation, and 1.5 or 3 for the IQR proximity rule.

If `capping_method='quantile'`, then `'fold'` indicates the percentile. So if `fold=0.05`, the limits will be the 95th and 5th percentiles.

Note: Outliers will be removed up to a maximum of the 20th percentiles on both sides. Thus, when `capping_method='quantile'`, then `'fold'` takes values between 0 and 0.20.

add_indicators: bool, default=False

Whether to add indicator variables to flag the capped outliers. If 'True', binary variables will be added to flag outliers on the left and right tails of the distribution. One binary variable per tail, per variable.

variables: list, default=None

The list of numerical variables to transform. If None, the transformer will automatically find and select all numerical variables.

missing_values: string, default='raise'

Indicates if missing values should be ignored or raised. If 'raise' the transformer will return an error if the the the datasets to `fit` or `transform` contain missing values. If 'ignore', missing data will be ignored when learning parameters or performing the transformation.

Methods of Winsorizer

fit(*X*, *y=None*)	Learn the values that will replace the outliers in The training input samples.
fit_transform(*X*, *y=None*, ***fit_params*)	Fit to data, then transform it. Fits transformer to X and y with optional parameters fit_params and returns a transformed version of X.
transform(X)	Cap the variables.

3.3 Data Transformation

Data transformation is also known as data wrangling. Data transformation refers to the process of converting data from one format or structure into another to make it more suitable for analysis, modeling, or visualization. This is a crucial step in data preprocessing, often required to ensure that data meets the assumptions and requirements of various analytical methods and machine learning algorithms.

Why is Data Transformation Important?

Improving Model Performance: Data transformation can enhance the accuracy and efficiency of machine learning models by aligning the data with the model's assumptions or by making it more interpretable.

Meeting Algorithm Requirements: Some algorithms require data in a specific format or scale. For instance, many machine learning algorithms assume that features are on the same scale.

Handling Non-Linearity: Transformation can help in dealing with non-linear relationships by changing the scale or distribution of the data.

Ensuring Data Quality: Transforming data can address issues such as missing values, outliers, and incorrect formats.

3.3.1 Encoding Techniques

Encoding refers to the process of transforming raw data into a numerical representation that can be understood and processed by machine learning algorithms. Since many machine learning algorithms rely on mathematical operations, they require data to be in a numerical format. In machine learning, encoding techniques are used to convert different types of data (e.g., categorical, text, image) into a numerical format that can be processed by machine learning algorithms. Here are some common encoding techniques along with examples for each:

One-Hot Encoding: One-hot encoding is used for categorical variables with multiple categories. It creates binary vectors for each category, where only one element is 1 (hot) and all others are 0 (cold). This encoding ensures that the model doesn't assume any ordinal relationship between categories.

Fruit	Apple	Orange	Banana
Apple	1	0	0
Orange	0	1	0
Banana	0	0	1

For example: Consider a "Fruit" variable with three categories: "Apple," "Orange," and "Banana." After one-hot encoding, the data will look like this:

Label Encoding: Label encoding is used for ordinal categorical variables, where there is a meaningful order between the categories. It assigns integer labels to each category based on their order.

Size	Encoded
Small	0
Medium	1
Large	2

For example: Consider a "Size" variable with categories: "Small," "Medium," and "Large." After label encoding, the data will look like this:

Note: While label encoding is simple, it might introduce an ordinal relationship where none exists.

Ordinal Encoding: Ordinal encoding is similar to label encoding, but it assigns numerical values based on the order and importance of categories.

Education_Level	Encoded
High School	1
Bachelor's	2
Master's	3
Ph.D.	4

For example: Consider a "Education_Level" variable with categories: "High School," "Bachelor's," "Master's," and "Ph.D." After ordinal encoding, the data will look like this:

Python libraries for encoding

"Sklearn" and "feature_engine" libraries have several encoding classes to handle categorical variables. Feature-engine's categorical encoders replace variable strings by estimated or arbitrary numbers.

Feature-engine's categorical encoders work only with categorical variables by default. Summary of Feature-engine's and sklearn encoders main characteristics are given in below tables

	Monotonic encoding	Suitable regression	Suitable Binary Classification	Suitable Multi-class Classification	Description
OneHotEncoder	√	√	√	√	Creates dummy/ binary variables from every category
CountFrequencyEncoder	×	√	√	√	Replaces categories by the count or frequency of observations
OrdinalEncoder	√ if ordered by target, × otherwise	√	√	√ if numbers assigned arbitrarily × otherwise	Replaces categories by integers arbitrarily or ordered by target mean value
MeanEncoder	√	√	√	× The transformer will return a value, but the mean of different classes does not have mathematical sense	Replaces categories by the target mean value per category
WoEEncoder	√	×	√	×	Replaces categories by the Weight of Evidence (WoE)
PRatioEncoder	√	×	√	×	Replaces categories by a ratio of probabilities
DecisionTreeEncoder	√	√	√	√	Replaces categories by the predictions of a decision tree
RareLabelEncoder	NA	√	√	√	Groups infrequent categories into a new category

Summary of Encoding class of feature_engine library

Summary of encoding classes of sklearn library

Encoding class	Description
LabelEncoder()	Encode target labels with value between 0 and n_classes-1.
OneHotEncoder(*[, categories, ...])	Encode categorical features as a one-hot numeric array.
OrdinalEncoder(*[, ...])	Encode categorical features as an integer array.

Syntaxes of Encoding classes are:

i. feature_engine.encoding.OneHotEncoder(top_categories=None, drop_last=False, drop_last_binary=False, variables=None, ignore_format=False)

ii. feature_engine.encoding.OrdinalEncoder(encoding_method='ordered', variables=None, ignore_format=False, errors='ignore')

iii. feature_engine.encoding.CountFrequencyEncoder(encoding_method='count', variables=None, ignore_format=False, errors='ignore')

iv. feature_engine.encoding.MeanEncoder(variables=None, ignore_format=False, errors='ignore')

v. feature_engine.encoding.DecisionTreeEncoder(encoding_method='arbitrary', cv=3, scoring='neg_mean_squared_error', param_grid=None, regression=True, random_state=None, variables=None, ignore_format=False)

vi. sklearn.preprocessing.OneHotEncoder(*, categories='auto', drop=None, sparse='deprecated', sparse_output=True, dtype=<class 'numpy.float64'>, handle_unknown='error', min_frequency=None, max_categories=None, feature_name_combiner='concat')

vii. sklearn.preprocessing.OrdinalEncoder(*, categories='auto', dtype=<class 'numpy.float64'>, handle_unknown='error', unknown_value=None, encoded_missing_value=nan, min_frequency=None, max_categories=None)

viii. sklearn.preprocessing.LabelEncoder()

3.3.2 Feature Scaling Techniques

Feature scaling is a preprocessing technique in machine learning used to standardize or normalize the range of independent features (variables) of a dataset. It is essential when the features in the dataset have different scales or units of measurement. Most machine learning algorithms assume that all features are on a similar scale, and when features are not scaled properly, it can negatively impact the performance and convergence of the model. We'll use two common feature scaling methods: standardization and normalization. The purpose of feature scaling is to ensure that each feature contributes equally to the model's performance, which can improve the effectiveness of the model, especially for algorithms that are sensitive to the scale of data.

Why Feature Scaling?

1. ***Algorithm Sensitivity:*** Many machine learning algorithms, especially those based on distance metrics (like K-Nearest Neighbors and Support Vector Machines) or gradient-based optimization (like Gradient Descent used in Neural Networks), are sensitive to the scale of the features. Features with larger ranges can disproportionately influence the model, leading to biased results.

2. ***Convergence Speed:*** For algorithms that use gradient-based optimization, like Logistic Regression and Neural Networks, feature scaling can significantly affect the convergence speed of the training process. Scaled features can help the algorithm converge faster by ensuring that the gradient descent steps are more uniform across features.

3. ***Distance Metrics:*** Algorithms that rely on distance metrics (like K-Means Clustering and K-Nearest Neighbors) assume that all features contribute equally to the distance calculation. If features are on different scales, the distance metrics can become skewed, leading to poor performance.

Scaling techniques

Standardization (Z-score normalization): Standardization transforms each feature such that it has zero mean and unit variance. It centers the data around 0, and the resulting values have a standard deviation of 1.The formula for standardization is:

standardized_value = (x - mean) / standard_deviation

Normalization (Min-Max scaling): Normalization scales each feature to a fixed range, typically [0, 1]. It is achieved by subtracting the minimum value of the feature and then dividing by the range (maximum - minimum).The formula for normalization is:

normalized_value = (x - min) / (max - min)

Robust scaling: Robust scaling is a method that scales the features by removing the median and scaling them according to the interquartile range (IQR). The formula for robust scaling is:

robust_scaled_value = (x - median) / IQR

Max Abs Scaling: Max Abs scaling scales the features to the range [-1, 1] by dividing each value by the maximum absolute value in the feature.The formula for max abs scaling is:

max_abs_scaled_value = x / max(abs(x))

Unit Vector Scaling (Vector normalization): Unit Vector Scaling scales each feature to have a Euclidean norm (magnitude) of 1.
The formula for unit vector scaling is:

unit_vector_scaled_value = x / ||x||

The choice of feature scaling technique depends on the nature of the data and the machine learning algorithm being used. It is essential to preprocess the data properly before training the model to ensure that all features are on a similar scale and to prevent any bias towards features with larger values.

Let's go through examples to illustrate the concept of feature scaling, for example Age and Income. Consider a dataset that contains information about individuals, including their age (ranging from 20 to 70) and annual income (ranging from $20,000 to $100,000). For this example, we calculate the mean and standard deviation of the age and income features and then standardize the values and we calculate the minimum and maximum values of the age and income features and then normalize the values.

```
# Sample data
     ages = [25, 35, 45, 55, 65]
     incomes = [30000, 50000, 70000, 80000, 60000]


# Standardization
mean_age = sum(ages) / len(ages)
std_dev_age = (sum((x - mean_age) ** 2 for x in ages) / len(ages)) ** 0.5
standardized_ages = [(x - mean_age) / std_dev_age for x in ages]
mean_income = sum(incomes) / len(incomes)
std_dev_income = (sum((x - mean_income) ** 2 for x in incomes) / len(incomes)) ** 0.5
standardized_incomes = [(x - mean_income) / std_dev_income for x in incomes]
print("Standardized ages:", standardized_ages)
print("Standardized incomes:", standardized_incomes)
# Normalization
min_age = min(ages)
max_age = max(ages)
normalized_ages = [(x - min_age) / (max_age - min_age) for x in ages]
min_income = min(incomes)
max_income = max(incomes)
normalized_incomes = [(x - min_income) / (max_income - min_income) for x in incomes]
print("Normalized ages:", normalized_ages)
print("Normalized incomes:", normalized_incomes)
```

Python libraries for feature scaling
The following classes are provided in the "sklearn" library for scaling the feature values:

preprocessing.MaxAbsScaler(*[, copy])	Scale each feature by its maximum absolute value.
preprocessing.MinMaxScaler([feature_range, ...])	Transform features by scaling each feature to a given range.
preprocessing.Normalizer([norm, copy])	Normalize samples individually to unit norm.
preprocessing.QuantileTransformer(*[, ...])	Transform features using quantiles information.
preprocessing.RobustScaler(*[, ...])	Scale features using statistics that are robust to outliers.
preprocessing.StandardScaler(*[, copy, ...])	Standardize features by removing the mean and scaling to unit variance.

preprocessing.maxabs_scale(X, *[, axis, copy])	Scale each feature to the [-1, 1] range without breaking the sparsity.
preprocessing.minmax_scale(X[, ...])	Transform features by scaling each feature to a given range.

preprocessing.normalize(X[, norm, axis, ...])	Scale input vectors individually to unit norm (vector length).
preprocessing.quantile_transform(X, *[, ...])	Transform features using quantiles information.
preprocessing.robust_scale(X, *[, axis, ...])	Standardize a dataset along any axis.
preprocessing.scale(X, *[, axis, with_mean, ...])	Standardize a dataset along any axis.

3.3.3 Future Transformation

Feature transformation in machine learning is a preprocessing step that modifies or creates new features from the original dataset to improve the performance of a model. This process helps to make the data more suitable for the machine learning algorithms by enhancing its quality, structure, and relevance.

Why Feature Transformation?

1. *Improve Model Performance:* By transforming features, you can help the model better capture patterns and relationships in the data, potentially leading to better predictive performance.
2. *Meet Model Assumptions:* Some machine learning models assume certain properties about the data (e.g., normal distribution). Feature transformations can help meet these assumptions.
3. *Enhance Interpretability:* Transformed features may be easier to interpret or visualize, making it easier to understand the model's behavior.
4. *Handle Skewed Data:* Transformation can help in stabilizing variance and normalizing skewed data, making it easier for models to learn effectively.

Handling skewed data

Handling skewed data is an important aspect of preprocessing in machine learning. Skewness in data refers to asymmetry in the distribution of

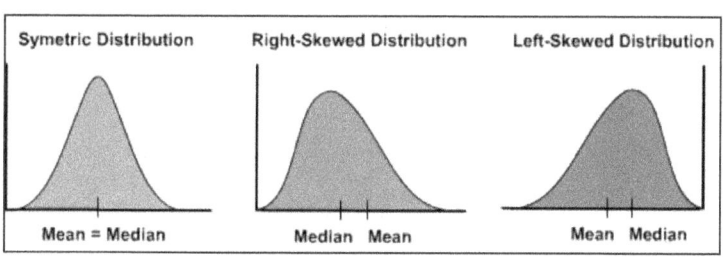

feature values, which can negatively impact model performance. Here's a detailed approach to handle skewed data effectively:

Identifying Skewed Data

1. *Visual Inspection:* Use histograms, box plots, or density plots to visually inspect the distribution of the data.

   Python code
   ```
   import matplotlib.pyplot as plt
   import seaborn as sns
   sns.histplot(data['feature'])
   plt.show()
   ```

2. *Statistical Measures:* Calculate skewness to quantify the degree of asymmetry in the data.

   Python code
   ```
   from scipy.stats import skew
   ```

```
skewness = skew(data['feature'])
print(f"Skewness: {skewness}")
```

Techniques to Handle Skewed Data
(a) Log transformation
- *Purpose:* Reduces positive skewness by compressing the range of feature values.
- *How It Works:* Applies the

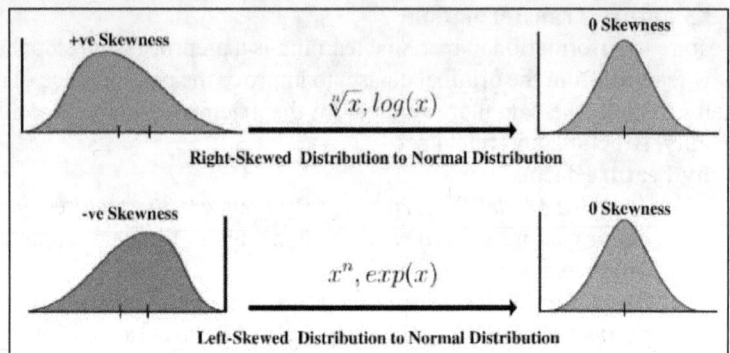

Right-Skewed Distribution to Normal Distribution

Left-Skewed Distribution to Normal Distribution

  logarithmic function to the feature values.
- *Python code:*
  ```
  import numpy as np
  data['feature_log'] = np.log1p(data['feature'])  # log1p handles log(1 + X) to avoid
  log(0)
  ```
(b) n^{th} root transformation
- *Purpose:* Reduces positive skewness and compresses the range of feature values.
- *How It Works:* Applies the nth root(square root,cube root, etc) function to the feature values.
- *Python code:*
  ```
  data['feature_sqrt'] = (data['feature'])**(1/n)
  ```

(c) n^{th} power transformation
- *Purpose:* Reduces negative skewness and compresses the range of feature values.
- *How It Works:* Applies the nth power(square,cube, etc) function to the feature values.
- *Python code:*
  ```
  data['feature'] = (data['feature'])**(1/n)
  ```
(d) exponential transformation
- *Purpose:* Reduces negative skewness and compresses the range of feature values.
- *How It Works:* Applies the e^x function to the feature values.
- *Python code:*
  ```
  Import numpy as np
  data['feature'] =np.exp (data['feature'])
  ```

(e) Box-Cox transformation
- *Purpose:* Stabilizes variance and makes data more normal-distribution-like.

- **How It Works:** Applies a power transformation. Requires data to be positive.

$$T(x) = \frac{x^\lambda - 1}{\lambda}; where \{-5 \leq \lambda \geq +5\}$$

- **Python code:**
from scipy import stats
stats.boxcox(data.Fare+0.01)
data['Age'],param=stats.boxcox(data.Age+1)
print('Delta=',param)
data["Age"].skew()

(f) **Yeo-Johnson transformation**
- **Purpose:** A generalization of Box-Cox that handles both positive and negative values.
- **How It Works:** Applies a power transformation similar to Box-Cox, but can handle zero and negative values.
- **Python code:**
from sklearn.preprocessing import PowerTransformer
transformer = PowerTransformer(method='yeo-johnson')
data['feature_yeojohnson'] = transformer.fit_transform(data[['feature']])

(g) **Quantile Transformation**
- **Purpose:** Transforms features to follow a uniform or normal distribution.
- **How It Works:** Maps feature values to uniform or normal quantiles.
- **Python code:**
from sklearn.preprocessing import QuantileTransformer
transformer = QuantileTransformer(output_distribution='normal')
data['feature_quantile'] = transformer.fit_transform(data[['feature']])

(h) **Binning**
- **Purpose:** Converts continuous features into categorical bins to reduce the effect of skewness.
- **How It Works:** Divides the range of feature values into discrete bins.
- **Python code:**
data['feature_binned'] = pd.cut(data['feature'], bins=10)

3.3.4 Discretization Techniques

Discretization refers to the process of converting continuous or numerical features into discrete or categorical ones. It involves dividing the range of a continuous variable into a set of intervals or bins, and then mapping each data point to the corresponding bin. This transformation is often necessary for certain algorithms that work only with categorical data or to simplify the representation of the data.

Let's explain discretization with an example in the context of machine learning,

For example: Age Discretization for Loan Approval:

Imagine a bank that wants to use machine learning to automate the loan approval process. One of the features they consider is the age of the loan applicants. However, most machine learning algorithms work better with discrete or categorical data, and they need to convert the continuous age values into categories. To use the age feature in the machine learning model, the bank decides to discretize the age into different bins. They choose three bins: "Young," "Middle-aged," and "senior." Here's how they do it:

"Young": Applicants aged 18 to 35

"Middle-aged": Applicants aged 36 to 55

"Senior": Applicants aged 56 and above

Now, each applicant's age will be mapped to one of the three categories based on the above bins. For example:

Applicant A: Age 25 -> "Young"

Applicant B: Age 42 -> "Middle-aged"

Applicant C: Age 60 -> "Senior"

Why Use Discretization?

1. *Simplify the Model:* Discretization can make complex continuous data easier to handle by reducing it to a smaller number of distinct categories.
2. *Improve Interpretability:* Discretized data can be easier to interpret because it simplifies continuous variables into understandable ranges or categories.
3. *Handle Non-Linearity:* By grouping similar values, discretization can help capture non-linear relationships in the data.
4. *Meet Algorithm Requirements:* Some machine learning algorithms, like decision trees or certain clustering methods, work better with categorical data.

Techniques for discretization

(a) Equal-Width Binning: Divides the range of the data into equal-width intervals or bins. Each bin has the same width.

Example: Suppose you have a feature with values ranging from 0 to 100 and you want to create 5 bins. Each bin will cover a width of 20.

Here, the bins are:

Bin 0: [0-20)

Bin 1: [20-40)

Bin 2: [40-60)

Bin 3: [60-80)

Bin 4: [80-100]

Python code:

```
import pandas as pd
# Sample data
data = pd.DataFrame({'feature': [5, 15, 25, 35, 45, 55, 65, 75, 85, 95]})
# Discretize into 5 equal-width bins
data['binned'] = pd.cut(data['feature'], bins=5, labels=False)
print(data)
```

(b) *Equal-Frequency Binning:* Divides the data into bins such that each bin contains approximately the same number of data points.

Example: Using the same feature with 10 data points and 3 bins, each bin will contain approximately 3 or 4 data points.

Here, the bins are:

Bin 0: [5, 25]

Bin 1: [35, 55]

Bin 2: [65, 95]

Python code:

```
# Discretize into 3 equal-frequency bins
data['binned'] = pd.qcut(data['feature'], q=3, labels=False)
print(data)
```

(c) *Custom Binning:* Defines bins based on specific criteria or domain knowledge, which may not be equal-width or equal-frequency.

Example: Suppose you want to bin age into specific ranges: [0-18), [19-35), [36-60), [61+].
Python code:
```
# Sample data
data = pd.DataFrame({'age': [10, 20, 30, 40, 50, 60, 70, 80]})
# Define custom bin edges and labels
bins = [0, 18, 35, 60, 100]
labels = ['0-18', '19-35', '36-60', '61+']
# Discretize with custom bins
data['age_group'] = pd.cut(data['age'], bins=bins, labels=labels)
print(data)
   age age_group
0  10    0-18
1  20    19-35
2  30    19-35
3  40    36-60
4  50    36-60
5  60    36-60
6  70    61+
7  80    61+
```

(d) ***Binning Based on Clustering:*** Uses clustering algorithms to create bins based on the natural groupings in the data.

Example: Apply K-Means clustering to bin the feature values into 3 clusters. Here, the clusters might represent different ranges of the feature values, such as:

Cluster 0: [5, 25]
Cluster 1: [35, 55]
Cluster 2: [65, 95]

Python code:
```
from sklearn.cluster import KMeans
import numpy as np
import pandas as pd
# Sample data
data = pd.DataFrame({'feature': [5, 15, 25, 35, 45, 55, 65, 75, 85, 95]})
# Reshape data for clustering
feature_values = data['feature'].values.reshape(-1, 1)
# Apply K-Means clustering with 3 clusters
kmeans = KMeans(n_clusters=3, random_state=0)
data['cluster'] = kmeans.fit_predict(feature_values)
print(data)
   feature  cluster
0     5       0
1    15       0
2    25       0
3    35       1
4    45       1
5    55       1
6    65       2
7    75       2
8    85       2
9    95       2
```

Python libraries for discretization

"sklearn" and "feature_engine" libraries have variaours classes for or performing discretization. The primary class used for discretization is KBinsDiscretizer. Feature-engine's discretisation transformers transform continuous variables into discrete features. This is accomplished, in general, by sorting the variable values into continuous intervals. Summary of discretization classes given in below tables:

Summary of discretization classes of feature_engine library

Transformer	Functionality
EqualFrequencyDiscretiser()	Sorts values into intervals with similar number of observations.
EqualWidthDiscretiser()	Sorts values into intervals of equal size.
ArbitraryDiscretiser()	Sorts values into intervals predefined by the user.
DecisionTreeDiscretiser()	Replaces values by predictions of a decision tree, which are discrete

Summary of discretization classes of sklearn library

Transformer	Functionality
preprocessing.KBinsDiscretizer([n_bins, ...])	Bin continuous data into intervals.
preprocessing.Binarizer(*[, threshold, copy])	Binarize data (set feature values to 0 or 1) according to a threshold.
preprocessing.LabelBinarizer(*[, neg_label, ...])	Binarize labels in a one-vs-all fashion.

Chapter 4: Supervised Learning

4.1 Supervised Learning

In supervised learning, the algorithm is trained on labeled data, where the input data is paired with the corresponding correct output. The algorithm learns from this labeled data and can make predictions or classify new, unseen data.

Supervised Machine Learning:

- In supervised learning, the computer is taught by example (called training data)
- It learns from past data and applies the learning to present data to predict future events.
- In this case, both input and desired output data help to predict future events.
- Supervised learning is a machine learning method in which models are trained using labeled data. In supervised learning, models need to find the mapping function to map the input variable (X) with the output variable (Y).
- Supervised learning needs supervision to train the model, which is similar to as a student learns things in the presence of a teacher

4.1.1 How Supervised Learning Works

In supervised learning, models are trained using labelled datasets, where the model learns about each type of data. Once the training process is completed, the model is tested on the basis of test data (a subset of the training set), and then it predicts the output. The working of Supervised learning can be easily understood by the below example and diagram:

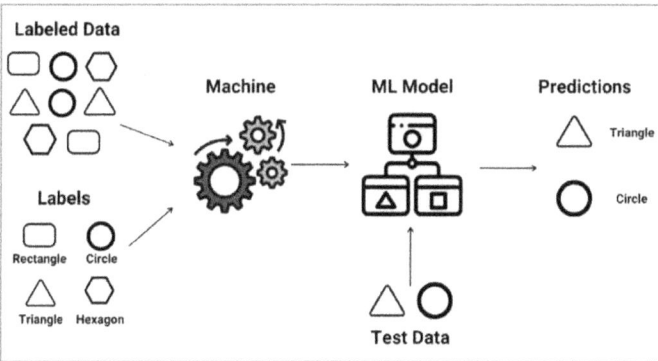

Suppose we have a dataset of different types of shapes which includes square, rectangle, triangle, and Polygon. Now the first step is that we need to train the model for each shape.

- If the given shape has four sides, and all the sides are equal, then it will be labelled as a **Square**.
- If the given shape has three sides, then it will be labelled as a **triangle**.
- If the given shape has six equal sides then it will be labelled as **hexagon**.

Now, after training, we test our model using the test set, and the task of the model is to identify the shape.

The machine is already trained on all types of shapes, and when it finds a new shape, it classifies the shape on the bases of a number of sides, and predicts the output.

Steps Involved in Supervised Learning:
Supervised learning is a type of machine learning where a model learns from labeled training data. The key steps involved in supervised learning are:

1. Data Collection
- Gather relevant labeled data (input-output pairs) for the problem.
- Ensure data quality, completeness, and diversity.

2. Data Preprocessing
- Handle missing values.
- Normalize or standardize numerical features.
- Encode categorical variables (e.g., one-hot encoding, label encoding).
- Split the dataset into training and testing sets.

3. Feature Selection & Engineering
- Identify the most relevant features to improve model performance.
- Create new features using domain knowledge (feature engineering).
- Reduce dimensionality (e.g., PCA) if needed.

4. Choose a Model
- Select an appropriate supervised learning algorithm based on the problem type:
  - **Regression** (e.g., Linear Regression, Decision Trees, Neural Networks) for continuous output.
  - **Classification** (e.g., Logistic Regression, SVM, Random Forest) for discrete output.

5. Train the Model
- Feed the training dataset to the chosen model.
- Adjust model parameters using optimization techniques (e.g., gradient descent).
- Minimize the error/loss function.

6. Evaluate the Model
- Use validation/testing data to measure model performance.
- Evaluate metrics such as accuracy, precision, recall, F1-score (for classification) or RMSE, R^2 (for regression).
- Detect underfitting or overfitting.

7. Hyperparameter Tuning
- Optimize model parameters using techniques like grid search, random search, or Bayesian optimization.
- Cross-validation is used to ensure model generalization.

8. Model Deployment
- Deploy the trained model to a production environment (e.g., cloud, mobile, web app).
- Ensure integration with real-world data sources.

9. Model Monitoring & Maintenance
- Continuously monitor model performance on new data.
- Retrain the model periodically to maintain accuracy.
- Address concept drift if the data distribution changes over time.

4.1.2 Applications of supervised learning algorithms
Supervised machine learning has a wide range of applications across various industries. Here are some key areas where it is used:

1. Healthcare
- **Disease Prediction & Diagnosis**: Models trained on medical records help diagnose diseases like cancer, diabetes, and COVID-19.
- **Medical Image Classification**: Detecting tumors in X-rays, MRIs, and CT scans using deep learning.

- **Drug Discovery**: Predicting drug effectiveness and side effects.

2. Finance & Banking
- **Fraud Detection**: Identifying fraudulent credit card transactions using anomaly detection.
- **Loan & Credit Scoring**: Assessing creditworthiness based on financial history.
- **Stock Market Prediction**: Forecasting stock prices using historical data.

3. Marketing & E-commerce
- **Customer Segmentation**: Categorizing customers based on purchasing behavior.
- **Recommendation Systems**: Suggesting products on platforms like Amazon, Netflix, and Spotify.
- **Churn Prediction**: Identifying customers likely to leave a service.

4. Natural Language Processing (NLP)
- **Spam Detection**: Filtering out spam emails using text classification.
- **Sentiment Analysis**: Analyzing customer reviews to understand public opinion.
- **Chatbots & Virtual Assistants**: Powering AI assistants like Siri, Alexa, and Google Assistant.

5. Autonomous Vehicles
- **Object Detection & Recognition**: Identifying pedestrians, traffic lights, and obstacles.
- **Lane Detection**: Assisting self-driving cars in staying within lanes.
- **Traffic Sign Recognition**: Helping vehicles obey road signs automatically.

6. Manufacturing & Quality Control
- **Defect Detection**: Identifying faulty products in production lines.
- **Predictive Maintenance**: Forecasting equipment failures before they happen.

7. Cybersecurity
- **Malware Detection**: Identifying malicious software based on patterns.
- **Intrusion Detection Systems (IDS)**: Detecting unauthorized access to networks.

8. Agriculture
- **Crop Disease Detection**: Using image classification to identify plant diseases.
- **Yield Prediction**: Forecasting crop productivity based on climate and soil conditions.

9. Human Resources
- **Resume Screening**: Automating candidate shortlisting based on job descriptions.
- **Employee Attrition Prediction**: Identifying employees likely to leave the company.

10. Speech Recognition
- **Voice Assistants**: Enabling speech-to-text in AI assistants.
- **Language Translation**: Converting spoken words between languages in real time.

4.1.3 Types of supervised Machine learning Algorithms
Supervised learning can be broadly categorized into two types: classification and regression.

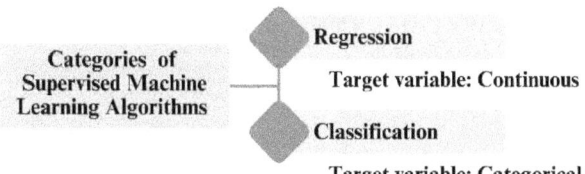

4.1.4 Regression versus Classification

Regression and classification are two main types of supervised learning, but they differ in their goals, outputs, and applications

Regression is used when the output (target variable) is continuous and numerical. It predicts a real-valued output based on input features.

Key Characteristics
- The target variable is continuous (e.g., price, temperature, age).
- The output can take any real number within a range.
- The model estimates a function that maps inputs to a continuous output.

Common Algorithms
- Linear Regression
- Polynomial Regression
- Decision Trees (for regression tasks)
- Random Forest Regression
- Support Vector Regression (SVR)
- Neural Networks (for regression tasks)

Example Use Cases
- Predicting house prices based on size, location, and features.
- Forecasting stock prices based on historical data.
- Estimating sales revenue for a company.
- Predicting temperature based on weather conditions.

Regression analysis is a statistical method to model the relationship between a dependent (target) variable and independent (predictor) variables with one or more independent variables. The goal of regression analysis is to develop a mathematical model or equation that represents the relationship between the independent variables and the target variable. This model can then be used to predict the target variable for new or unseen data points based on their feature values.

For examples
- In an advertising and sales scenario, a machine learning model should predict the sales value when an amount is spent on advertising.
- In the GRE rank and GATE rank scenario, the machine learning model should predict the GATE rank given the student's GRE rank.
- In the speed and time scenario, the machine learning model needs to predict the time it will take to achieve a certain speed. See above three scenario's sample data sets are given below:

Advertisement Rs	Sales Rs	GRE Rank	GATE Rank	Speed Km/hr	Time Hr
2000	1,00,000	80	300	80	200
2500	1,30,000	90	200	90	196
3000	1,80,000	200	330	200	142
3100	1,93,000	320	460	320	125
3300	??	400	??	400	??
3500	??	500	??	500	??

4.2 Regression Analysis

Regression analysis is a statistical method that describes the relationship between a dependent variable (target variable) and one or more independent variables (predictor variables or features). The goal of a regression model is to estimate the parameters or coefficients that represent the relationship between the independent variables and the dependent variable, allowing for predictions or inference about the target variable based on the values of the predictors.

The general form of a regression model can be represented as:

$$Y = \beta_0 + \beta_1 X_1 + \beta_2 X_2 + ... + \beta_p X_p + \varepsilon$$

where

Y is the dependent variable (target variable) to be predicted.

$X_1, X_2, ..., X_p$ are the independent variables (predictor variables or features).

$\beta_0, \beta_1, \beta_2, ..., \beta_p$ are the regression coefficients, representing the impact of each independent variable on the dependent variable.

ε is the error term, representing the unexplained variation in the dependent variable.

The regression coefficients ($\beta_0, \beta_1, \beta_2, ..., \beta_p$) are estimated during the model training process, typically using optimization techniques that minimize the difference between the predicted values and the actual values of the dependent variable.

4.2.1 Regression Line

In linear regression, the regression line is a line that best represents the relationship between the dependent variable and one or more independent variables. It's the line that minimizes the discrepancies between the observed values and the values predicted by the model. It is the line that minimizes the difference between the predicted values and the actual values of the dependent variable. It is used to predict the value of dependent variable Y of the known value of independent variable X. The regression line is often visualized in a scatter plot, where the observed data points are plotted, and the line is drawn to best fit the pattern of the data. The line is positioned to minimize the vertical distance between the data points and the line, representing the residuals or errors.

Line of best fit

The term "best fitting" refers to the quality of the fit between the regression model and the observed data points. It indicates how well the regression model captures the underlying relationship between the independent variable(s) and the dependent variable. A "best fitting" regression model is one that minimizes the discrepancy between the predicted values from the model and the actual values of the dependent variable. The goal is to find the regression coefficients (intercept and slope) that produce the smallest difference between the predicted values and the observed values.

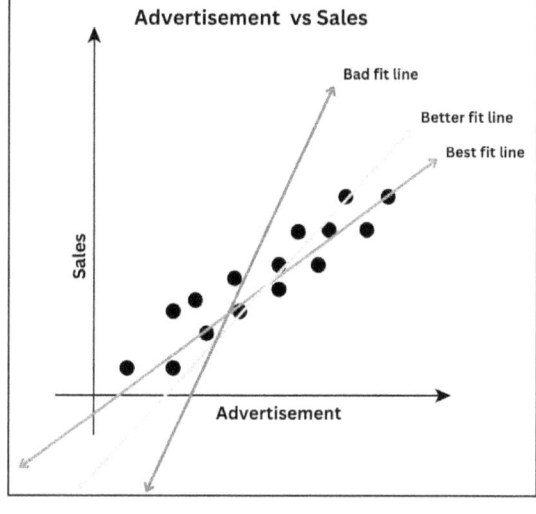

Overfitting vs underfitting

Overfitting: Overfitting occurs when a model learns the training data too well, to the point that it captures noise and random fluctuations in the data instead of the true underlying pattern. An overfit model performs extremely well on the training data but fails to generalize well to new, unseen data. Signs of overfitting include excessively low training error but high testing error.

Causes of overfitting:

Using a complex model with a high number of parameters relative to the amount of training data.

- Insufficient regularization or lack of constraints on the model's complexity.
- Presence of outliers or noise in the training data.
- Training on too few data points or using a highly specific subset of the data.

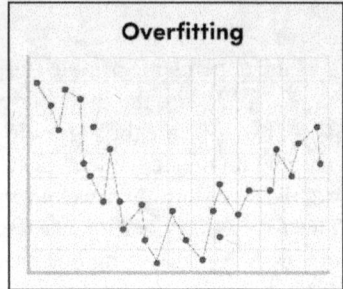

Effects of overfitting:

- Poor performance on new data.
- High variance in predictions.
- Difficulty in interpreting the model due to excessive complexity.

Methods to address overfitting:

i.   Reduce model complexity by using simpler models or reducing the number of features.
ii.   Regularize the model by adding regularization terms, such as L1 or L2 regularization, to the objective function.
iii. Gather more training data to provide a better representation of the underlying population.
iv.   Use techniques like cross-validation and early stopping to identify the optimal training duration and prevent overfitting.

Underfitting: Underfitting occurs when a model is too simple to capture the underlying patterns in the training data. It fails to capture the complexity of the relationship between the features and the target variable. An underfit model performs poorly on both the training and testing data and shows high bias.

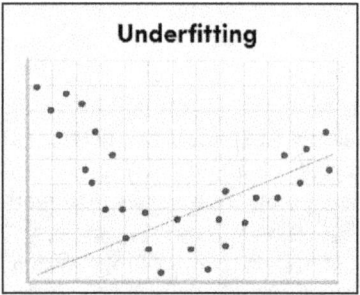

Causes of underfitting:

- Using an overly simple model that cannot capture the complexity of the data.
- Insufficient training or not allowing the model enough iterations to learn from the data.
- Ignoring relevant features or not incorporating enough information from the data.

Effects of underfitting:

- High bias and poor performance on both training and testing data.
- Inability to capture the underlying patterns and relationships in the data.

Methods to address underfitting:

- Increase model complexity by using more powerful models or adding more features.
- Gather more relevant data or engineer additional informative features.
- Use techniques like boosting, bagging, or ensemble methods to combine multiple models and capture more complex patterns.

The aim in machine learning is to strike a balance between overfitting and underfitting by finding the optimal level of model complexity that generalizes well to new, unseen data.

This is achieved through techniques like regularization, feature engineering, model selection, and hyper parameter tuning.

4.3 Least Squared Method

The Least Squares method is a statistical technique used to find the equation of the best-fitting curve or line to a set of data points by minimizing the sum of the squared differences between the observed values and the values predicted by the model. The method works by minimizing the sum of the offsets or residuals of points from the plotted curve. Least squares regression is used to predict the behavior of dependent variables.

The least square regression method is a technique commonly used in regression analysis. It is a mathematical method used to find the best-fit line that represents the relationship between the dependent variable and an independent variable in such a way that the error is minimized

The line of the best fit is drawn across a scatter plot of data points in order to represent the relationship between those data points

The general form of the regression line is:

$$Y = \beta_0 + \beta_1 X$$

Where

Y is the dependent variable, X is the independent variable, β_1 is the slope of the regression line and β_0 is the Y-intercept

- The regression line $Y = \beta_0 + \beta_1 X$ which intercepts the Y axis at β_0 i.e $(0, \beta_0)$ and passes through means of variables $\bar{X}$(independent) and $\bar{Y}$(dependent) that means it passes through $(\bar{X}, \bar{Y})$
- Let us the below table and graph to understand the sample data set and regression line

Independent Variable-X	Dependent Variable-Y
--	--
--	--
--	--
Mean $\bar{X}$	Mean $\bar{Y}$

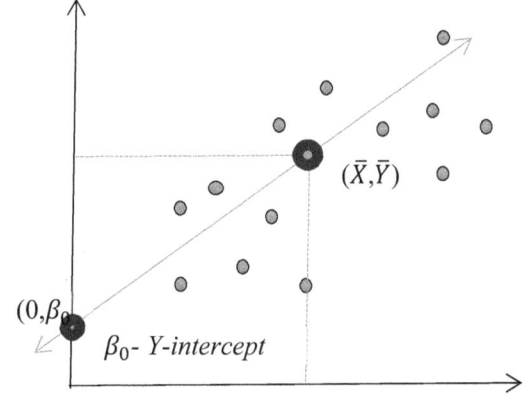

68

Residuals

residuals are the differences between the observed values and the values predicted by the regression model.

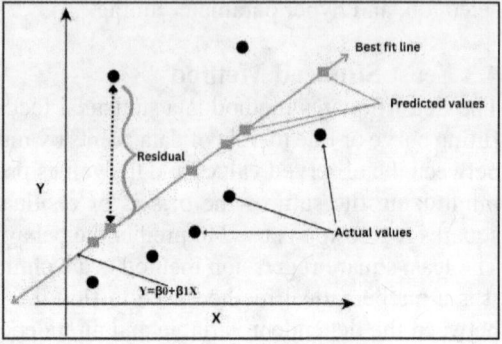

Understanding Residuals

1. **Observed Value:** This is the actual value from the dataset, denoted as y_i for the ith data point.

2. **Predicted Value:** This is the value predicted by the regression model for the ith data point, denoted as $\hat{y}_i$

3. **Residual:** The residual for the ith data point is the difference between the observed value and the predicted value, denoted by e_i:

$$Residual_i = y_i - \hat{y}_i$$

Or

$$e_{i=}y_i - \hat{y}_i$$

Key Points About Residuals

- **Interpretation:** Residuals indicate how far off the model's predictions are from the actual data. A residual of zero means the model's prediction perfectly matches the observed value for that data point.

- **Positive Residual:** If $y_i > \hat{y}_i$, the residual is positive, meaning the model's prediction is too low.

- **Negative Residual:** If $y_i < \hat{y}_i$, the residual is negative, meaning the model's prediction is too high.

Uses of Residuals

1. **Model Fit:** Residuals help in assessing how well the regression model fits the data. A good model will have residuals that are randomly scattered around zero, with no discernible pattern.

2. **Diagnostics:** Analyzing residuals can reveal issues such as non-linearity, heteroscedasticity (non-constant variance of residuals), or outliers. For example:
   - **Patterned Residuals:** If residuals show a pattern (e.g., a curve), it suggests the model may not adequately capture the relationship between variables.
   - **Heteroscedasticity:** If the variance of residuals increases or decreases systematically with the fitted values, it may indicate issues with the model's assumptions.

3. **Goodness-of-Fit:** Metrics like the **Residual Sum of Squares (RSS)**, which is the sum of the squared residuals, are used to quantify how well the model fits the data. Lower RSS values indicate a better fit.

Sum of the Squares of Residuals(SSR)

The Sum of Squared Residuals (SSR), also known as the Sum of Squared Errors (SSE) or the Residual Sum of Squares (RSS), is a key metric in regression analysis that quantifies how well a regression model fits a dataset. It measures the total discrepancy between the observed values and the values predicted by the model.

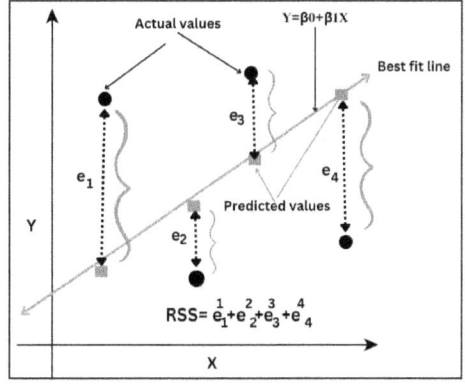

The Sum of Squared Residuals is calculated by taking the residuals (differences between observed and predicted values), squaring each residual to eliminate negative values, and then summing these squared residuals.

Formula

For a set of n data points, where y_i is the observed/actual value and $\hat{y}_i$ is the predicted value for the ith data point, the Sum of Squared Residuals is given by:

$$SSR = \sum_{i=1}^{n}(y_i - \hat{y}_i)^2 \ \ or \ \ \sum_{i=1}^{n} e_i^2$$

4.3.1 Regression Evaluation Metrics

A regression evaluation metric is a quantitative measure used to assess the performance of a regression model. These metrics help determine how well the model predicts the dependent variable (target) based on the independent variables (features). They are crucial for understanding the accuracy, reliability, and usefulness of the model.

1. Mean Absolute Error (MAE)

- *Description:* MAE measures the average magnitude of the errors in a set of predictions. It gives the average absolute difference between the observed actual outcomes and the predictions, without considering the direction of the error.
- *Formula:* $MAE = \frac{1}{n}\sum_{i=1}^{n}|y_i - \hat{y}_i|$
  Where
  y_i is the actual value for observation i.
  $\hat{y}_i$ is the predicted value for observation i.
  n is the number of observations.
- *Interpretation:* Lower MAE values indicate better model performance. MAE is easy to interpret as it provides errors in the same units as the target variable.

2. Mean Squared Error (MSE)

- *Description:* MSE measures the average of the squared differences between the actual values and the predicted values. It emphasizes larger errors more than smaller ones due to the squaring of differences.
- *Formula:* $MSE = \frac{1}{n}\sum_{i=1}^{n}(y_i - \hat{y}_i)^2$
  where
  y_i is the actual value for observation i.
  $\hat{y}_i$ is the predicted value for observation i.
  n is the number of observations.
- Interpretation: Lower MSE values indicate better model performance. MSE is useful for highlighting models that have fewer large errors.

3. Root Mean Squared Error (RMSE)
- *Description:* RMSE is the square root of the MSE and provides a measure of the average magnitude of the errors, in the same units as the target variable.
- *Formula:* RMSE$=\sqrt{\frac{1}{n}\sum_{i=1}^{n}(y_i - \hat{y}_i)^2}$

where
> y_i is the actual value for observation i.
> $\hat{y}_i$ is the predicted value for observation i.
> n is the number of observations.

- Interpretation: Lower RMSE values indicate better model performance. RMSE is useful for understanding the standard deviation of the residuals.

4. R-squared (Coefficient of Determination)
- *Description:* R-squared represents the proportion of the variance in the dependent variable that is predictable from the independent variables. It indicates how well the model explains the variability of the target variable.
- *Formula:* R2$=1 - \frac{SSR}{SST}$

Where
> SSR is the Sum of Squares of Residuals: $\sum_{i=1}^{n}(y_i - \hat{y}_i)^2$
> SST is the Total Sum of Squares: $\sum_{i=1}^{n}(y_i - \bar{y}_i)^2$
> $\bar{y}_i$ is the mean of the actual values.

- *Interpretation:* R^2 values range from 0 to 1, where a value of 1 means the model explains all the variance in the target variable, and a value of 0 means it explains none.

  $R^2=1$: This indicates that the model explains all the variance in the dependent variable. The predictions perfectly match the actual values, meaning there is no residual error.

  $R^2=0$: This indicates that the model explains none of the variance in the dependent variable. The model's predictions are no better than simply using the mean of the dependent variable as the prediction.

  $0<R^2<1$: This range indicates that the model explains some portion of the variance. The closer R^2 is to 1, the better the model explains the variability of the dependent variable.

5. Adjusted R-squared
- *Description:* Adjusted R-squared adjusts the R-squared value for the number of predictors in the model. It accounts for the fact that adding more predictors can increase R-squared even if those predictors are not truly relevant.
- *Formula:* Adjusted R2$=1 - \left(\frac{(1-R^2)(n-1)}{n-p-1}\right)$

where
> n is the number of observations.
> p is the number of predictors in the model.
> R^2 is the R-squared value.

- *Interpretation:* Adjusted R^2 can decrease if additional predictors do not improve the model significantly. It is useful for comparing models with different numbers of predictors.

  Range: Like R^2, the Adjusted R^2 value ranges from 0 to 1. However, unlike R^2, Adjusted R^2 can be negative if the model is poorly fitting the data (i.e., if the model performs worse than a horizontal line representing the mean of the dependent variable).

Comparison: Adjusted R^2 is particularly useful when comparing models with different numbers of predictors. A higher Adjusted R^2 indicates a model that explains a higher proportion of the variance in the dependent variable, adjusted for the number of predictors.

Model Improvement: An increase in Adjusted R^2 when adding a predictor suggests that the new predictor is contributing valuable information. Conversely, if Adjusted R^2 decreases, it indicates that the additional predictor does not improve the model or might even be worsening the fit.

High Adjusted R^2: A higher Adjusted R^2 value indicates a better model fit after adjusting for the number of predictors. For many applications, an Adjusted R^2 above 0.7 is considered good, but this can vary by field and context.

6. Mean Absolute Percentage Error (MAPE)

- *Description:* MAPE measures the prediction accuracy as a percentage of the actual values. It provides a normalized measure of error.
- *Formula:* $MAPE = \frac{1}{n} \sum_{i=1}^{n} \left| \frac{y_i - \hat{y}_i}{y_i} \right| \times 100\%$

  Where

  > y_i is the actual value for observation i.
  > $\hat{y}_i$ is the predicted value for observation i.
  > n is the number of observations.

- *Interpretation:* Lower MAPE values indicate better model performance. MAPE is useful for understanding errors in percentage terms, which can be easier to interpret relative to the size of the actual values.

7. F-statistic

- *Description:* The F-statistic evaluates the overall significance of the regression model by comparing it with a model with no predictors (intercept only). It tests whether at least one predictor variable has a non-zero coefficient.
- *Formula:* $F = \frac{(SSR/p)}{(SSE/(n-p-1))}$

  where:

  > SSR is the Sum of Squares due to Regression (explained variance):
  > $\sum_{i=1}^{n} (y_i - \bar{y}_i)^2$
  > SSE is the Sum of Squares due to Error (residual variance):
  > $\sum_{i=1}^{n} (y_i - \hat{y}_i)^2$
  > p is the number of predictors.
  > n is the number of observations.

- *Interpretation:* A higher F-statistic value indicates that the model explains a significant amount of the variance in the dependent variable relative to the variance unexplained by the model.

Summary

These metrics each provide unique insights into the performance of a regression model. They help you understand the model's accuracy, its fit, and how well it generalizes to new data. Choosing the right metric often depends on the specific goals and context of your analysis.

4.4 Regression Algorithms

4.5.1 Linear Regression

Linear regression is a fundamental statistical and machine learning technique used to model the relationship between a dependent variable and one or more independent variables. It is widely employed for predictive modeling, trend analysis, and forecasting. **Linear regression** is a method for modeling the relationship between a continuous dependent variable Y and one or more independent variables X. The goal is to find the best-fitting linear relationship between the variables.

Objectives of Linear Regression

1. *Predictive Modeling:* To predict the value of the dependent variable Y based on the values of independent variables X.
2. *Trend Analysis:* To identify and understand the trends and relationships between variables.
3. *Estimation of Relationships:* To estimate the magnitude and direction of the relationship between dependent and independent variables.

Assumptions of Linear Regression

1. *Linearity:* The relationship between the dependent variable and the independent variables is linear.
2. *Independence:* The residuals (errors) are independent of each other.
3. *Homoscedasticity:* The residuals have constant variance at all levels of the independent variables.
4. *Normality:* The residuals are normally distributed (mainly important for inference).

How Linear Regression Works

1. *Model Fitting:* The goal is to find the line (in simple linear regression) or hyperplane (in multiple linear regression) that best fits the data. This is typically done by minimizing the sum of the squared residuals (errors) between the observed values and the values predicted by the model.
2. *Estimation of Parameters:* The coefficients $\beta 0, \beta 1, ..., \beta p$ are estimated using methods such as Ordinary Least Squares (OLS), which minimizes the sum of squared errors.
3. *Prediction:* Once the model is trained, it can be used to predict the dependent variable Y for new values of the independent variables X.

4.4.1.1 Simple Linear Regression

Purpose: Models the relationship between one dependent variable and one independent variable.

Formula:

$$y = \beta 0 + \beta 1 x + \epsilon$$

where

- y is the dependent variable.
- x is the independent variable.
- β_0 is the y-intercept (the value of y when x=0).
- β_1 is the slope of the line (the change in y for a one-unit change in x).
- ϵ is the error term (the difference between the observed and predicted values).

Example: Predicting a person's weight based on their height.

Python code Simple Linear regression model implementation

```
# Importing Necessary Libraries
import numpy as np
import pandas as pd
import seaborn as sns
```

```
import matplotlib.pyplot as plt
%matplotlib inline
```
#Loading dataset
#Download the real time project dataset from kaggle.com and load the dataset as below code:
```
ad=pd.read_csv("L:\\DataScienceBook\\CONTENT\\ Advertising.csv")
print(ad) # print dataframe "ad"
```
DataFrame which consists of 200 rows and 4 co

	TV	radio	newspaper	sales
0	230.1	37.8	69.2	22.1
1	44.5	39.3	45.1	10.4
2	17.2	45.9	69.3	9.3
3	151.5	41.3	58.5	18.5
4	180.8	10.8	58.4	12.9

Data Preprocessing
Information about Data set
```
ad.info()
```

```
<class 'pandas.core.frame.DataFrame'>
RangeIndex: 200 entries, 0 to 199
Data columns (total 4 columns):
 #   Column     Non-Null Count   Dtype
---  ------     --------------   -----
 0   TV         200 non-null     float64
 1   radio      200 non-null     float64
 2   newspaper  200 non-null     float64
 3   sales      200 non-null     float64
dtypes: float64(4)
memory usage: 6.4 KB
```

checking the Null values in data set
```
Ad.isnull.sum()
```

```
TV         0
radio      0
newspaper  0
sales      0
```

Correlation coefficients
```
sns.heatmap(ad.corr(),annot=True)
plt.show()
```

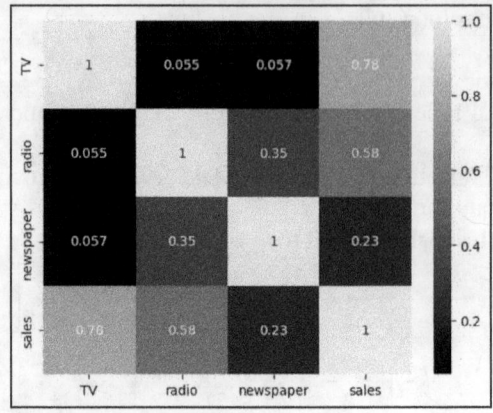

```
#creating single new column for input variables
ad['invest']=ad['TV']+ad['radio']+ad['newspaper']
print(ad)
```

	TV	radio	newspaper	sales	invest
0	230.1	37.8	69.2	22.1	337.1
1	44.5	39.3	45.1	10.4	128.9
2	17.2	45.9	69.3	9.3	132.4
3	151.5	41.3	58.5	18.5	251.3
4	180.8	10.8	58.4	12.9	250.0

```
# checking outliers in data set
sns.boxplot(x=ad.invest)
plt.title("Outlier in Invest")
plt.show()
```

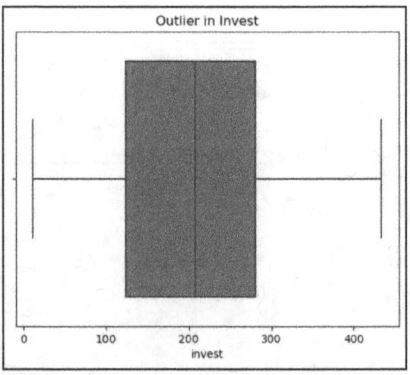

```
#Splitting train set and test set
x=ad.drop(columns=['TV','radio','newspaper','sales'])
# Droping all varaibles except  input variable(invest)
y=ad.drop(columns=['TV','radio','newspaper','invest'])# target variable only
print(x)
print(y)
```

	invest
0	337.1
1	128.9
2	132.4
3	251.3
4	250.0

	sales
0	22.1
1	10.4
2	9.3
3	18.5
4	12.9

Data Spitting for training and testing

x: invest (Input/Independent)	y:sales (Output/Target/Dependent)
80 % Train Data	80 % Train Data
20 % Test Data	20 % Test Data

```
from sklearn.model_selection import train_test_split
x_train,x_test,y_train,y_test=train_test_split(x,y,test_size=0.2,random_state=50)
print(x_train.size,x_test.size)   160 40
print(y_train.size,y_test.size) )   160 40
```

```
# Single linear regression  model building
# One input and one Output variable
# Model  Y = β0 + β1X + ε
```

```
from sklearn.linear_model import LinearRegression
model=LinearRegression()
```

```
print(model.intercept_)    # Y Intercept: β0
        array([4.02779389])
print(model.coef_) # Line Slope: β1
        array([[0.05033333]])
```

```
# Model: Y=0.05033*X+4.02779389
```

```
#Predictions
train_predictions=model.predict(x_train)
test_predictions=model.predict(x_test)
```

```
#Evaluation Metrices
from sklearn.metrics import mean_squared_error
```

```
test_RMSE=np.sqrt(mean_squared_error(y_test,test_predictions))
train_RMSE=np.sqrt(mean_squared_error(y_train,train_predictions))
print(train_RMSE,test_RMSE)
        2.58295787615846   2.6376721538828325
print(model.score(x_train,y_train))
        0.7779513559724153
print(model.score(x_test,y_test))
        0.5113516313797599
# So, finally  the model got 77 % accuracy in   training  data and 51 % accuracy in  testing
```

4.4.1.2 Multiple Linear Regression

In multiple linear regression, the goal is to fit a linear equation to the data that minimizes the difference between the observed values of the dependent variable and the predicted values. The equation for a multiple linear regression model can be written as:

$$Y = \beta_0 + \beta_1 X_1 + \beta_2 X_2 + ... + \beta_p X_p + \varepsilon$$

Where:

Y is the dependent variable or the variable to be predicted.

X_1, X_2, ..., X_p are the independent variables or predictors.

β_0, β_1, β_2, ..., β_p are the regression coefficients or parameters that determine the relationship between the independent variables and the dependent variable.

ε is the error term, representing the unexplained variation in the dependent variable.

The regression coefficients represent the change in the dependent variable for a one-unit change in the corresponding independent variable, assuming all other independent variables are held constant.

To estimate the regression coefficients, the model uses a method called least squares, which minimizes the sum of the squared differences between the observed and predicted values. The coefficients can be estimated using various techniques, such as ordinary least squares (OLS), gradient descent, or matrix methods.

Multiple linear regression is commonly used for prediction, forecasting, and understanding the relationships between variables in fields such as economics, finance, social sciences, and machine learning. Before fitting a multiple linear regression model, it is important to check assumptions, such as linearity, independence, and normality of errors, to ensure the validity of the model and interpret the results correctly.

Python code to implement Multiple Linear Regression

```
# Importing Necessary Libraries
import numpy as np
import pandas as pd
import seaborn as sns
import matplotlib.pyplot as plt
%matplotlib inline
#Loading dataset
#Download the real time project dataset from kaggle.com and load the dataset as below
code:
ad=pd.read_csv("L:\\DataScienceBook\\CONTENT\\ Advertising.csv")

#Dataset splitting
X=ad.drop(columns="sales")
y=ad["sales"]
from sklearn.model_selection import train_test_split
X_train,X_test,y_train,y_test=train_test_split(X,y,test_size=0.3,random_state=99)
# Multiple linear regression  model building
from sklearn.linear_model import LinearRegression
model=LinearRegression()
model.fit(X_train,y_train)
print(model.intercept_)   #  y intercept
        2.576941878933358
 print(model.coef_)_  # Coefficients
[0.04648032, 0.18594407, 0.00556825]
```

```
#Predictions
train_predictions=model.predict(X_train)
test_predictions=model.predict(X_test)

#Evaluation Metrics
from sklearn.metrics import mean_squared_error
test_rmse=np.sqrt(mean_squared_error(y_test,test_predictions))
train_rmse=np.sqrt(mean_squared_error(y_train,train_predictions))
print(train_rmse,test_rmse)
      1.7735313528169045  1.435542628944345
Print(model.score(X_train,y_train))
 0.8850092451204061

print(model.score(X_test,y_test))
0.9197848691418977
```

So, finally the model got 88 % accuracy in training data and 91 % accuracy in testing

4.4.2 Polynomial Regression
Polynomial regression is an extension of linear regression that models the relationship between a dependent variable and one or more independent variables as an nnn-th degree polynomial. Unlike linear regression, which assumes a linear relationship between the variables, polynomial regression can capture more complex relationships by fitting a polynomial equation to the data.

Polynomial regression allows for a nonlinear relationship between the independent variable(s) and the dependent variable by fitting a polynomial equation. It is particularly useful when the data exhibits curvature or nonlinear trends that a simple linear model cannot adequately capture.

Polynomial Regression Model
In polynomial regression, the relationship between the dependent variable y and the independent variable x is modeled as:

$$y=\beta_0 + \beta_1 x + \beta_2 x^2 + \beta_3 x^3 + \cdots + \beta_n x^n + \epsilon$$

where:
- β_0 is the intercept.
- $\beta_1, \beta_2, \ldots, \beta_n$ are the coefficients for the polynomial terms.
- $x^2, x^3, \ldots, x^n$ are the polynomial terms of the independent variable.
- ϵ epsilon is the error term (the difference between observed and predicted values).

Need for Polynomial Regression:
The need of Polynomial Regression in ML can be understood in the below points:
- o   If we apply a linear model on a linear dataset, then it provides us a good result as we have seen in Simple Linear Regression, but if we apply the same model without any modification on a non-linear dataset, then it will produce a drastic output. Due to which loss function will increase, the error rate will be high, and accuracy will be decreased.
- o   So for such cases, where data points are arranged in a non-linear fashion, we need the Polynomial Regression model. We can understand it in a better way using the below comparison diagram of the linear dataset and non-linear dataset.

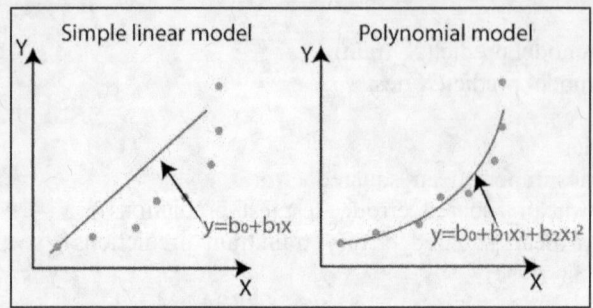

- o In the above image, we have taken a dataset which is arranged non-linearly. So if we try to cover it with a linear model, then we can clearly see that it hardly covers any data point. On the other hand, a curve is suitable to cover most of the data points, which is of the Polynomial model.
- o Hence, *if the datasets are arranged in a non-linear fashion, then we should use the Polynomial Regression model instead of Simple Linear Regression.*

A Polynomial Regression algorithm is also called Polynomial Linear Regression because it does not depend on the variables, instead, it depends on the coefficients, which are arranged in a linear fashion

Key Concepts
1. *Polynomial Degree:*
   - o The degree of the polynomial (n) determines the complexity of the model. A higher degree allows the model to fit more complex curves, but it also increases the risk of overfitting.
2. *Overfitting:*
   - o Overfitting occurs when the model becomes too complex and starts capturing noise in the data rather than the underlying trend. This can lead to poor generalization to new data.
3. *Feature Engineering:*
   - o In polynomial regression, the independent variable is transformed into polynomial features (e.g., x^2, x^3). These features are used to fit the polynomial model.

Applications of Polynomial Regression
- *Curve Fitting:* When data shows a nonlinear trend, polynomial regression can provide a better fit than linear regression.
- *Economics:* Modeling nonlinear economic trends or relationships.
- *Engineering:* Analyzing complex systems where relationships between variables are not linear.
- *Biology:* Modeling growth curves or other nonlinear biological phenomena.

Choosing the Degree of Polynomial
- *Low Degree*: Captures simple trends but may underfit if the true relationship is complex.
- *High Degree:* Captures complex trends but may overfit, especially if the dataset is small.

Polynomial regression is a powerful tool for modeling nonlinear relationships and can be particularly useful when the underlying relationship between variables is more complex than a simple linear trend. However, care must be taken to choose the appropriate polynomial degree to balance model complexity and generalization performance

Python code to implement Polynomial regression

```
#Importing the libraries
import numpy as np
import matplotlib.pyplot as plt
import pandas as pd
#Importing the dataset
dataset = pd.read_csv('Position_Salaries.csv')
X = dataset.iloc[:, 1:-1].values
y = dataset.iloc[:, -1].values
#Training the Linear Regression model on the whole dataset
from sklearn.linear_model import LinearRegression
lin_reg = LinearRegression()
lin_reg.fit(X, y)
LinearRegression(copy_X=True, fit_intercept=True, n_jobs=None, normalize=False)
#Training the Polynomial Regression model on the whole dataset
from sklearn.preprocessing import PolynomialFeatures
poly_reg = PolynomialFeatures(degree = 4)
X_poly = poly_reg.fit_transform(X)
lin_reg_2 = LinearRegression()
lin_reg_2.fit(X_poly, y)
LinearRegression(copy_X=True, fit_intercept=True, n_jobs=None, normalize=False)
#Visualising the Linear Regression results
plt.scatter(X, y, color = 'red')
plt.plot(X, lin_reg.predict(X), color = 'blue')
plt.title('Truth or Bluff (Linear Regression)')
plt.xlabel('Position Level')
plt.ylabel('Salary')
plt.show()
```

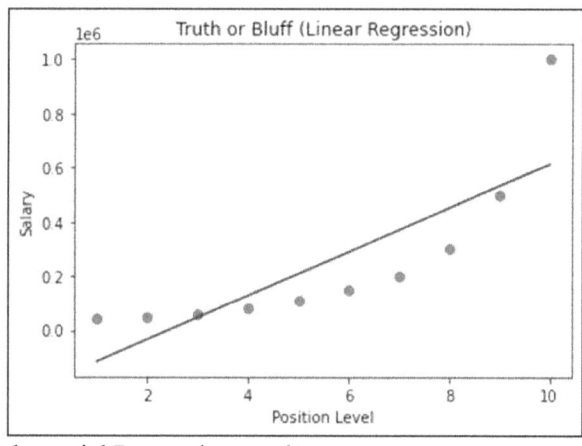

```
Visualising the Polynomial Regression results
plt.scatter(X, y, color = 'red')
plt.plot(X, lin_reg_2.predict(poly_reg.fit_transform(X)), color = 'blue')
plt.title('Truth or Bluff (Polynomial Regression)')
plt.xlabel('Position level')
plt.ylabel('Salary')
plt.show()
```

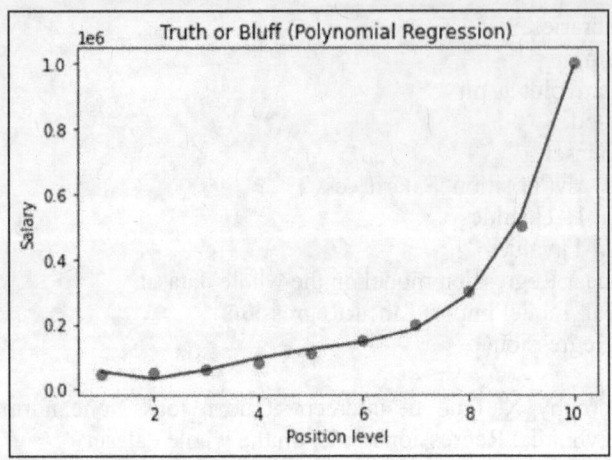

Visualising the Polynomial Regression results (for higher resolution and smoother curve)
X_grid = np.arange(min(X), max(X), 0.1)
X_grid = X_grid.reshape((len(X_grid), 1))
plt.scatter(X, y, color = 'red')
plt.plot(X_grid, lin_reg_2.predict(poly_reg.fit_transform(X_grid)), color = 'blue')
plt.title('Truth or Bluff (Polynomial Regression)')
plt.xlabel('Position level')
plt.ylabel('Salary')
plt.show()

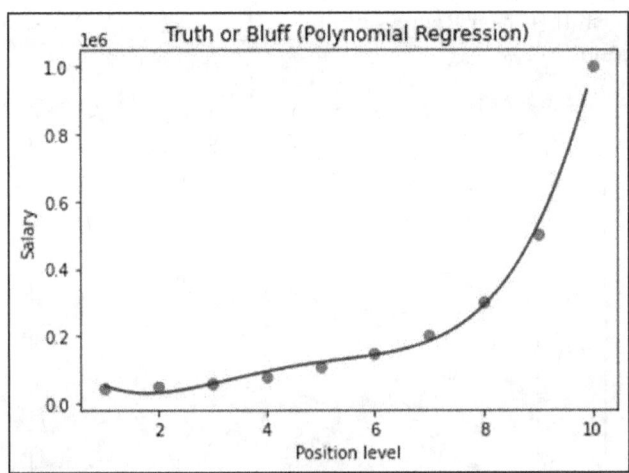

# Predicting a new result with Linear Regression
lin_reg.predict([[6.5]])
        array([330378.78787879])
#Predicting a new result with Polynomial Regression
lin_reg_2.predict(poly_reg.fit_transform([[6.5]]))
        array([158862.45265155])

4.5 Regularization

Regularization is a technique used in machine learning and statistics to improve the performance and generalization ability of a model by preventing overfitting. Overfitting occurs when a model learns the noise or random fluctuations in the training data rather than the underlying pattern, leading to poor performance on new, unseen data. Regularization helps address this issue by adding a penalty to the model's complexity.

Regularization aims to Reduce Model Complexity by discouraging overly complex models (e.g., with large coefficients), regularization helps to simplify the model, making it more robust to variations in the data. Improve Generalization: A regularized model is less likely to fit the noise in the training data and thus performs better on unseen data. Regularization is a set of methods for reducing overfitting in machine learning models. Typically, regularization trades a marginal decrease in training accuracy for an increase in generalizability. Regularization encompasses a range of techniques to correct for overfitting in machine learning models. In general, regularization is a process in which an additional penalty function is introduced to solve an ill-posed problem or prevent overfitting of the model

What with regularization

1. *Complexity Control:* Regularization helps control model complexity by preventing overfitting to training data, resulting in better generalization to new data.
2. *Preventing Overfitting:* One way to prevent overfitting is to use regularization, which penalizes large coefficients and constrains their magnitudes, thereby preventing a model from becoming overly complex and memorizing the training data instead of learning its underlying patterns.
3. *Balancing Bias and Variance:* Regularization can help balance the trade-off between model bias (underfitting) and model variance (overfitting) in machine learning, which leads to improved performance.
4. *Feature Selection:* Some regularization methods, such as L1 regularization (Lasso), promote sparse solutions that drive some feature coefficients to zero. This automatically selects important features while excluding less important ones.
5. *Handling Multicollinearity:* When features are highly correlated (multicollinearity), regularization can stabilize the model by reducing coefficient sensitivity to small data changes.
6. *Generalization:* Regularized models learn underlying patterns of data for better generalization to new data, instead of memorizing specific examples.

Benefits of Regularization

1. Regularization improves model generalization by reducing overfitting. Regularized models learn underlying patterns, while overfit models memorize noise in training data.
2. Regularization techniques such as L1 (Lasso) L1 regularization simplifies models and improves interpretability by reducing coefficients of less important features to zero.
3. Regularization improves model performance by preventing excessive weighting of outliers or irrelevant features.
4. Regularization makes models stable across different subsets of the data. It reduces the sensitivity of model outputs to minor changes in the training set.
5. Regularization prevents models from becoming overly complex, which is especially important when dealing with limited data or noisy environments.
6. Regularization can help handle multicollinearity (high correlation between features) by reducing the magnitudes of correlated coefficients.
7. Regularization introduces hyperparameters (e.g., alpha or lambda) that control the strength of regularization. This allows fine-tuning models to achieve the right balance between bias and variance.
8. Regularization promotes consistent model performance across different datasets. It reduces the risk of dramatic performance changes when encountering new data.

4.5.1 Regularization techniques

Regularization is a technique used to reduce errors by fitting the function appropriately on the given training set and avoiding overfitting. The commonly used regularization techniques are :

1. Lasso Regularization – L1 Regularization
2. Ridge Regularization – L2 Regularization
3. Elastic Net Regularization – L1 and L2 Regularization

4 .5.2 Bias and Variance

In machine learning, an error is a measure of how accurately an algorithm can make predictions for the previously unknown dataset. if the machine learning model is not accurate, it can make predictions errors, and these prediction errors are usually known as Bias and Variance. In machine learning, these errors will always be present as there is always a slight difference between the model predictions and actual predictions. The main aim of ML/data science analysts is to reduce these errors in order to get more accurate results. On the basis of these errors, the machine learning model is selected that can perform best on the particular dataset. There are mainly two types of errors in machine learning, which are:

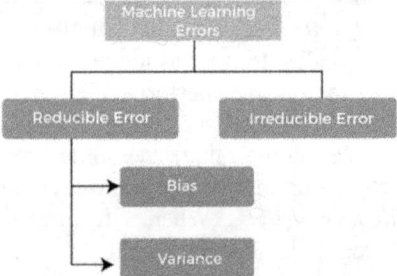

Reducible errors: These errors can be reduced to improve the model accuracy. Such errors can further be classified into bias and Variance.

Irreducible errors: These errors will always be present in the model

a) *Bias:* In general, a machine learning model analyses the data, find patterns in it and make predictions. While training, the model learns these patterns in the dataset and applies them to test data for prediction. While making predictions, a difference occurs between prediction values made by the model and actual values/expected values, and this difference is known as bias errors or Errors due to bias. It can be defined as an inability of machine learning algorithms such as Linear Regression to capture the true relationship between the data points. Each algorithm begins with some amount of bias because bias occurs from assumptions in the model, which makes the target function simple to learn. A model has either:

o *Low Bias:* A low bias model will make fewer assumptions about the form of the target function.

o *High Bias:* A model with a high bias makes more assumptions, and the model becomes unable to capture the important features of our dataset. A high bias model also cannot perform well on new data.

Generally, a linear algorithm has a high bias, as it makes them learn fast. The simpler the algorithm, the higher the bias it has likely to be introduced. Whereas a nonlinear algorithm often has low bias.Some examples of machine learning algorithms with low bias are Decision Trees, k-Nearest Neighbours and Support Vector Machines. At the same time, an algorithm with high bias is Linear Regression, Linear Discriminant Analysis and Logistic Regression.

Let Y be the true value of a parameter, and let $\hat{Y}$ be an estimator of Y based on a sample of data. Then, the bias of the estimator $\hat{Y}$ is given by:

$$\text{Bias } (\bar{Y}) = E(\hat{Y}) - Y$$

where $E(\hat{Y})$ is the expected value of the estimator $\hat{Y}$. It is the measurement of the model that how well it fits the data.

Ways to reduce High Bias:
High bias mainly occurs due to a much simple model. Below are some ways to reduce the high bias:
- o   Increase the input features as the model is underfitted.
- o   Decrease the regularization term.
- o   Use more complex models, such as including some polynomial features.

b)   ***Variance:*** The variance would specify the amount of variation in the prediction if the different training data was used. In simple words, variance tells that how much a random variable is different from its expected value. Ideally, a model should not vary too much from one training dataset to another, which means the algorithm should be good in understanding the hidden mapping between inputs and output variables. Variance errors are either of low variance or high variance.

Low variance means there is a small variation in the prediction of the target function with changes in the training data set. At the same time, High variance shows a large variation in the prediction of the target function with changes in the training dataset.

A model that shows high variance learns a lot and perform well with the training dataset, and does not generalize well with the unseen dataset. As a result, such a model gives good results with the training dataset but shows high error rates on the test dataset.

Since, with high variance, the model learns too much from the dataset, it leads to overfitting of the model. A model with high variance has the below problems:
- o   A high variance model leads to overfitting.
- o   Increase model complexities.

Usually, nonlinear algorithms have a lot of flexibility to fit the model, and have high variance.

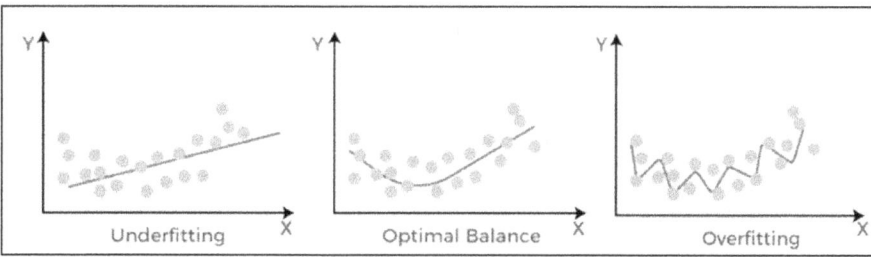

Let Y be the actual values of the target variable, and $\hat{Y}$ be the predicted values of the target variable. Then the variance of a model can be measured as the expected value of the square of the difference between predicted values and the expected value of the predicted values

$$\text{Variance} = E[(\hat{Y} - E[\hat{Y}])^2]$$

Where $E[\hat{Y}]$ is the expected value of the predicted values. Here, the expected value is averaged over all the training data.

Some examples of machine learning algorithms with low variance are, Linear Regression, Logistic Regression, and Linear discriminant analysis. At the same time, algorithms with high variance are decision tree, Support Vector Machine, and K-nearest neighbours.

Ways to Reduce High Variance:

○ Reduce the input features or number of parameters as a model is overfitted.
○ Do not use a much complex model.
○ Increase the training data.
○ Increase the Regularization term.

Different Combinations of Bias-Variance

There are four possible combinations of bias and variances, which are represented by the below diagram:

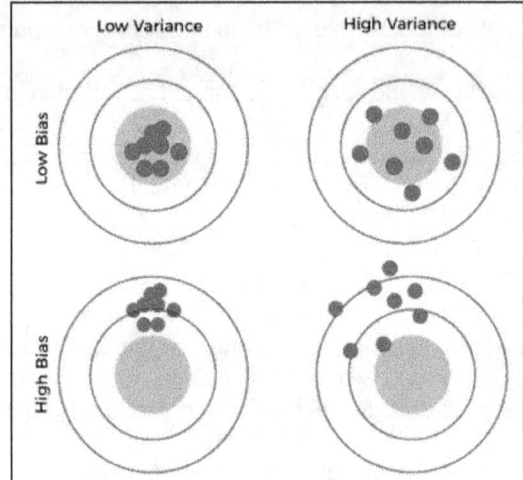

(a) ***High Bias, Low Variance:*** A model that has high bias and low variance is considered to be underfitting.
- **Model**: Simple model (e.g., linear regression on complex data).
- **Training Error**: High.
- **Testing Error**: High.
- **Performance**: Underfitting.

(b) ***High Variance, Low Bias:*** A model that has high variance and low bias is considered to be overfitting.
- **Model**: Complex model (e.g., high-degree polynomial regression).
- **Training Error**: Low.
- **Testing Error**: High.
- **Performance**: Overfitting

(c) ***High-Bias, High-Variance:*** A model with high bias and high variance cannot capture underlying patterns and is too sensitive to training data changes. On average, the model will generate unreliable and inconsistent predictions.

(d) ***Low Bias, Low Variance:*** A model with low bias and low variance can capture data patterns and handle variations in training data. This is the perfect scenario for a machine learning model where it can generalize well to unseen data and make consistent, accurate predictions. However, in reality, this is not feasible.
- **Model**: Well-chosen model with the right complexity (e.g., proper regularization and model selection).
- **Training Error**: Low.

- **Testing Error**: Low.
- **Performance**: Optimal.

4.5.3 Bias Variance tradeoff

The bias-variance tradeoff is a fundamental concept in machine learning. It refers to the balance between bias and variance, which affect predictive model performance. Finding the right tradeoff is crucial for creating models that generalize well to new data.

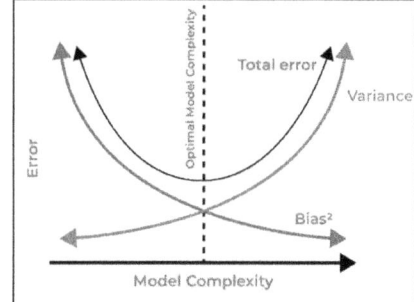

- The bias-variance tradeoff demonstrates the inverse relationship between bias and variance. When one decreases, the other tends to increase, and vice versa.
- Finding the right balance is crucial. An overly simple model with high bias won't capture the underlying patterns, while an overly complex model with high variance will fit the noise in the data.

4.6 Classification

Classification is used when the output (target variable) is **categorical**. It predicts **which category** or class an input belongs to.

Key Characteristics
- The target variable is **discrete** (e.g., "spam" or "not spam", "cat" or "dog").
- The output is a **class label** (not a continuous value).
- The model learns a function that assigns an input to one or more categories.

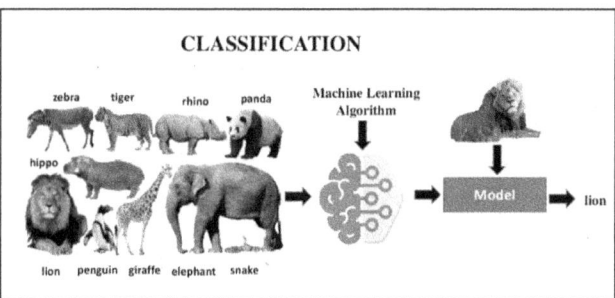

Common Algorithms
- Logistic Regression
- Decision Trees
- Random Forest Classifier
- Support Vector Machine (SVM)
- Naïve Bayes
- K-Nearest Neighbors (KNN)
- Neural Networks (for classification tasks)

Example Use Cases
- **Spam detection**: Classifying emails as spam or not spam.
- **Disease diagnosis**: Predicting if a patient has cancer (yes/no).
- **Sentiment analysis**: Categorizing customer reviews as positive, negative, or neutral.
- **Face recognition**: Identifying individuals in images.

Key points

Labeled Data: The algorithm is trained on a dataset where each example is paired with a label or class. For instance, in a dataset of emails, each email might be labeled as "spam" or "not spam."

Training Phase: During training, the algorithm analyzes the features (attributes or variables) of the data and learns to associate these features with the corresponding labels. For example, the algorithm might learn that certain words or phrases are strong indicators of spam.

Prediction Phase: After training, the algorithm can predict the class label for new, unseen data. For example, when you receive a new email, the algorithm can use what it has learned to classify it as either "spam" or "not spam."

For instance, an algorithm can learn to predict whether a given email is spam or ham (no spam), as illustrated below.

Key Differences Between Regression & Classification

Feature	Regression	Classification
Output Type	Continuous values (e.g., price, temperature)	Categorical values (e.g., Yes/No, Dog/Cat)
Nature of Output	Infinite possibilities	Limited, predefined categories
Example Algorithms	Linear Regression, SVR, Random Forest Regression	Logistic Regression, SVM, Decision Trees
Example Applications	House price prediction, sales forecasting	Spam detection, disease diagnosis

4.6.1 Lazy Learners Versus Eager Learners

In supervised machine learning, classification algorithms can be broadly categorized into two types based on how they approach learning and prediction: **lazy learners** and **eager learners**. Here's a clear explanation of both:

Lazy Learners: Lazy learners do not build a model during the training phase. Instead, they store the training data and perform computation only when a prediction is requested.

How They Work:
- **Training Phase**: Simply involves storing the training data.
- **Prediction Phase**: When a prediction is needed, the algorithm performs computation by looking at the stored training data. This often involves comparing the new data with the training examples.

Characteristics:
- **Delayed Computation**: Computation is deferred until a prediction is needed.
- **Memory-Based**: They rely on the entire training dataset to make predictions.
- **Simple Training**: Training is fast as it mainly involves storing data.
- **Potentially Expensive Predictions**: Prediction can be slow and computationally expensive because it involves processing the entire training set.

Examples:
- **k-Nearest Neighbors (k-NN)**: During training, it simply stores the data. For prediction, it calculates the distance between the new data point and all stored data points to determine the nearest neighbors and classify the new data based on them.

Eager Learners: Eager learners build a model during the training phase. They generalize from the training data to create a model that can then be used to make predictions.

How They Work:
- **Training Phase**: Involves creating a model or function that summarizes the training data.
- **Prediction Phase**: Uses the built model to make predictions on new data.

Characteristics:

- **Precomputed Model**: The model is built and stored during the training phase.
- **Efficient Predictions**: Predictions are generally faster and more efficient because they only involve using the precomputed model.
- **Potentially Expensive Training**: Training can be computationally intensive as it involves model creation and optimization.

Examples:
- **Decision Trees**: During training, a decision tree is built by recursively splitting the data based on feature values to create a tree structure. Prediction involves traversing this tree.
- **Support Vector Machines (SVM)**: Builds a hyperplane or set of hyperplanes during training to separate classes. Predictions are made by determining which side of the hyperplane the new data falls on.
- **Logistic Regression**: During training, it finds the best-fitting parameters for a logistic function that describes the relationship between features and class labels. Predictions involve applying this function.

Comparison
- **Training Time**: Lazy learners often have faster training times as they only store data. Eager learners can have longer training times due to model creation and optimization.
- **Prediction Time**: Lazy learners can be slower at prediction since they must compare new data against all training examples. Eager learners are usually faster at prediction because they use a pre-built model.
- **Storage**: Lazy learners require more memory to store training data. Eager learners need memory for the model, which can be less than storing the entire dataset.

Lazy learners and eager learners represent two different approaches to learning from data. Lazy learners store the training data and compute predictions on the fly, while eager learners build a model from the training data and use this model for fast predictions. The choice between them depends on the specific needs of the application, including considerations of training time, prediction speed, and memory usage.

4.6.2 Different Types of Classification Tasks in Machine Learning
In supervised learning, there are several types of classification algorithms based on the nature of the target variable or the number of classes they can predict. Here are some common types of classifications in supervised learning:

1. Binary Classification: The task involves classifying data into one of two classes. This type of classification involves predicting one of two possible classes or categories. Examples include spam detection (spam or not spam), disease diagnosis (healthy or diseased), and credit card fraud detection (fraudulent or non-fraudulent).

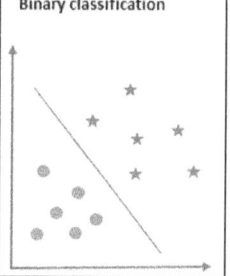
Binary classification

Examples:
- **Spam Detection**: Classify emails as "spam" or "not spam."
- **Medical Diagnosis**: Predict whether a patient has a disease ("disease" or "no disease").
- **Sentiment Analysis**: Determine whether a piece of text is "positive" or "negative."

Characteristics:
- **Output**: Two distinct classes.
- **Evaluation Metrics**: Accuracy, precision, recall, F1-score, ROC-AUC.

2. Multiclass Classification: The task involves classifying data into one of three or more classes. In this type, the target variable can have more than two classes. The goal is to assign each data instance to one of the multiple mutually exclusive classes. Examples include image recognition (classifying images into different objects or categories), sentiment analysis (classifying text into positive, negative, or neutral), and document classification (assigning documents to various topics or classes).

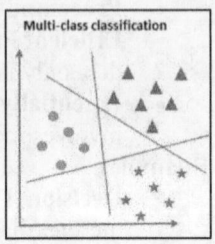

Examples:
- **Image Recognition**: Classify an image into one of several categories, such as "cat," "dog," "car," etc.
- **Handwriting Recognition**: Recognize digits (0-9) from handwritten text.
- **Topic Classification**: Assign news articles to topics such as "sports," "politics," "technology," etc.

Characteristics:
- **Output**: More than two classes.
- **Evaluation Metrics**: Accuracy, precision, recall, F1-score (per class or averaged), confusion matrix.

3. Multilabel Classification: Each instance can be assigned multiple labels simultaneously. Unlike multiclass classification where each instance belongs to one and only one class, multilabel classification allows for multiple class assignments per instance. In multi-label classification, each data instance can belong to multiple classes simultaneously. The goal is to predict a set of labels

or categories for each instance. For example, in a news article categorization task, a single article can be assigned to multiple topics such as politics, sports, and entertainment.

Examples:
- **Text Classification**: Assign multiple tags to a document (e.g., "science," "technology," "AI").
- **Image Annotation**: Tag images with multiple labels (e.g., an image of a dog in a park might be tagged as "dog," "park," and "outdoors").

Characteristics:
- **Output**: Each instance can belong to multiple classes.
- **Evaluation Metrics**: Hamming loss, precision, recall, F1-score (micro, macro, or per-label).

4. Hierarchical Classification: The task involves classifying instances into a hierarchy of classes, where classes are organized into a tree-like structure.

Hierarchical classification involves organizing classes into a hierarchical structure. The classes are arranged in a tree-like structure, where each class can have sub-classes. The goal is to predict the most appropriate class in the hierarchy. Examples include topic classification in large document collections and species classification in biology.

Examples:
- **Document Classification**: Categorize documents into a hierarchy such as "Science" → "Biology" → "Genetics."
- **Product Classification**: Assign products to categories and subcategories, such as "Electronics" → "Computers" → "Laptops."

Characteristics:
- **Output**: Instances are classified into a hierarchy of classes.

- **Evaluation Metrics**: Can be more complex due to the hierarchical nature; often includes metrics adapted for hierarchical structures.

5. *Ordinal Classification:* The task involves classifying instances into categories that have a meaningful order but the intervals between categories may not be uniform.

Ordinal classification deals with data where the classes have a natural order or hierarchy. The goal is to predict the relative ordering of the classes. For instance, in movie rating prediction, the classes can be "poor," "average," "good," and "excellent," with an inherent order.

Examples:
- **Rating Systems**: Classify customer reviews as "poor," "fair," "good," "excellent."
- **Medical Scales**: Categorize patients into stages of a disease (e.g., "mild," "moderate," "severe").

Characteristics:
- **Output**: Ordered categories.
- **Evaluation Metrics**: Accuracy, ordinal-specific metrics like Spearman's rank correlation.

6. Imbalanced Classification: The classification task where some classes are significantly underrepresented compared to others, makes it difficult for the model to learn the minority class effectively.

Imbalanced classification refers to a scenario where the classes in the dataset are not represented equally. One class may have significantly more instances than the others. This type of classification often requires specialized techniques to handle the class imbalance, such as oversampling, undersampling, or using class weighting techniques.

Examples:
- **Fraud Detection**: Detecting fraudulent transactions where fraud cases are much less frequent than non-fraud cases.
- **Rare Disease Diagnosis**: Identifying patients with a rare disease.

Characteristics:
- **Output**: Imbalance between class distributions.
- **Evaluation Metrics**: Precision-recall curves, F1-score, balanced accuracy, methods to handle imbalance like resampling or cost-sensitive learning.

Summary

Different types of classification tasks require different approaches and evaluation metrics. Choosing the right type depends on the nature of your data and the specific problem you are addressing. Each type of classification task also presents its own set of challenges and requires different strategies for model training and evaluation.

4.6.3 Applications of Classification Algorithms

Classification algorithms in machine learning have a wide range of applications across various fields. Here are some notable applications:

1. Email and Spam Filtering
- **Application**: Automatically classify incoming emails as "spam" or "not spam."
- **Algorithms**: Naive Bayes, Support Vector Machines (SVM), k-Nearest Neighbors (k-NN), Logistic Regression.

2. Medical Diagnosis
- **Application**: Predict whether a patient has a particular disease based on medical test results and symptoms.
- **Algorithms**: Decision Trees, Random Forests, Neural Networks, Logistic Regression.

3. Image and Video Recognition
- **Application**: Identify objects, people, or activities within images and videos.

- **Algorithms**: Convolutional Neural Networks (CNNs), Support Vector Machines (SVM), k-Nearest Neighbors (k-NN).

4. Speech Recognition
- **Application**: Convert spoken language into text by classifying audio signals.
- **Algorithms**: Recurrent Neural Networks (RNNs), Long Short-Term Memory Networks (LSTMs), Transformer models.

5. Sentiment Analysis
- **Application**: Determine the sentiment expressed in a piece of text, such as positive, negative, or neutral.
- **Algorithms**: Naive Bayes, Support Vector Machines (SVM), Recurrent Neural Networks (RNNs), Transformer models.

6. Credit Scoring and Fraud Detection
- **Application**: Assess the creditworthiness of individuals and detect fraudulent transactions.
- **Algorithms**: Decision Trees, Random Forests, Gradient Boosting Machines, Neural Networks.

7. Customer Churn Prediction
- **Application**: Predict which customers are likely to stop using a service or product.
- **Algorithms**: Logistic Regression, Random Forests, Gradient Boosting Machines.

8. Document Classification
- **Application**: Automatically categorize documents into predefined topics or genres.
- **Algorithms**: Naive Bayes, Support Vector Machines (SVM), Neural Networks, k-Nearest Neighbors (k-NN).

9. Recommendation Systems
- **Application**: Recommend products, movies, or services to users based on their preferences and behavior.
- **Algorithms**: Collaborative Filtering, Content-Based Filtering, Neural Networks.

10. Face Recognition
- **Application**: Identify or verify individuals based on facial features.
- **Algorithms**: Convolutional Neural Networks (CNNs), Deep Learning models.

11. Disease Outbreak Prediction
- **Application**: Predict and track the spread of diseases based on various factors such as location, time, and symptoms.
- **Algorithms**: Decision Trees, Random Forests, Neural Networks.

12. Genomic Data Analysis
- **Application**: Classify genetic sequences and predict gene functions or disease susceptibility.
- **Algorithms**: Random Forests, Support Vector Machines (SVM), Neural Networks.

13. Social Media Analysis
- **Application**: Classify posts, comments, or tweets for trends, sentiment, or topics.
- **Algorithms**: Naive Bayes, Support Vector Machines (SVM), Transformer models.

14. Autonomous Vehicles
- **Application**: Classify objects, pedestrians, and other vehicles for navigation and safety.
- **Algorithms**: Convolutional Neural Networks (CNNs), Object Detection models, Sensor Fusion techniques.

15. Text Classification

- **Application**: Categorize text data into different classes, such as topic categorization, language detection, or intent classification.
- **Algorithms**: Naive Bayes, Support Vector Machines (SVM), Recurrent Neural Networks (RNNs), Transformers.

16. Anomaly Detection
- **Application**: Identify unusual or unexpected behavior in various datasets, such as network security or manufacturing.
- **Algorithms**: Isolation Forests, One-Class SVM, Autoencoders.

Summary

Classification algorithms are versatile and widely used in many fields due to their ability to categorize data into meaningful classes or labels. Each application may require different algorithms and techniques based on the nature of the data and the specific problem being addressed.

4.6.4 Types of Classification algorithms

In supervised learning, classification algorithms are used to predict the category or class of a given data point. Here are some common types of classification algorithms:

1. **Logistic Regression**: A statistical method for predicting binary outcomes based on one or more predictor variables.
2. **K-Nearest Neighbors (KNN)**: A non-parametric method that classifies data points based on their proximity to other data points in the feature space.
3. **Support Vector Machines (SVM)**: A powerful classification method that finds the optimal hyperplane separating different classes in the feature space.
4. **Naive Bayes**: A probabilistic classifier based on Bayes' theorem, assuming independence between predictors.
5. **Decision Trees**: A tree-like model of decisions, where each internal node represents a test on an attribute, each branch represents the outcome of the test, and each leaf node represents a class label.
6. **Random Forest**: An ensemble method that uses multiple decision trees to improve classification performance and reduce overfitting.
7. **Gradient Boosting Machines (GBM)**: An ensemble technique that builds models sequentially, each correcting the errors of its predecessor, often resulting in highly accurate models.
8. **Neural Networks**: Models inspired by the human brain, consisting of layers of interconnected nodes that can learn complex patterns in data.
9. **Linear Discriminant Analysis (LDA)**: A method that finds a linear combination of features that best separates two or more classes.
10. **Quadratic Discriminant Analysis (QDA)**: Similar to LDA but allows for a quadratic decision boundary, making it more flexible for certain datasets.
11. **XGBoost**: An optimized implementation of gradient boosting that is particularly effective for large datasets and competitions.
12. **AdaBoost**: An ensemble method that combines multiple weak classifiers to create a strong classifier, focusing on misclassified instances.
13. **Multinomial Logistic Regression**: An extension of logistic regression for multiclass classification problems.

Each of these algorithms has its strengths and weaknesses, and the choice of algorithm often depends on the specific characteristics of the dataset and the problem at hand.

4.7 Evaluation Metrics of Classification Algorithms

classification evaluation metric is a measure used to assess the performance of a classification model. These metrics provide insight into how well the model is making predictions, particularly in distinguishing between different classes. They help evaluate various aspects of model performance, such as accuracy, error rates, and the ability to handle imbalanced datasets. Let's dive into the classification evaluation metrics with explanations, formulas, and example calculations.

4.7.1 Confusion Matrix

A confusion matrix is a table used to evaluate the performance of a classification model. It summarizes the results of a classification algorithm by showing the number of correct and incorrect predictions categorized by their actual and predicted classes. It provides a comprehensive view of how well the model performs, particularly in distinguishing between classes.

Components of a Confusion Matrix

For a binary classification problem, the confusion matrix is structured as follows:

		Predicted	
		Positive	Negative
Actual	Positive	True Positive (TP)	False Negative (FN)
	Negative	False Positive (FP)	True Negative (TN)

True Positives (TP): The number of instances that are correctly predicted as positive.

False Positives (FP): The number of instances that are incorrectly predicted as positive (i.e., actual negative instances incorrectly classified as positive).

True Negatives (TN): The number of instances that are correctly predicted as negative.

False Negatives (FN): The number of instances that are incorrectly predicted as negative (i.e., actual positive instances incorrectly classified as negative).

4.7.2 Accuracy

Definition: Accuracy is the ratio of correctly predicted instances to the total number of instances. It gives a general sense of how often the model is correct.

Formula: $\text{Accuracy} = \dfrac{No.of\ Correct\ predictions}{Total\ no.of\ predictions}$

4.7.3 Precision

Definition: Precision measures the accuracy of positive predictions. It is the ratio of true positives to the sum of true positives and false positives.

Formula: $\text{Precision} = \dfrac{True\ Positives}{True\ Positives + Palse\ Positives}$

4.7.4 Recall (Sensitivity or True Positive Rate)

Definition: Recall measures the ability of the model to find all the positive instances. It is the ratio of true positives to the sum of true positives and false negatives.

Formula: $\text{Recall} = \dfrac{True\ Positives}{True\ Positives + Fa\quad Negatives}$

4.7.5 F1 Score
Definition: The F1 Score is the harmonic mean of precision and recall. It provides a single metric that balances both precision and recall.

Formula: F1 Score$=2\frac{Precision.Recall}{Precision+Recall}$

4.7.6 ROC Curve and AUC
ROC Curve: The ROC curve plots the true positive rate (recall) against the false positive rate at various threshold settings.

AUC (Area Under the Curve): AUC measures the overall ability of the model to distinguish between classes. It ranges from 0 to 1, with 1 being perfect and 0.5 being no better than random guessing.

Example Calculation: Assuming you have the ROC curve and calculate the AUC using software tools or libraries (e.g., scikit-learn in Python), if the AUC is 0.85, it means the model has good discriminatory power.

4.7.7 Matthews Correlation Coefficient (MCC)
Definition: MCC is a measure of the quality of binary classifications. It considers all four categories of the confusion matrix and provides a balanced measure even if classes are imbalanced.

Formula: MCC$=\frac{TP.TN-FP.FN}{\sqrt{(TP+FP)(TP+FN)(TN+FP)(TN+FN)}}$

4.7.8 Specificity (True Negative Rate)
Definition: Specificity measures the proportion of actual negatives that are correctly identified.

Formula: Specificity$=\frac{True\ Negatives}{True\ Negatives+Fal\quad Positives}$

4.7.9 Average Precision (AP)
Definition: AP is the mean of precision scores at different recall levels. It is especially useful in cases with imbalanced datasets.

Example Calculation: AP is typically calculated using precision-recall curves and is often computed using libraries such as scikit-learn. If you have a precision-recall curve, you can integrate precision values over recall levels to get AP.

4.7.10 Log Loss (Logarithmic Loss)
Definition: Log Loss evaluates the probabilistic predictions of a model. Lower log loss values indicate better performance.

Formula: Log Loss$=-\frac{1}{N}\sum_{i=1}^{N}\left[y_i.\log\left(p_i\right)+(1-y_i).\log\left(1-p_i\right)\right]$

4.8 Classification Algorithms
4.8.1 Logistic Regression
Logistic regression is a statistical method used for binary classification problems, where the outcome or dependent variable is categorical and typically has two possible outcomes (e.g., "yes" or "no," "spam" or "not spam"). Despite its name, logistic regression is used for classification rather than regression tasks.

Logistic Regression is a method to predict a dependent variable, given a set of independent variables, such that the dependent variable is categorical

Dependent variable (Y): The response binary variable holding values like - 0 or 1, YES or NO, Male or Female, True or False, etc

Independent variable(X): The predictor variable used to predict the response variable Y-is the probability of an event to happen that you are trying to predict

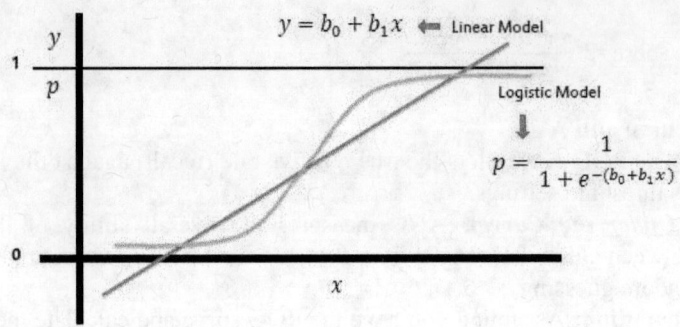

In logistic regression, instead of fitting a regression line, we fit an "S" shaped logistic function, which predicts the values. Logistic regression can be used to classify the observations using different types of data and can easily determine the most effective variables used for the classification

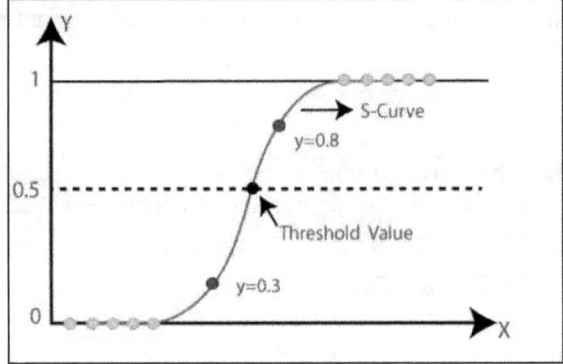

Model the probability of an event occurring depending on the values of the independent variables, which can be categorical or numerical. Estimate the probability that an event occurs for randomly selected observations versus the probability that the event does not occur. Predict the effect of the series of variables on binary response variables classify observations by estimating (Threshold value) the probability that an observation is in a particular category (such as YES or NO)

CGPA	Admission
X	Y
4.2	0
5.1	0
5.5	0
8.2	1
9.0	1
9.1	1

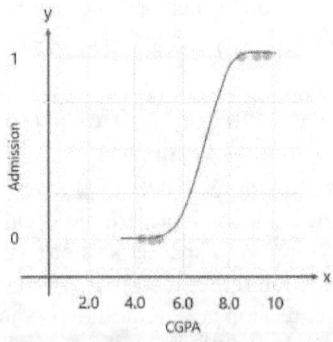

Logistic Function (Sigmoid Function):
The *sigmoid function* is a mathematical function used to map the predicted values to probabilitiesIt maps any real value into another value within a range of 0 and 1.

The value of the logistic regression must be between 0 and 1, which cannot go beyond this limit, so it forms a curve like the *"S" form*.

The *S-form* curve is called the *Sigmoid function* or the *logistic function*.

In logistic regression, we use the concept of the threshold value, which defines the probability of either 0 or 1. Such as values above the threshold value tends to 1, and a value below the threshold values tends to 0

$$E(y) = \frac{1}{1 + e^{-y}}$$

Decision boundary

Our current prediction function returns a probability score between 0 and 1.

In order to map this to a discrete class (true/false, cat/dog), we select a threshold value or tipping point above which we will classify values into class 1, and below which we classify values into class 2.

If $E(y) \geq 0.5$, then it classified as class=1 or True or Yes

If $E(y) < 0.5$, then it classified class=0 or False or No

Python code to implement Logistic regression

```
#Importing the libraries
import numpy as np
import matplotlib.pyplot as plt
import pandas as pd
#Importing the dataset
dataset = pd.read_csv('Social_Network_Ads.csv')
#Splitting the dataset into the Training set and Test set
X = dataset.iloc[:, [2, 3]].values
y = dataset.iloc[:, -1].values
from sklearn.model_selection import train_test_split
X_train, X_test, y_train, y_test = train_test_split(X, y, test_size = 0.25, random_state = 0)
#Feature Scaling
from sklearn.preprocessing import StandardScaler
sc = StandardScaler()
X_train = sc.fit_transform(X_train)
X_test = sc.transform(X_test)
#Training the Logistic Regression model on the Training set
from sklearn.linear_model import LogisticRegression
classifier = LogisticRegression(random_state = 0)
classifier.fit(X_train, y_train)
LogisticRegression(C=1.0, class_weight=None, dual=False, fit_intercept=True,
          intercept_scaling=1, l1_ratio=None, max_iter=100,
          multi_class='auto', n_jobs=None, penalty='l2',
          random_state=0, solver='lbfgs', tol=0.0001, verbose=0,
          warm_start=False)
#Predicting the Test set results
y_pred = classifier.predict(X_test)
Making the Confusion Matrix
from sklearn.metrics import confusion_matrix
cm = confusion_matrix(y_test, y_pred)
print(cm)
       [[65  3]
       [ 8 24]]
```

```
#Visualising the Training set results
from matplotlib.colors import ListedColormap
X_set, y_set = X_train, y_train
X1, X2 = np.meshgrid(np.arange(start = X_set[:, 0].min() - 1, stop = X_set[:, 0].max() +
1, step = 0.01),
                np.arange(start = X_set[:, 1].min() - 1, stop = X_set[:, 1].max() + 1, step =
0.01))
plt.contourf(X1, X2, classifier.predict(np.array([X1.ravel(),
X2.ravel()]).T).reshape(X1.shape),
        alpha = 0.75, cmap = ListedColormap(('red', 'green')))
plt.xlim(X1.min(), X1.max())
plt.ylim(X2.min(), X2.max())
for i, j in enumerate(np.unique(y_set)):
    plt.scatter(X_set[y_set == j, 0], X_set[y_set == j, 1],
            c = ListedColormap(('red', 'green'))(i), label = j)
plt.title('Logistic Regression (Training set)')
plt.xlabel('Age')
plt.ylabel('Estimated Salary')
plt.legend()
plt.show()
```

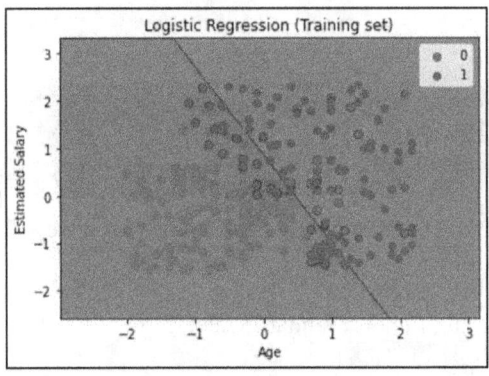

```
#Visualising the Test set results
In [9]:
from matplotlib.colors import ListedColormap
X_set, y_set = X_test, y_test
X1, X2 = np.meshgrid(np.arange(start = X_set[:, 0].min() - 1, stop = X_set[:, 0].max() +
1, step = 0.01),
                np.arange(start = X_set[:, 1].min() - 1, stop = X_set[:, 1].max() + 1, step =
0.01))
plt.contourf(X1, X2, classifier.predict(np.array([X1.ravel(),
X2.ravel()]).T).reshape(X1.shape),
        alpha = 0.75, cmap = ListedColormap(('red', 'green')))
plt.xlim(X1.min(), X1.max())
plt.ylim(X2.min(), X2.max())
for i, j in enumerate(np.unique(y_set)):
    plt.scatter(X_set[y_set == j, 0], X_set[y_set == j, 1],
            c = ListedColormap(('red', 'green'))(i), label = j)
plt.title('Logistic Regression (Test set)')
```

plt.xlabel('Age')
plt.ylabel('Estimated Salary')
plt.legend()
plt.show()

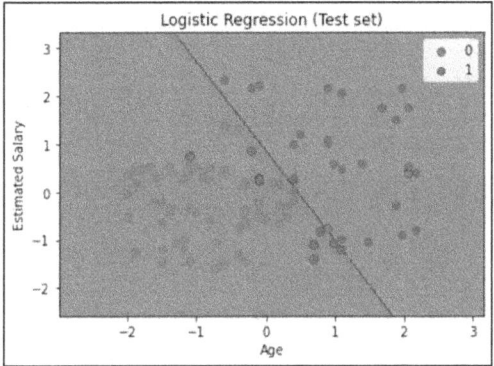

4.8.1.1 Linear Regression versus Logistic Regression

Linear regression and logistic regression are both statistical methods used for predicting outcomes, but they are used in different contexts and have distinct characteristics.

1. Purpose and Type of Outcome:
- **Linear Regression:**
  - **Purpose:** Used for predicting a continuous numeric outcome.
  - **Outcome:** The dependent variable is continuous and can take any value within a range (e.g., predicting house prices, temperature, or weight).
  - **Example:** Predicting the price of a house based on features like size, location, and age.
- **Logistic Regression:**
  - **Purpose:** Used for predicting categorical outcomes, specifically binary outcomes.
  - **Outcome:** The dependent variable is categorical, often binary (e.g., yes/no, true/false, or 0/1). It predicts the probability of the occurrence of an event.
  - **Example:** Predicting whether a customer will buy a product (yes/no) based on their age, income, and other features.

2. Model Equation:
- **Linear Regression:**
  - **Equation:** $Y=\beta 0+\beta_1 X_1+\beta_2 X_2+\cdots+\beta_n X_n$
  - Here, Y is the dependent variable, $X_1, X_2, \ldots, X_n$ are the independent variables, β_0 is the intercept, $\beta_1, \beta_2, \ldots, \beta_n$ are the coefficients, and ϵ is the error term.
  - The relationship is linear, meaning the model predicts Y as a linear combination of the input variables.
- **Logistic Regression:**
  - **Equation:** $\text{logit}(p)=\beta 0+\beta_1 X_1+\beta_2 X_2+\cdots+\beta_n X_n$
  - Where p is the probability of the dependent event occurring, and $\text{logit}(p)$ is the log-odds of the probability.
  - The probability p is then computed using the logistic function:
  $$p=\frac{1}{1+e^{(\beta 0+\beta 1 X 1+\beta 2 X 2+\cdots+\beta n X n)}}$$
  - This transformation ensures that the predicted probabilities are between 0 and 1.

3. Assumptions:
- **Linear Regression:**
  - Assumes linear relationship between the independent variables and the dependent variable.
  - Assumes homoscedasticity (constant variance of the error terms).
  - Assumes normal distribution of error terms.
- **Logistic Regression:**
  - Does not assume a linear relationship between the independent variables and the dependent variable. Instead, it models the log-odds of the probability.
  - Assumes that the log-odds of the dependent variable is linearly related to the independent variables.
  - Does not require homoscedasticity or normally distributed error terms.

4. Error Measurement:
- **Linear Regression:**
  - Uses metrics like Mean Squared Error (MSE) or Root Mean Squared Error (RMSE) to measure the accuracy of the predictions.
- **Logistic Regression:**
  - Uses metrics like Accuracy, Precision, Recall, F1 Score, and Log-Loss to evaluate model performance.

5. Interpretation of Coefficients:
- **Linear Regression:**
  - Coefficients represent the change in the dependent variable for a one-unit change in the independent variable.
- **Logistic Regression:**
  - Coefficients represent the change in the log-odds of the dependent variable for a one-unit change in the independent variable. Exponentiating the coefficients can give the odds ratios.

In summary, linear regression is used for predicting continuous outcomes with a linear relationship, while logistic regression is used for predicting binary outcomes and models the probability of an event occurring.

4.8.2 K-Nearest Neighbors (KNN)

K-Nearest Neighbors (KNN) algorithm is a supervised machine learning algorithm used for both classification and regression tasks but mostly it is used for Classification problems. It is a non-parametric algorithm, meaning it doesn't make any assumptions about the underlying data distribution.

For example, Suppose, we have an image of a creature that looks similar to cat and dog, but we want to know either it is a cat or a dog. So for this identification, we can use the KNN algorithm, as it works on a similarity measure. Our KNN model will find the similar features of the new data set to the cats and dogs images and based on the most similar features it will put it in either cat or dog category.

Why do we need a K-NN Algorithm?

Suppose there are two categories, i.e., Category A and Category B, and we have a new data point x1, so this data point will lie in which of these categories? To solve this type of problem, we need a K-NN algorithm. With the help of K-NN, we can easily identify the category or class of a particular dataset. Consider the below diagram:

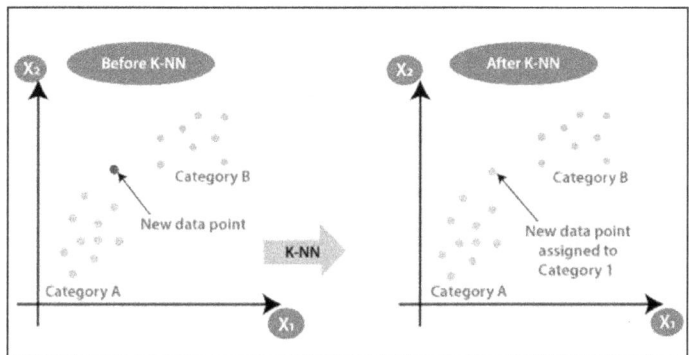

In KNN, the "K" refers to the number of nearest neighbors considered for making predictions. The algorithm works as follows:

Data preparation: KNN requires labeled training data, where each data point is associated with a specific class or category (for classification) or a numerical value (for regression). The data should be in a numerical format, and it's important to normalize or scale the features to ensure they contribute equally to the distance calculations. We have the labeled training data with known species. We'll use the sepal length and sepal width as numerical features.

Here's a simplified version of the dataset:

Object	Sepal Length	Sepal Width	Species
1	5.1	3.5	Setosa
2	4.9	3.0	Setosa
3	6.2	2.9	Virginica
4	5.5	4.2	Setosa
5	6.3	2.8	Virginica

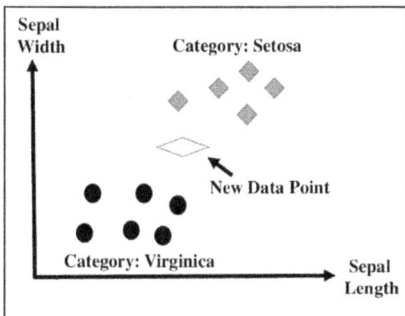

Calculating distances: For a given test data point, the algorithm calculates the distances to all the training data points based on a chosen distance metric (e.g., Euclidean distance, Manhattan distance). The distance metric determines how "close" or "similar" two data points are in the feature space.

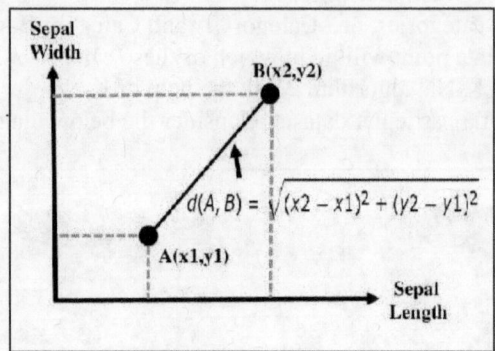

For the new flower, let's say it has a sepal length of 5.8 and a sepal width of 3.4. We calculate the Euclidean distance between this point and all the training data points.

The distances between the new flower and the training examples are:

Distance to Object 1: $sqrt((5.1 - 5.8)^2 + (3.5 - 3.4)^2) = 0.707$
Distance to Object 2: $sqrt((4.9 - 5.8)^2 + (3.0 - 3.4)^2) = 1.13$
Distance to Object 3: $sqrt((6.2 - 5.8)^2 + (2.9 - 3.4)^2) = 0.7$
Distance to Object 4: $sqrt((5.5 - 5.8)^2 + (4.2 - 3.4)^2) = 0.943$
Distance to Object 5: $sqrt((6.3 - 5.8)^2 + (2.8 - 3.4)^2) = 0.616$

Finding nearest neighbors: The algorithm identifies the K nearest neighbors to the test data point based on the calculated distances. These neighbors are the data points with the smallest distances to the test point.

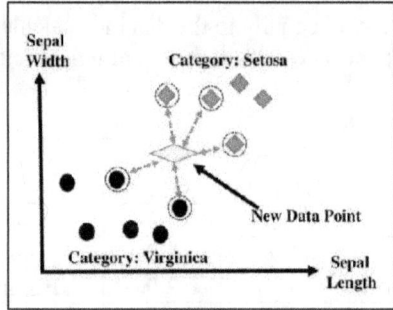

Let's assume we choose K = 3. The three nearest neighbors to the new flower are Object 3, 5, and 1, as they have the smallest distances.

Majority voting (classification) or averaging (regression): For classification tasks, the algorithm determines the majority class among the K nearest neighbors and assigns that class to the test data point. In regression tasks, the algorithm computes the average value of the target variables of the K nearest neighbors and assigns it as the predicted value for the test data point.

Since we are performing classification, we consider the species of the K nearest neighbors. Among the three neighbors, Object 3 is Virginica, Object 5 is Virginica, and Object 1 is Setosa.

Now, we count the occurrences of each species:

Virginica: 2
Setosa: 1

Based on the majority voting, the predicted species for the new flower is Virginica. In this example, the KNN algorithm predicted the species of the new flower as Virginica based on the majority vote of the three nearest neighbors.

How to select the value of K in the K-NN Algorithm?

Below are some points to remember while selecting the value of K in the K-NN algorithm: There is no particular way to determine the best value for "K", so we need to try some values to find the best out of them. The most preferred value for K is 5.A very low value for K such as K=1 or K=2, can be noisy and lead to the effects of outliers in the model. Large values for K are good, but it may find some difficulties.

The choice of the value K is important and can impact the algorithm's performance. A smaller K value makes the model more sensitive to local variations in the data, potentially leading to overfitting. A larger K value can smooth out the decision boundary or regression line but may lead to underfitting.

KNN has several advantages, such as its simplicity, ease of implementation, and ability to handle multi-class classification and regression tasks. However, it can be computationally expensive for large datasets since it requires calculating distances between the test point and all training data points.

Furthermore, KNN assumes that nearby data points tend to have similar labels or values, which may not always hold true if there are irrelevant or noisy features in the dataset. Feature selection and dimensionality reduction techniques can be applied to mitigate such issues.

Overall, KNN is a versatile algorithm that can be effective for various machine learning tasks, especially in situations where the decision boundary or regression line is complex or non-linear.

Advantages of KNN Algorithm:

It is simple to implement.

It is robust to the noisy training data

It can be more effective if the training data is large.

Disadvantages of KNN Algorithm:

Always needs to determine the value of K which may be complex sometimes.

The computation cost is high because of calculating the distance between the data points for all the training samples.

Python code to implement K-NN algorithm

```
#Importing the libraries
import numpy as np
import matplotlib.pyplot as plt
import pandas as pd
#Importing the dataset
dataset = pd.read_csv('Social_Network_Ads.csv')
X = dataset.iloc[:, [2, 3]].values
y = dataset.iloc[:, -1].values
#Splitting the dataset into the Training set and Test set
from sklearn.model_selection import train_test_split
X_train, X_test, y_train, y_test = train_test_split(X, y, test_size = 0.25, random_state = 0)
#Feature Scaling
from sklearn.preprocessing import StandardScaler
sc = StandardScaler()
X_train = sc.fit_transform(X_train)
X_test = sc.transform(X_test)
#Training the K-NN model on the Training set
```

```
#from sklearn.neighbors import KNeighborsClassifier
classifier = KNeighborsClassifier(n_neighbors = 5, metric = 'minkowski', p = 2)
classifier.fit(X_train, y_train)
KNeighborsClassifier(algorithm='auto', leaf_size=30, metric='minkowski',
metric_params=None, n_jobs=None, n_neighbors=5, p=2,weights='uniform')
#Predicting the Test set results
y_pred = classifier.predict(X_test)
#Making the Confusion Matrix
from sklearn.metrics import confusion_matrix
cm = confusion_matrix(y_test, y_pred)
print(cm)
                [[64  4]
                 [ 3 29]]
#Visualising the Training set results
from matplotlib.colors import ListedColormap
X_set, y_set = X_train, y_train
X1, X2 = np.meshgrid(np.arange(start = X_set[:, 0].min() - 1, stop = X_set[:, 0].max() +
1, step = 0.01),np.arange(start = X_set[:, 1].min() - 1, stop = X_set[:, 1].max() + 1, step =
0.01))
plt.contourf(X1, X2, classifier.predict(np.array([X1.ravel(),
X2.ravel()]).T).reshape(X1.shape),  alpha = 0.75, cmap = ListedColormap(('red',
'green')))
plt.xlim(X1.min(), X1.max())
plt.ylim(X2.min(), X2.max())
for i, j in enumerate(np.unique(y_set)):
    plt.scatter(X_set[y_set == j, 0], X_set[y_set == j, 1],
            c = ListedColormap(('red', 'green'))(i), label = j)
plt.title('K-NN (Training set)')
plt.xlabel('Age')
plt.ylabel('Estimated Salary')
plt.legend()
plt.show()
```

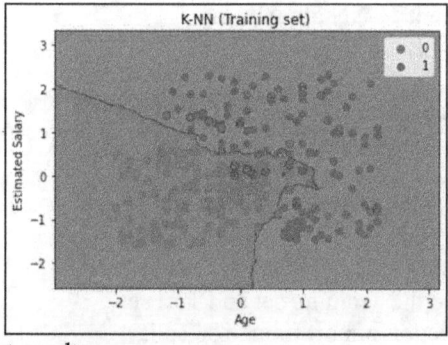

```
#Visualizing the Test set results
from matplotlib.colors import ListedColormap
X_set, y_set = X_test, y_testX1, X2 = np.meshgrid(np.arange(start = X_set[:, 0].min() -
1,  stop = X_set[:, 0].max() + 1, step = 0.01),np.arange(start = X_set[:, 1].min() - 1, stop
= X_set[:, 1].max() + 1, step = 0.01))
plt.contourf(X1, X2, classifier.predict(np.array([X1.ravel(),
X2.ravel()]).T).reshape(X1.shape),alpha = 0.75, cmap = ListedColormap(('red', 'green')))
plt.xlim(X1.min(), X1.max())
plt.ylim(X2.min(), X2.max())
```

```
for i, j in enumerate(np.unique(y_set)):
    plt.scatter(X_set[y_set == j, 0], X_set[y_set == j, 1], c = ListedColormap(('red',
'green'))(i), label = j)
plt.title('K-NN (Test set)')
plt.xlabel('Age')
plt.ylabel('Estimated Salary')
plt.legend()
plt.show()
```

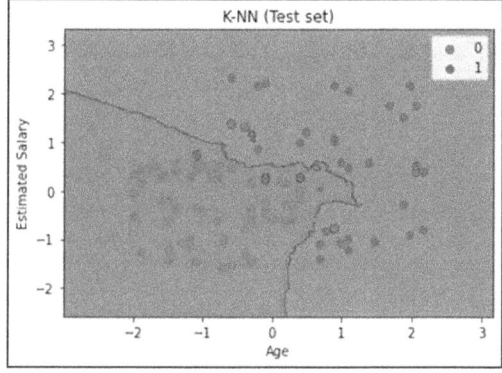

4.8.3 Decision Tree Algorithm

Decision Tree is a Supervised learning technique that can be used for both classification and Regression problems, but mostly it is preferred for solving Classification problems.

A decision tree or tree diagram is a decision support tool that uses a tree-like graph or model of decisions and their possible consequences, including change event outcomes, resource costs, and utility. A decision tree is a classification schema that generates a tree and a set of rules representing the model of different classes from a given data set. The following diagram shows the formation of a decision tree for given datasets, the compute function computes the decision tree with high accuracy.

It is a tree-structured classifier, where internal nodes represent the features of a dataset, branches represent the decision rules and each leaf node represents the outcome.

In a Decision tree, there are two nodes, which are the Decision Node and the Leaf Node. Decision nodes are used to make any decision and have multiple branches, whereas Leaf nodes are the output of those decisions and do not contain any further branches. The decisions or the tests are performed on the basis of 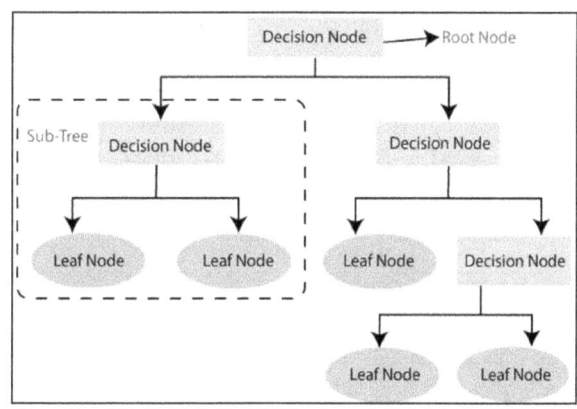 features of the given database. A decision tree can contain categorical data (YES/NO) as well as numeric data

- **Root Node:** Root node is from where the decision tree starts. It represents the entire dataset, which further gets divided into two or more homogeneous sets.
- **Leaf Node:** Leaf nodes are the final output node, and the tree cannot be segregated further after getting a leaf node.

- **Splitting:** Splitting is the process of dividing the decision node/root node into sub-nodes according to the given conditions.
- **Branch/Sub Tree:** A tree formed by splitting the tree.
- Pruning: Pruning is the process of removing the unwanted branches from the tree to get the out come
- **Parent/Child node:** The root node of the tree is called the parent node, and other nodes are called the child nodes.

- The set of records available for developing classification methods is generally divided into two disjoint sub sets.

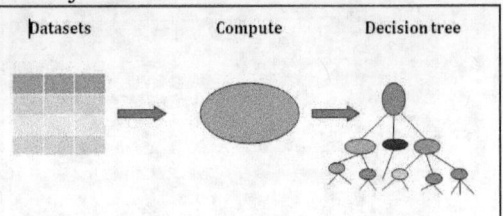

Some decision trees can only deal with binary-valued target classes. Others are able to assign records to an arbitrary number of classes, but are error-prone when the number of training examples per class gets small. This can happen rather quickly in a tree with many levels and/or many branches per node.
node.
The process of growing a decision tree is computationally expensive. At each node, each candidate splitting filed is explained before is best split can be found. We find the decision tree from that data.

S.NO	OUTLOOK	TEMPERATURE	HUMIDITY	WINDY	PLAY
1	Sunny	Hot	High	False	N
2	Sunny	Hot	High	True	N
3	Overcast	Hot	High	False	Y
4	Rainy	Mild	High	False	Y
5	Rainy	Cool	Normal	False	Y
6	Rainy	Cool	Normal	True	N
7	Overcast	Cool	Normal	True	Y
8	Sunny	Mild	High	False	N
9	Sunny	Cool	Normal	False	Y
10	Rainy	Mild	Normal	False	Y
11	Sunny	Mild	Normal	True	Y
12	Overcast	Mild	High	True	Y
13	Overcast	Hot	Normal	False	Y
14	Rainy	Mild	High	True	N

The goal of the classification is to build a concise model that can be used to predict the class of the records whose class label is not known. If the target attribute (or variable or class label) whose domain is a nominal/categorical attribute we call the tree as classification tree and if continues then the tree is called regression tree.
The attributes outlook, temperature, humidity, and windy, are categorical attributes, that is, they cannot be ordered. Based on the training data set, we want to find a set of rules to know what values of outlook, temperature, humidity and windy, determine whether or not to play golf. One possible Decision tree for above data set is given below as

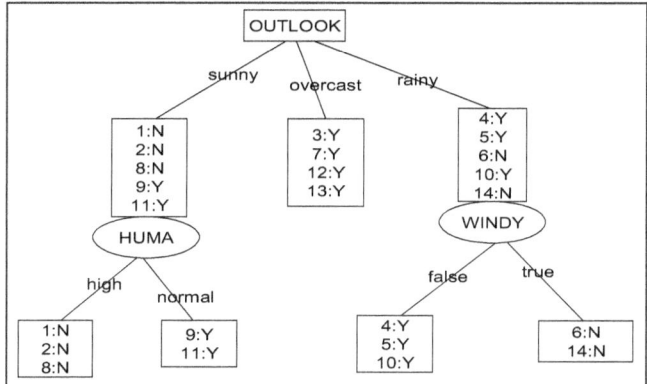

In the Decision tree, each leaf node represents a rule. Classification of an unknown input vector is done by traversing the tree from the root node to the leaf node. We have the following rules corresponding to the above decision tree as

Rule 1: If OUTLOOK (sunny) & HUMA (high) then N (not play)
Rule 2: If OUTLOOK (sunny) & HUMA(normal) then Y (play)
Rule 3: If OUTLOOK (overcast) then Y (play)
Rule 4: If OUTLOOK (rainy)&WINDY (false) then Y (play)
Rule 5: If OUTLOOK (rainy)&WINDY (true), then N (not play)

Splitting Of Decision Tree

Splitting of decision tree for above training data set, we may split many ways. In the decision tree at root node we may choose any attribute from OUTLOOK, HUMADITY, TEMPERATURE, & WINDY except the class variable. Now we split the leaf by taking appropriate childs. The process is continued until all attributes. Some of the possible splitting criteria are shown below

Example possible decision tree 1 :

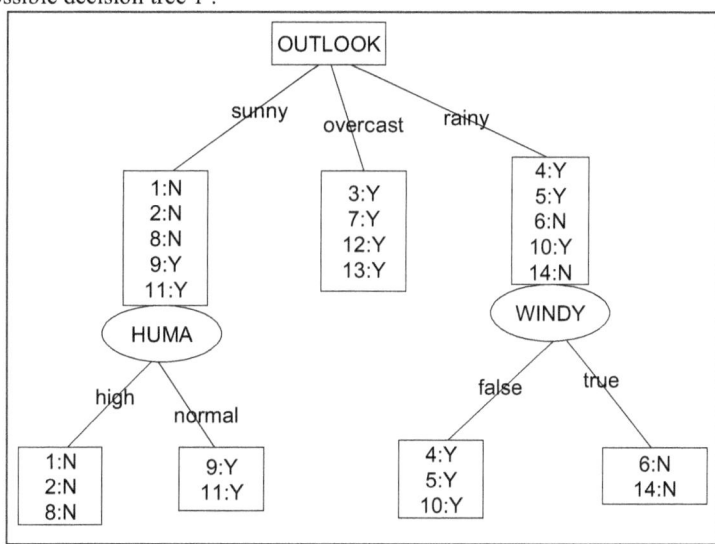

Example possible decision tree 2:

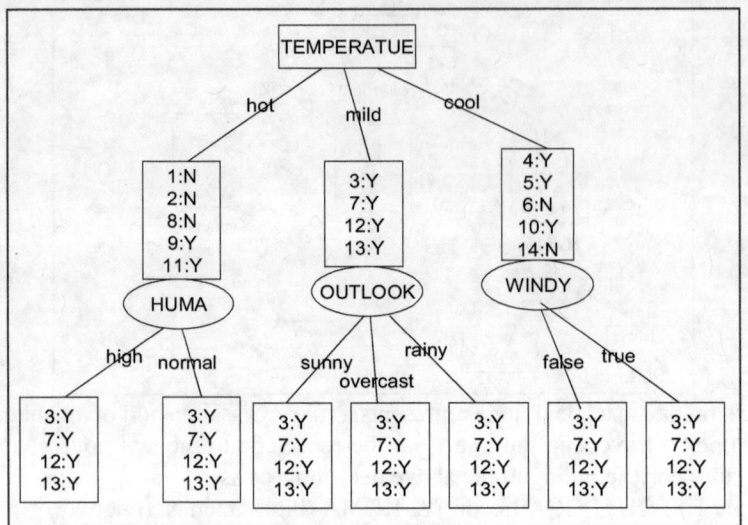

Example possible decision tree 3:

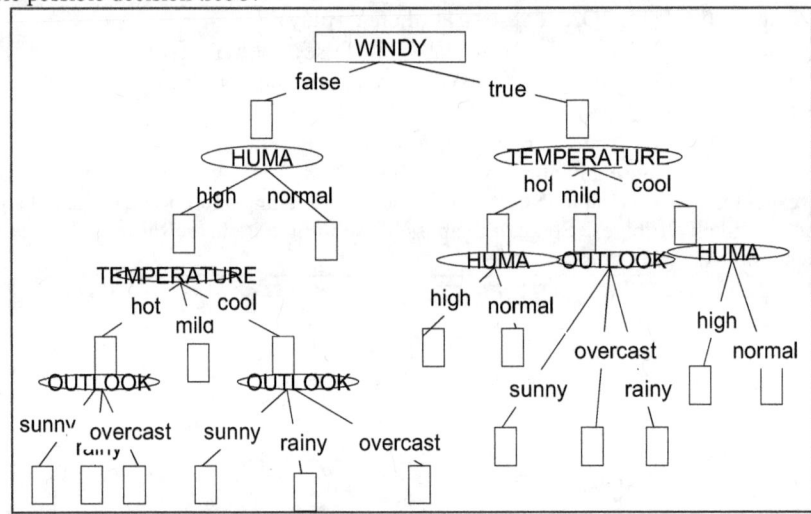

Example possible decision tree 4:

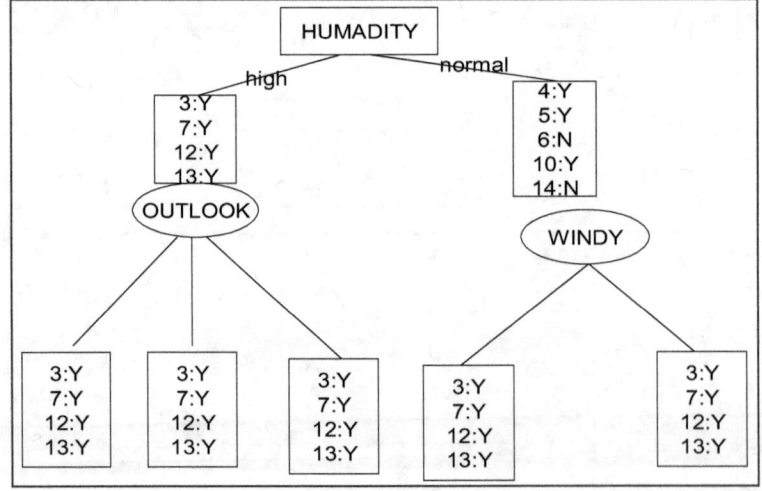

Best Splitting of Decision Tree

To made rules with accuracy and very high support. Support refers to percentage number of data points that satisfy the rule. To select node that means which attribute is to split in the decision tree is based on the information theory and information entropy , gain and gain_ration. There are explained with formulae as given below.

Entropy

Entropy provides an information theoretic approach to measure the goodness of a split. It is also measure of the disorder present in a system. In the decision tree construction process, definition of entropy as a measure of disorder suits well.

We want to choose an attribute that split the data such that class value (yes or no) of the data in daughter nodes are mostly same (low order). If the class values of the data in a node is equally divided among possible values of class value, we say entropy(disorder) of the node is maximum. If the class values of the in a node is same for all data, entropy is minimum. If we are given probability distribution $P = (p1, p2, ..., pn)$ then

$$Entropy(P) = -p_1 \log_2 p_1 - p_2 \log_2 p_2 - ...... - p_n \log_2 p_n$$

In the context of decision tree, if the outcomes of a node is to classify the records into two classes, C1 and C2, the outcome can be viewed as a message that is being generated and the entropy gives the measure of information for a message to be C1 or C2.

If a set of records T is partitioned into a set of disjoint exhaustive classes, C1,C2,....Cn, on the basis of the value of the class attribute, then the information needed to indentify the class of an element of T is as

$$Info(T) = Entropy(P)$$

Where P is the probability distribution of the partion $C_1, C_2, ..., C_n$. P is computed based on their relative frequencies, i.e..,

$$P = (|C_1|/|T|, |C_2|/|T|, ... |C_n|/|T|)$$

Information for a Partition on X

If T is portioned on the value of non-class attribute X, into sets $T_1, T_2, ... T_n$, then the information needed to identify the class of an element of T becomes the weighted average of the information to identify the class of the elements of T_i, i.e., the weighted average of Info(T_i) is

$$Info(X,T) = \sum_{i=0}^{n} \left(\frac{|T_i|}{|T|} Info(T_i) \right)$$

Gain

The information gain due to a split on attribute X as

$$Gain(X, T) = Info(T) - Info(X,T)$$

The information gain represents the difference between the information needed to identify an element of T and the information needed to identify an element of T after the value of attribute X obtained. That is the information due to attribute X.

Gain Ratio

$$Gain\_ratio(X, T) = \frac{Gain(X,T)}{Info(X,T)}$$

Gini Index

If a data set T contains n classes, then gini(T) is defined as

$$Gini(T) = 1 - \sum p_i 2$$

where pi is the relative frequency of class i in T. If the split divides T into T_1 and T_2, then the index of the divided data is given as

$$ginisplit(T) = n_1/n \; gini(T_1) + {}_n2/ngini(T_2)$$

Python code to implement the Decision tree algorithm
```
#importing libraries
import numpy as np
import pandas as pd
import seaborn as sns
import matplotlib.pyplot as plt
#importing dataset
df=pd.read_csv("L:\\DataScienceBook\\CONTENT\\penguins_size.csv")
df.shape    OUTPUT: (344, 7)
```

	species	island	culmen_length_mm	culmen_depth_mm	flipper_length_mm	body_mass_g	sex
0	Adelie	Torgersen	39.1	18.7	181.0	3750.0	MALE
1	Adelie	Torgersen	39.5	17.4	186.0	3800.0	FEMALE
2	Adelie	Torgersen	40.3	18.0	195.0	3250.0	FEMALE
3	Adelie	Torgersen	NaN	NaN	NaN	NaN	NaN
4	Adelie	Torgersen	36.7	19.3	193.0	3450.0	FEMALE

```
#Missing Values Finding
df.isnull().sum()
        species               0
        island                0
        culmen_length_mm      2
        culmen_depth_mm       2
        flipper_length_mm     2
        body_mass_g           2
        sex                  10
                dtype: int64
```

```
#Replacing null values manually
df['culmen_length_mm']=df['culmen_length_mm'].fillna(df['culmen_length_mm'].mean(
))
df['culmen_depth_mm']=df['culmen_depth_mm'].fillna(df['culmen_depth_mm'].mean())
df['flipper_length_mm']=df['flipper_length_mm'].fillna(df['flipper_length_mm'].mean())
df['body_mass_g']=df['body_mass_g'].fillna(df['body_mass_g'].mean())
X=pd.get_dummies(df.drop('species',axis=1),drop_first=True)
y=df[['species']]
```

	culmen_length_mm	culmen_depth_mm	flipper_length_mm	body_mass_g	island_Dream	island_Torgersen	sex_MALE
0	39.10000	18.70000	181.000000	3750.000000	0	1	1
1	39.50000	17.40000	186.000000	3800.000000	0	1	0
2	40.30000	18.00000	195.000000	3250.000000	0	1	0
3	43.92193	17.15117	200.915205	4201.754386	0	1	1
4	36.70000	19.30000	193.000000	3450.000000	0	1	0
...	...	...	...	...	...	...	...
339	43.92193	17.15117	200.915205	4201.754386	0	0	1
340	46.80000	14.30000	215.000000	4850.000000	0	0	0
341	50.40000	15.70000	222.000000	5750.000000	0	0	1
342	45.20000	14.80000	212.000000	5200.000000	0	0	0
343	49.90000	16.10000	213.000000	5400.000000	0	0	1

344 rows × 7 columns

```
#Data set Splitting
from sklearn.model_selection import train_test_split
X_train,X_test,y_train,y_test=train_test_split(X,y,test_size=0.3,random_state=101)
```

```
#Model with Default Hyperparameters
from sklearn.tree import DecisionTreeClassifier
model=DecisionTreeClassifier()
model.fit(X_train,y_train)
```

```
#Prediction
test_pred=model.predict(X_test)
train_pred=model.predict(X_train)
```

```
#Evaluation
from sklearn.metrics import classification_report,confusion_matrix,accuracy_score
accuracy_score(y_train,train_pred)
accuracy_score(y_test,test_pred)
print(confusion_matrix(y_test,test_pred)
```

```
[[41  0  0]
 [ 0 25  1]
 [ 2  0 35]]
```

```
# criterion=gini
model=DecisionTreeClassifier(criterion='gini')
model.fit(X_train,y_train)
test_pred=model.predict(X_test)
train_pred=model.predict(X_train)
print("Train Accuracy:",accuracy_score(y_train,train_pred))
        Train Accuracy: 1.0
print("Test Accuracy:",accuracy_score(y_test,test_pred))
        Test Accuracy: 0.9615384615384616
# Tree Visualization
plt.figure(figsize=(20,15),dpi=300)
plot_tree(model,filled=True,feature_names=X.columns)
```

110

plt.show()

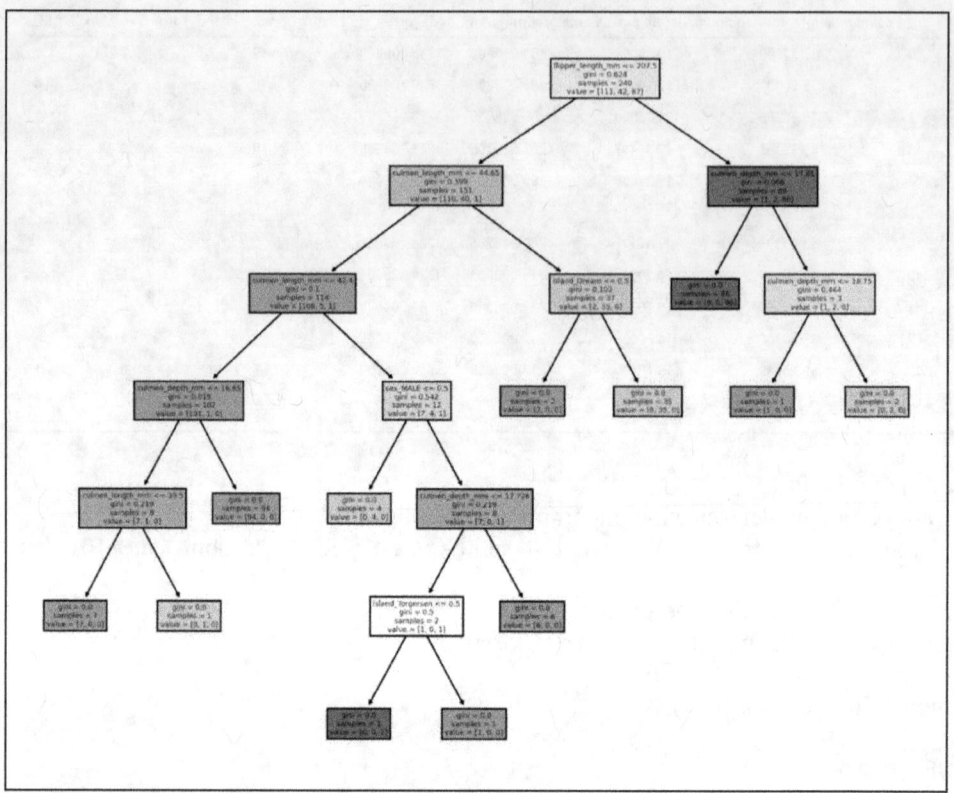

```
#criterion=entropy
model=DecisionTreeClassifier(criterion='entropy')
model.fit(X_train,y_train)
# Prediction
test_pred=model.predict(X_test)
train_pred=model.predict(X_train)
print("Train Accuracy:",accuracy_score(y_train,train_pred))
print("Test Accuracy:",accuracy_score(y_test,test_pred))
        Train Accuracy: 1.0
        Test Accuracy: 0.9903846153846154
print(confusion_matrix(y_test,test_pred))
```

```
[[40  1  0]
 [ 0 26  0]
 [ 0  0 37]]
```

```
plt.figure(figsize=(10,8),dpi=300)
plot_tree(model,filled=True,feature_names=X.columns)
plt.show()
```

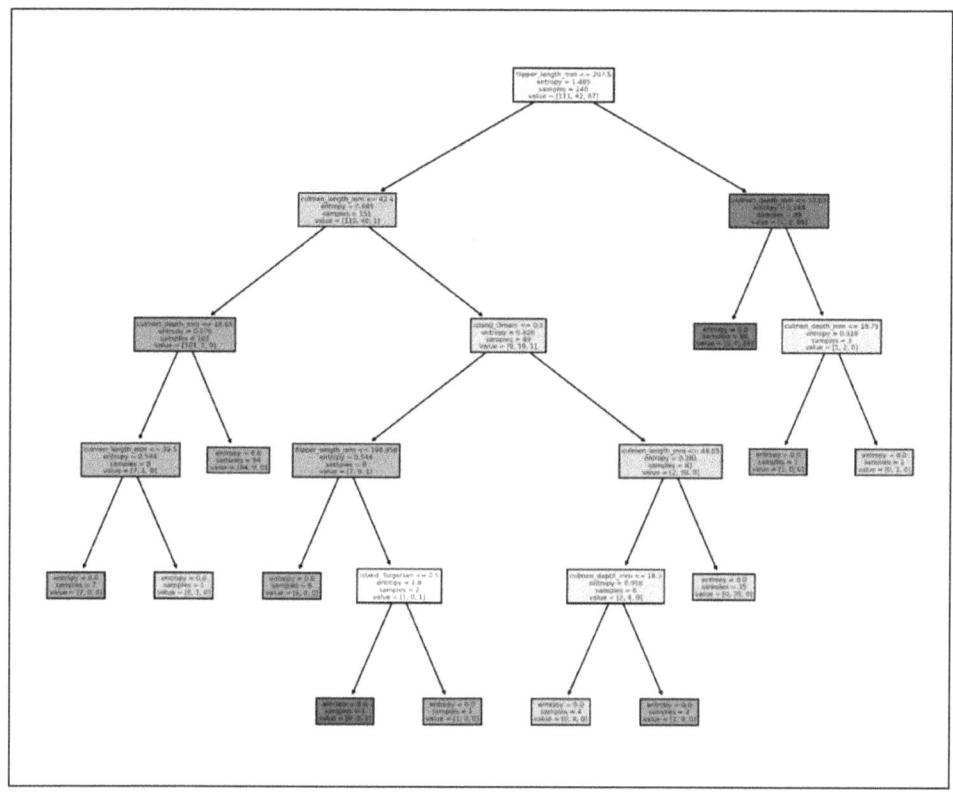

4.8.4 Random Forest Algorithm

Random Forest is a supervised machine learning algorithm that is used for both classification and regression tasks. It is a type of ensemble learning that combines multiple decision trees to produce a more robust model, In machine learning, an ensemble is a collection of models whose predictions are averaged (or aggregated in some way).

Random Forest is another ensemble machine learning algorithm that follows the bagging technique. It is an extension of the bagging estimator algorithm. The base estimators in the random forest are decision trees. Unlike bagging meta estimator, random forest randomly selects a set of features that are used to decide the best split at each node of the decision tree.

How does the random forest algorithm work?

Step by step, the Random forest model does:

1. Random subsets are created from the original dataset (bootstrapping).

2. At each node in the decision tree, only a random set of features is considered to decide the best split.

3. A decision tree model is fitted on each of the subsets.

4. The final prediction is calculated by averaging the predictions from all decision trees.

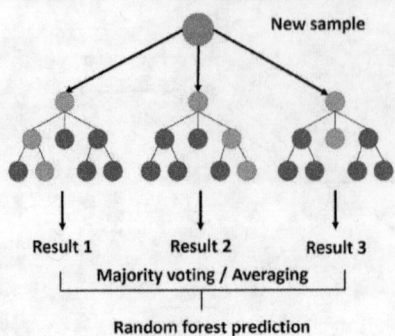

Random forest prediction

Steps:
1. Split the dataset into subsets

A random forest is an ensemble of decision trees. To create many decision trees, we must divide the dataset we have into subsets.

There are two main ways to do this: you can randomly choose on which features to train each tree (random feature subspaces) and take a sample with replacement from the features chosen (bootstrap sample).

2. Train decision trees

After we have split the dataset into subsets, we train decision trees on these subsets. The process of training is the same as it would be for training an individual tree – we just make a lot more of them.

It might be interesting to know that this training process is very scalable: since the trees are independent, you can parallelize the training process easily.

3. Aggregate the results

Each individual tree contains one result that depends on the tree's initial data. To get rid of the dependence on the initial data and produce a more accurate estimation, we combine their output into one result.

Different methods of aggregating the results can be used. For example, in the case of classification, voting by performance is used quite often, whereas for regression, averaging models are applied.

4. Validate the model

After we complete the training procedure with the training data and run the tests with the test dataset, we perform the hold-out validation procedure. This involves training a new model with the same hyperparameters. In particular, these include the number of trees, the pruning and training procedures, the split function, etc.

Note that the objective of training is not to find the specific model instance that is most suitable for us. The goal is to develop a general model without pre-trained parameters and find the most appropriate training procedure in terms of metrics: accuracy, overfitting resistance, memory, and other generic parameters.

The hold-out validation procedure is required for model evaluation purposes only. Another common method to avoid overfitting is k-fold cross-validation. It is based on the same principle: validation of hyperparameters using metrics and overfitting resistance, followed by training a new model on the entire dataset.

Decision trees versus Random forests

A decision tree model takes some input data and follows a series of if-then steps until it reaches one of the predefined output values.

In contrast, a random forest model is a combination of many individual decision trees, trained on subsets of initial data.

As an example, if you wanted to use a single decision tree to predict how often certain customers would use a particular service provided by the bank, you would collect data on how often clients have visited the bank in the past and what services they have used. You would specify certain characteristics that determine the customer's choice. The decision tree would create rules that help you predict whether or not a customer will use the services.

If you put the same data into a random forest, the algorithm would create several trees from randomly selected groups of customers. The output of the forest would be the combination of the individual results of all those trees.

Decision tree	Random forest
An algorithm that generates a tree-like set of rules for classification or regression.	An algorithm that combines many decision trees to produce a more accurate outcome.
When a dataset with certain features is ingested into a decision tree, it generates a set of rules for prediction.	Builds decision trees on random samples of data and averages the results.
High dependency on the initial data set; low accuracy of prediction in the real world as a result.	High precision and reduced bias of results.
Prone to overfitting because of the possibility to adapt to the initial data set too much.	The use of many trees allows the algorithm to avoid and/or prevent overfitting.

Benefits and challenges of the random forest algorithm
Random forest has its advantages and drawbacks. The former, however, outweigh the latter.

Benefits
- Cost-effective. RF is much cheaper and faster to train when compared to neural networks. At the same time, it doesn't suffer much in accuracy. For this reason, random forest modeling is used in mobile applications, for example.
- Robust against overfitting. If one tree makes an inaccurate prediction due to an outlier in its training set, another will most likely compensate for that prediction with the opposite outlier. Thus, a set of uncorrelated trees performs better than any of the individual ones taken separately.
- High coverage rates and low bias. The above makes random forest classifier ideal for situations where there may be some missing values in your dataset or if you want to understand how much variance there is between different types of data output (e.g., college undergraduates who are likely to finish their studies and leave, proceed to master's degree, or drop out).
- Applicable for classification and regression. RF has proven equally accurate results for both types of tasks.
- Can handle missing values in features without introducing bias into predictions.
- Easy to interpret. Every tree in the forest makes predictions independently, so you can look at any individual tree to understand its prediction.

Challenges
There are some challenges associated with random forest classifiers as well:

- Random forests are more complicated than decision trees, where just following the route of the tree is enough for making a decision.
- The RF classifiers tend to be slower than some other types of machine learning models, so they might not be suitable for some applications.
- They work best with large datasets and when there is sufficient training data available.

Applications of random forest

This algorithm is used to forecast behavior and outcomes in a number of sectors, including banking and finance, e-commerce, and healthcare. It has been increasingly employed thanks to its ease of application, adaptability, and ability to perform both classification and regression tasks.

Advantages of a Random Forest

- We can use Random Forests for both classification and regression problems.
- The predictions by random forests are easily understandable.
- It can handle large datasets efficiently.
- A highly accurate and robust method, as there are several Decision Trees in the process.
- It eliminates or reduces over-fitting of data science model by taking the average of all the predictions, canceling the biases.
- It can handle missing values by using median values to replace continuous variables and computing the proximity-weighted average of missing values.
- Random Forest uses the application of feature importance, helping to determine the most contributing features.

Disadvantages of a Random Forest

- The whole process of Random Forest is very slow at generating predictions due to the multiple trees. Moreover, it is a time-consuming algorithm.
- Compared to Decision Trees, the Random Forest model is difficult to interpret and make quick decisions.
- The process also takes more time than Decision Trees.

Applications Where Random Forest is Preferable

The Random Forest algorithm excels in various applications where it is considered among the best approaches. This is due to its versatility, ease of use, and robust performance. Here are a few scenarios where Random Forest can be particularly effective:

1. **Biomedical Fields**: For medical diagnoses, we can use the Random Forest algorithm to classify the patient's disease as malignant or benign based on their medical records.
2. **Banking Industry**: It is useful in detecting customers who are more likely to be safe or risky for loans or to detect fraudulent activity based on patterns of transactions.
3. **E-Commerce**: Random Forest helps recommend products to users based on their past purchasing history and behavior on the site.
4. **Stock Market Analysis**: It can predict stock price movements and trends, aiding investment decision-making.
5. **Quality Control**: In manufacturing, it can predict the failure of a product or a manufacturing process.
6. **Remote Sensing**: The algorithm is adept at classifying different land cover types in satellite images.

The key reasons why Random Forest is a good choice for these applications include its ability to handle large datasets with higher dimensionality, its robustness to noise, and its capability to run in parallel, which speeds up the training process. Moreover, it provides a good estimate of the importance of features, which helps understand the factors driving the prediction, making it valuable for real-world applications.

Example to understand the random forests

Consider the fruit basket as the data as shown in the figure below. Now n number of samples are taken from the fruit basket and an individual decision tree is constructed for each sample. Each decision tree will generate an output as shown in the figure. The final output is considered based on majority voting. In the below figure you can see that the majority decision tree gives output as an apple when compared to a banana, so the final output is taken as an apple.

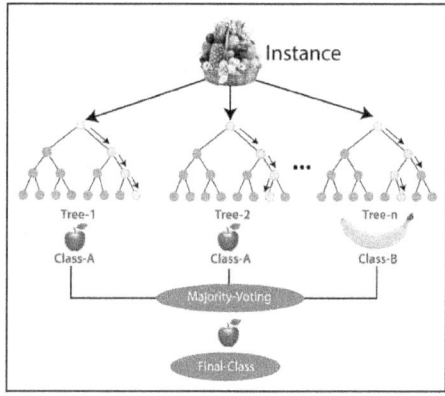

Python code to implement the Random Forest algorithms

```
# Importing the libraries
import numpy as np
import matplotlib.pyplot as plt
import pandas as pd
#Importing the dataset
dataset = pd.read_csv('Social_Network_Ads.csv')
X = dataset.iloc[:, [2, 3]].values
y = dataset.iloc[:, -1].values
# Splitting the dataset into the Training set and Test set
from sklearn.model_selection import train_test_split
X_train, X_test, y_train, y_test = train_test_split(X, y, test_size = 0.25, random_state = 0)

#Training the Random Forest Classification model on the Training set

from sklearn.ensemble import RandomForestClassifier
classifier = RandomForestClassifier(n_estimators = 10, criterion = 'entropy', random_state = 0)
classifier.fit(X_train, y_train)
y_pred = classifier.predict(X_test)
#Confusion Matrix
from sklearn.metrics import confusion_matrix
cm = confusion_matrix(y_test, y_pred)
print(cm)
            [[63  5]
             [ 4 28]]

# Visualising the Training set results
from matplotlib.colors import ListedColormap
X_set, y_set = X_train, y_train
```

```
X1, X2 = np.meshgrid(np.arange(start = X_set[:, 0].min() - 1, stop = X_set[:, 0].max() +
1, step = 0.01),np.arange(start = X_set[:, 1].min() - 1, stop = X_set[:, 1].max() + 1, step =
0.01))
plt.contourf(X1, X2, classifier.predict(np.array([X1.ravel(),
X2.ravel()]).T).reshape(X1.shape), alpha = 0.75, cmap = ListedColormap(('red',
'green')))
plt.xlim(X1.min(), X1.max())
plt.ylim(X2.min(), X2.max())
for i, j in enumerate(np.unique(y_set)):
    plt.scatter(X_set[y_set == j, 0], X_set[y_set == j, 1],
            c = ListedColormap(('red', 'green'))(i), label = j)
plt.title('Random Forest Classification (Training set)')
plt.xlabel('Age')
plt.ylabel('Estimated Salary')
plt.legend()
plt.show()
```

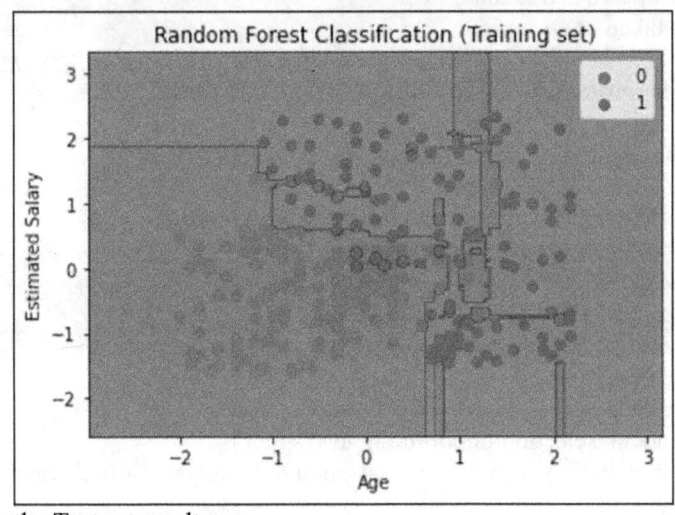

```
# Visualising the Test set results
from matplotlib.colors import ListedColormap
X_set, y_set = X_test, y_test
X1, X2 = np.meshgrid(np.arange(start = X_set[:, 0].min() - 1, stop = X_set[:, 0].max() +
1, step = 0.01),
                np.arange(start = X_set[:, 1].min() - 1, stop = X_set[:, 1].max() + 1, step =
0.01))
plt.contourf(X1, X2, classifier.predict(np.array([X1.ravel(),
X2.ravel()]).T).reshape(X1.shape),
        alpha = 0.75, cmap = ListedColormap(('red', 'green')))
plt.xlim(X1.min(), X1.max())
plt.ylim(X2.min(), X2.max())
for i, j in enumerate(np.unique(y_set)):
    plt.scatter(X_set[y_set == j, 0], X_set[y_set == j, 1],
            c = ListedColormap(('red', 'green'))(i), label = j)
plt.title('Random Forest Classification (Test set)')
plt.xlabel('Age')
plt.ylabel('Estimated Salary')
plt.legend()
```

plt.show()

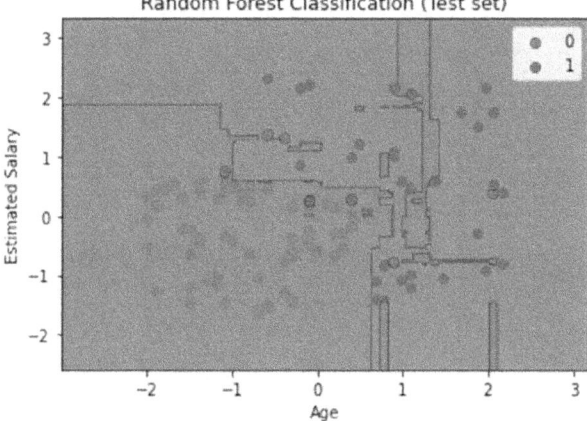

4.8.5 Support Vector Machine Algorithm

A Support Vector Machine (SVM) is a supervised learning algorithm used for classification and regression tasks. It is widely used in machine learning and has proven to be effective in various applications. SVM can be used for Regression and classification The main idea behind SVM is to find an optimal hyperplane that separates the data into different classes. In the case of binary classification, the hyperplane represents a decision boundary that maximizes the margin between the two classes. The margin is defined as the distance between the hyperplane and the nearest data points from each class, known as support vectors.

SVMs can handle both linearly separable and non-linearly separable data by using different kernel functions. A kernel function transforms the input data into a higher-dimensional feature space, where it may become linearly separable. This allows SVMs to capture complex relationships and handle non-linear decision boundaries.

The training process of an SVM involves finding the optimal hyperplane by solving an optimization problem. The objective is to maximize the margin while minimizing the classification error. This optimization problem can be solved using various algorithms, such as the Sequential Minimal Optimization (SMO) or the Quadratic Programming (QP) method.Once the SVM is trained, it can be used to predict the class labels of new, unseen data points. The decision boundary determined during training is used to classify the new instances.

The goal of the SVM algorithm is to create the best line or decision boundary that can segregate n-dimensional space into classes so that we can easily put the new data point in the correct category in the future. This best decision boundary is called a hyperplane.

Types of SVM

SVM can be of two types:

Linear SVM: Linear SVM is used for linearly separable data, which means if a dataset can be classified into two classes by using a single straight line, then such data is termed as linearly separable data, and classifier is used called as Linear SVM classifier.

Non-linear SVM(Kernel SVM): Non-Linear SVM is used for non-linearly separated data, which means if a dataset cannot be classified by using a straight line, then such data is termed as non-linear data and classifier used is called as Non-linear SVM classifier.

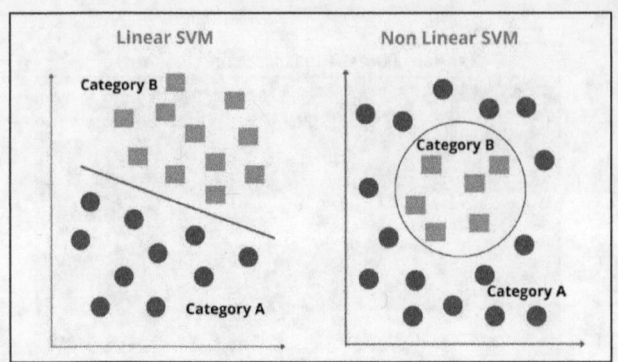

Let's walk through the steps of the Support Vector Machine (SVM) algorithm using an example in binary classification. Suppose we have a dataset of flower samples with two features: sepal length and sepal width. The dataset contains two classes: *Setosa* and *Versicolor*. Our goal is to train an SVM model to classify new flowers based on these two features

Object	Sepal Length	Sepal Width	Species
1	5.1	3.5	Setosa
2	4.9	3.0	Setosa
3	6.2	2.9	Virginica
4	5.5	4.2	Setosa
5	6.3	2.8	Virginica

The SVM algorithm helps to find the best line or decision boundary; this best boundary or region is called as a hyperplane. SVM algorithm finds the closest point of the lines from both the classes. These points are called support vectors. The distance between the vectors and the hyperplane is called as margin. And the goal of SVM is to maximize this margin. The hyperplane with maximum margin is called the optimal hyperplane.

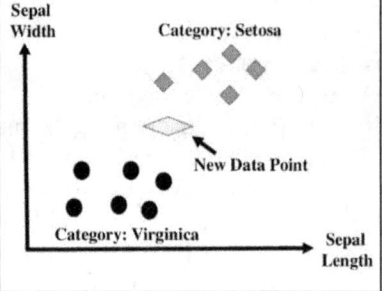

The goal of the SVM algorithm is to create the best line or decision boundary that can segregate n-dimensional space into classes so that we can easily put the new data point in the correct category in the future. This best decision boundary is called a hyperplane.

SVM chooses the extreme points/vectors that help in creating the hyperplane. These extreme cases are called as support vectors, and hence algorithm is termed as Support Vector Machine. Consider the below diagram in which there are two different categories that are classified using a decision boundary or hyperplane:

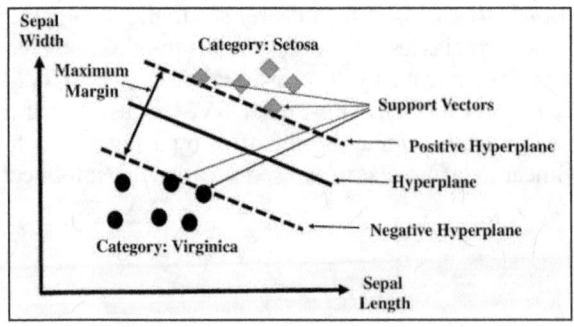

Hyperplane and Support Vectors in the SVM algorithm:

Hyperplane: There can be multiple lines/decision boundaries to segregate the classes in n-dimensional space, but we need to find out the best decision boundary that helps to classify the data points. This best boundary is known as the hyperplane of SVM.

The dimensions of the hyperplane depend on the features present in the dataset, which means if there are 2 features (as shown in image), then hyperplane will be a straight line. And if there are 3 features, then hyperplane will be a 2-dimension plane.

We always create a hyperplane that has a maximum margin, which means the maximum distance between the data points.

*Support Vectors:*The data points or vectors that are the closest to the hyperplane and which affect the position of the hyperplane are termed as Support Vector. Since these vectors support the hyperplane, hence called a Support vector.

How SVM works:

- **Linear SVM**: The working of the SVM algorithm can be understood by using an example. Suppose we have a dataset that has two tags (green and blue), and the dataset has two features x1 and x2. We want a classifier that can classify the pair(x1, x2) of coordinates in either green or blue. Consider the below image:

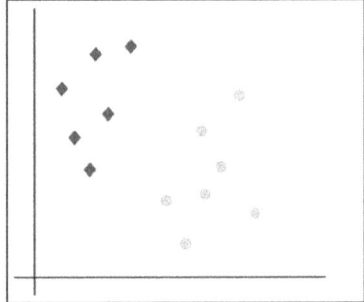

  So as it is 2-d space so by just using a straight line, we can easily separate these two classes. But there can be multiple lines that can separate these classes. Consider the below image:

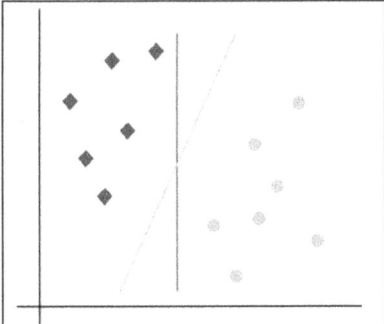

  Hence, the SVM algorithm helps to find the best line or decision boundary; this best boundary or region is called as a hyperplane. SVM algorithm finds the closest point of the lines from both the classes. These points are called support vectors. The distance between the vectors and the hyperplane is called as margin. And the goal of SVM is to maximize this margin. The hyperplane with maximum margin is called the optimal hyperplane

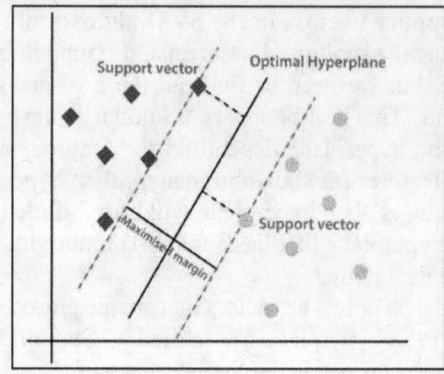

- **Non-Linear SVM:**If data is linearly arranged, then we can separate it by using a straight line, but for non-linear data, we cannot draw a single straight line. Consider the below image:

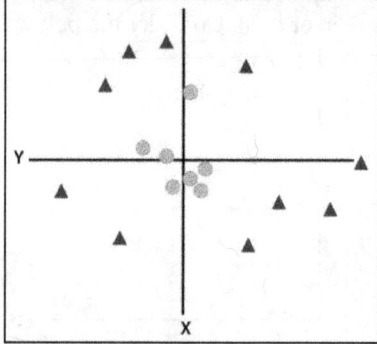

So to separate these data points, we need to add one more dimension. For linear data, we have used two dimensions x and y, so for non-linear data, we will add a third dimension z. It can be calculated as:

$$z=x^2 +y^2$$

By adding the third dimension, the sample space will become as below image:

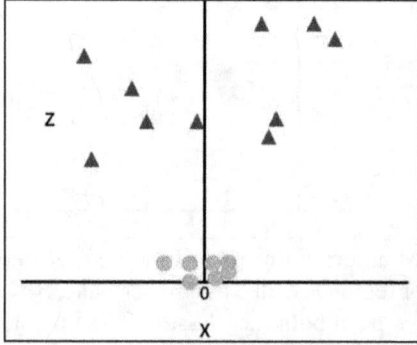

So now, SVM will divide the datasets into classes in the following way. Consider the below image:

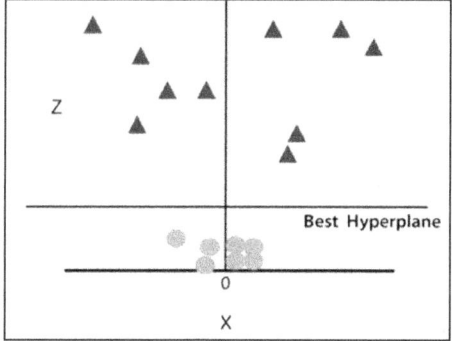

Since we are in 3-d Space, hence it is looking like a plane parallel to the x-axis. If we convert it in 2d space with z=1, then it will become as:

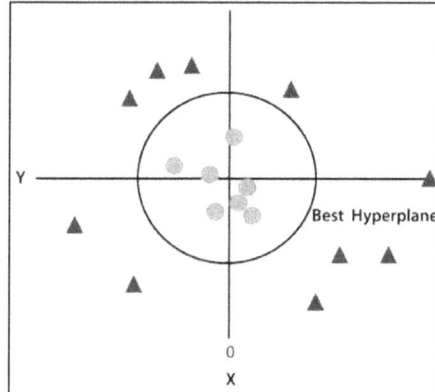

Hence we get a circumference of radius 1 in case of non-linear data.

Python code to implement SVM model

```
#Importing the libraries
import numpy as np
import matplotlib.pyplot as plt
import pandas as pd
#Importing the dataset
dataset = pd.read_csv('Social_Network_Ads.csv')
X = dataset.iloc[:, [2, 3]].values
y = dataset.iloc[:, -1].values
#Splitting the dataset into the Training set and Test set
from sklearn.model_selection import train_test_split
X_train, X_test, y_train, y_test = train_test_split(X, y, test_size = 0.25, random_state =
0)
# Training the SVM model on the Training set
from sklearn.svm import SVC
classifier = SVC(kernel = 'linear', random_state = 0)
classifier.fit(X_train, y_train)
SVC(C=1.0, break_ties=False, cache_size=200, class_weight=None, coef0=0.0,
    decision_function_shape='ovr', degree=3, gamma='scale', kernel='linear',
    max_iter=-1, probability=False, random_state=0, shrinking=True, tol=0.001,
    verbose=False)
#Predicting the Test set results
y_pred = classifier.predict(X_test)
#Making the Confusion Matrix
```

```
from sklearn.metrics import confusion_matrix
cm = confusion_matrix(y_test, y_pred)
print(cm)
                    [[66  2]
                     [ 8 24]]
# Visualising the Training set results
from matplotlib.colors import ListedColormap
X_set, y_set = X_train, y_train
X1, X2 = np.meshgrid(np.arange(start = X_set[:, 0].min() - 1, stop = X_set[:, 0].max() +
1, step = 0.01),
                np.arange(start = X_set[:, 1].min() - 1, stop = X_set[:, 1].max() + 1, step =
0.01))
plt.contourf(X1, X2, classifier.predict(np.array([X1.ravel(),
X2.ravel()]).T).reshape(X1.shape),
        alpha = 0.75, cmap = ListedColormap(('red', 'green')))
plt.xlim(X1.min(), X1.max())
plt.ylim(X2.min(), X2.max())
for i, j in enumerate(np.unique(y_set)):
    plt.scatter(X_set[y_set == j, 0], X_set[y_set == j, 1],
            c = ListedColormap(('red', 'green'))(i), label = j)
plt.title('SVM (Training set)')
plt.xlabel('Age')
plt.ylabel('Estimated Salary')
plt.legend()
plt.show()
```

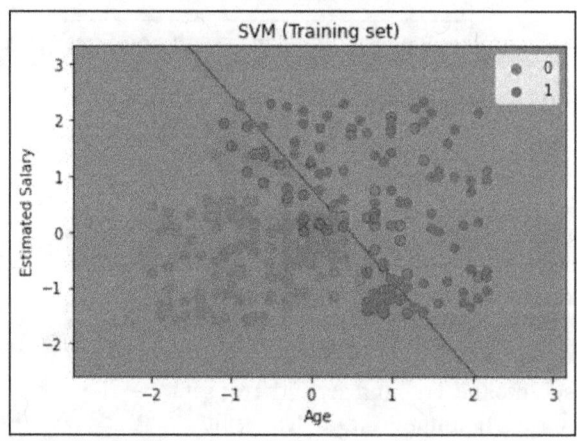

```
# Visualising the Test set results
from matplotlib.colors import ListedColormap
X_set, y_set = X_test, y_test
X1, X2 = np.meshgrid(np.arange(start = X_set[:, 0].min() - 1, stop = X_set[:, 0].max() +
1, step = 0.01),np.arange(start = X_set[:, 1].min() - 1, stop = X_set[:, 1].max() + 1, step =
0.01))
plt.contourf(X1, X2, classifier.predict(np.array([X1.ravel(),
X2.ravel()]).T).reshape(X1.shape), alpha = 0.75, cmap = ListedColormap(('red',
'green')))
plt.xlim(X1.min(), X1.max())
plt.ylim(X2.min(), X2.max())
for i, j in enumerate(np.unique(y_set)):
    plt.scatter(X_set[y_set == j, 0], X_set[y_set == j, 1],
```

```
              c = ListedColormap(('red', 'green'))(i), label = j)
plt.title('SVM (Test set)')
plt.xlabel('Age')
plt.ylabel('Estimated Salary')
plt.legend()
plt.show()
```

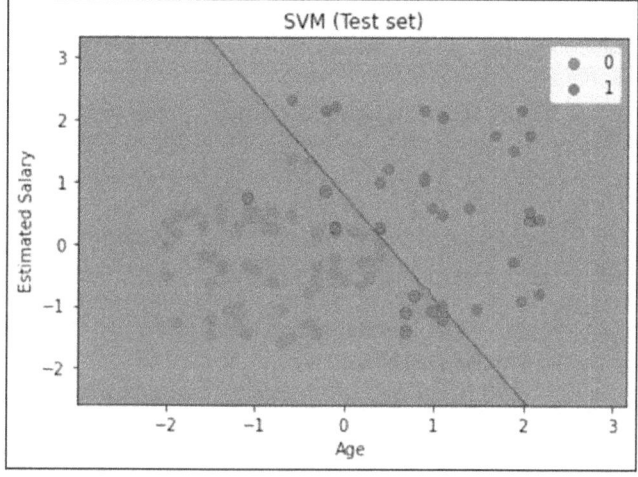

4.8.6 Naive Bays Theorem

The Bayes classification algorithm, often referred to as **Naive Bayes**, is a family of simple yet powerful probabilistic classifiers based on Bayes' Theorem. Despite its simplicity, Naive Bayes classifiers are surprisingly effective for a variety of tasks, especially in text classification, spam filtering, and sentiment analysis.

Key Concepts of Naive Bayes:

1. **Bayes' Theorem**: Bayes' Theorem is the mathematical foundation of the Naive Bayes classifier. It describes the probability of an event occurring based on prior knowledge of conditions related to the event. Bayes' theorem is also known as Bayes' Rule or Bayes' law, which is used to determine the probability of a hypothesis with prior knowledge. It depends on the conditional probability. The formula for Bayes' theorem is given as:

$$P(A|B) = \frac{P(B|A)P(A)}{P(B)}$$

Where,

P(A|B) is Posterior probability: Probability of hypothesis A on the observed event B.

P(B|A) is Likelihood probability: Probability of the evidence given that the probability of a hypothesis is true.

P(A) is Prior Probability: Probability of hypothesis before observing the evidence.

P(B) is Marginal Probability: Probability of Evidence.

Naïve Bayes algorithm is a supervised learning algorithm, which is based on Bayes theorem and used for solving classification problems.

It is mainly used in text classification that includes a high-dimensional training dataset.

Naïve Bayes Classifier is one of the simple and most effective Classification algorithms which helps in building the fast machine learning models that can make quick predictions.

It is a probabilistic classifier, which means it predicts on the basis of the probability of an object.

Some popular examples of Naïve Bayes Algorithm are spam filtration, Sentimental analysis, and classifying articles.

Why is it called Naïve Bayes?

The Naïve Bayes algorithm is comprised of two words Naïve and Bayes, Which can be described as:

Naïve: It is called Naïve because it assumes that the occurrence of a certain feature is independent of the occurrence of other features. Such as if the fruit is identified on the bases of color, shape, and taste, then red, spherical, and sweet fruit is recognized as an apple. Hence each feature individually contributes to identify that it is an apple without depending on each other.

Bayes: It is called Bayes because it depends on the principle of Bayes' Theorem.

2. **Naive Assumption**: The "naive" part of Naive Bayes comes from the assumption that the features (predictors) are conditionally independent of each other given the class label. This assumption simplifies the computation of the posterior probabilities and is what makes the algorithm computationally efficient.

Despite this strong assumption of independence, Naive Bayes often performs well in practice, particularly when dealing with large datasets.

3. **Types of Naive Bayes Classifiers**:
    1. **Gaussian Naive Bayes**: Assumes that the continuous values associated with each feature are distributed according to a Gaussian (normal) distribution.
    2. **Multinomial Naive Bayes**: Typically used for discrete data, such as word counts in text classification. It assumes that the features follow a multinomial distribution.
    3. **Bernoulli Naive Bayes**: Used for binary/boolean features. It assumes that the features follow a Bernoulli distribution.

How Naive Bayes Works:

1. **Training Phase**:
    o The algorithm calculates the prior probability for each class.
    o It then computes the likelihood of each feature given each class.
    o These probabilities are stored for later use in the prediction phase.
2. **Prediction Phase**:
    o For a given instance, the algorithm calculates the posterior probability for each class using Bayes' Theorem.
    o The class with the highest posterior probability is chosen as the predicted class for that instance.

Python code to implement Naïve Bayesian algorithm

```
#Importing the libraries
import numpy as np
import matplotlib.pyplot as plt
import pandas as pd
#Importing the dataset
dataset = pd.read_csv('Social_Network_Ads.csv')
X = dataset.iloc[:, [2, 3]].values
y = dataset.iloc[:, -1].values
Splitting the dataset into the Training set and Test set
from sklearn.model_selection import train_test_split
X_train, X_test, y_train, y_test = train_test_split(X, y, test_size = 0.25, random_state = 0)
#Feature Scaling
```

```
from sklearn.preprocessing import StandardScaler
sc = StandardScaler()
X_train = sc.fit_transform(X_train)
X_test = sc.transform(X_test)
#Training the Naive Bayes model on the Training set
from sklearn.naive_bayes import GaussianNB
classifier = GaussianNB()
classifier.fit(X_train, y_train)
GaussianNB(priors=None, var_smoothing=1e-09)
#Predicting the Test set results
y_pred = classifier.predict(X_test)
#Making the Confusion Matrix
from sklearn.metrics import confusion_matrix
cm = confusion_matrix(y_test, y_pred)
print(cm)
[[65  3]
 [ 7 25]]
#Visualising the Training set results
from matplotlib.colors import ListedColormap
X_set, y_set = X_train, y_train
X1, X2 = np.meshgrid(np.arange(start = X_set[:, 0].min() - 1, stop = X_set[:, 0].max() +
1, step = 0.01),
            np.arange(start = X_set[:, 1].min() - 1, stop = X_set[:, 1].max() + 1, step =
0.01))
plt.contourf(X1, X2, classifier.predict(np.array([X1.ravel(),
X2.ravel()]).T).reshape(X1.shape),
        alpha = 0.75, cmap = ListedColormap(('red', 'green')))
plt.xlim(X1.min(), X1.max())
plt.ylim(X2.min(), X2.max())
for i, j in enumerate(np.unique(y_set)):
    plt.scatter(X_set[y_set == j, 0], X_set[y_set == j, 1],
            c = ListedColormap(('red', 'green'))(i), label = j)
plt.title('Naive Bayes (Training set)')
plt.xlabel('Age')
plt.ylabel('Estimated Salary')
plt.legend()
plt.show()
```

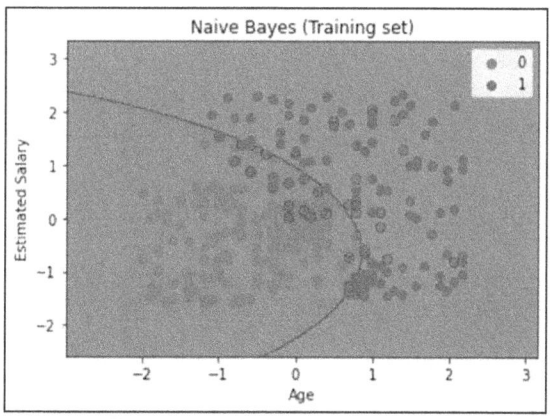

#Visualising the Test set results

```
from matplotlib.colors import ListedColormap
X_set, y_set = X_test, y_test
X1, X2 = np.meshgrid(np.arange(start = X_set[:, 0].min() - 1, stop = X_set[:, 0].max() +
1, step = 0.01),
            np.arange(start = X_set[:, 1].min() - 1, stop = X_set[:, 1].max() + 1, step =
0.01))
plt.contourf(X1, X2, classifier.predict(np.array([X1.ravel(),
X2.ravel()]).T).reshape(X1.shape),
        alpha = 0.75, cmap = ListedColormap(('red', 'green')))
plt.xlim(X1.min(), X1.max())
plt.ylim(X2.min(), X2.max())
for i, j in enumerate(np.unique(y_set)):
    plt.scatter(X_set[y_set == j, 0], X_set[y_set == j, 1],
            c = ListedColormap(('red', 'green'))(i), label = j)
plt.title('Naive Bayes (Test set)')
plt.xlabel('Age')
plt.ylabel('Estimated Salary')
plt.legend()
plt.show()
```

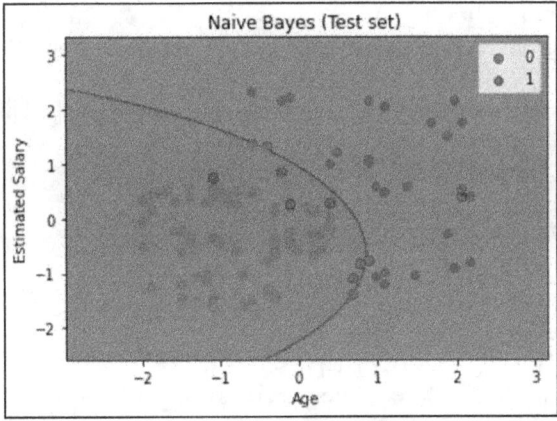

Chapter 5: Unsupervised Learning

5.1 Unsupervised Learning
What is Unsupervised Learning?

Unsupervised learning is a type of machine learning where a model is trained on unlabeled data (i.e., data without predefined categories or target values). The algorithm explores the structure of the data and identifies patterns, relationships, or groupings without explicit supervision.

Key Characteristics

- No labeled data (only input features, no target values).
- Finds hidden structures, relationships, or clusters.
- Used for **data exploration, pattern recognition, and dimensionality reduction**.

5.1.1 Categories of Unsupervised Machine Learning

1. Clustering

Clustering algorithms group similar data points together based on shared characteristics.

Common Clustering Algorithms:

- K-Means Clustering
- Hierarchical Clustering
- DBSCAN (Density-Based Spatial Clustering)
- Gaussian Mixture Models (GMM)

Example Applications:

- **Customer segmentation** in marketing (e.g., grouping customers based on buying behavior).
- **Anomaly detection** in cybersecurity (e.g., detecting fraud in transactions).
- **Image segmentation** (e.g., separating objects in images).

2. Dimensionality Reduction

This technique reduces the number of input variables while retaining the most important information.

Common Dimensionality Reduction Algorithms:

- Principal Component Analysis (PCA)
- t-Distributed Stochastic Neighbor Embedding (t-SNE)
- Autoencoders (Neural Networks for feature learning)

Example Applications:

- **Data visualization** (reducing high-dimensional data to 2D or 3D for easier interpretation).
- **Feature extraction** to improve supervised learning models.
- **Noise reduction** in image and text processing.

Real-World Applications of Unsupervised Learning

- **Recommendation Systems** (e.g., Netflix, Amazon) – Suggesting content based on user behavior.
- **Anomaly Detection** – Fraud detection in banking.
- **Genetics & Biology** – Identifying gene patterns.
- **Self-Driving Cars** – Recognizing road objects and scenes.

5.1.2 Clustering

Clustering is an **unsupervised learning** technique used to **group similar data points** together based on patterns or similarities. It helps in understanding the hidden structure of data without any predefined labels.

Key Characteristics of Clustering:

No labeled data – The algorithm learns patterns without predefined categories.

Groups similar data points – Items in the same cluster are more similar to each other than to those in different clusters.

Helps in data exploration – Useful for customer segmentation, anomaly detection, and more.

Clustering or cluster analysis is a machine learning technique, which groups the unlabeled dataset. It can be defined as "A way of grouping the data points into different clusters, consisting of similar data points. The objects with the possible similarities remain in a group that has less or no similarities with another group."

It does it by finding some similar patterns in the unlabeled dataset such as shape, size, color, behavior, etc., and divides them as per the presence and absence of those similar patterns.

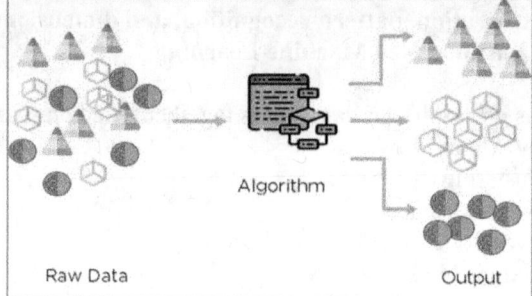

It is an unsupervised learning method, hence no supervision is provided to the algorithm, and it deals with the unlabeled dataset.

Clustering is somewhere similar to the classification algorithm, but the difference is the type of dataset that we are using. In classification, we work with the labeled data set, whereas in clustering, we work with the unlabeled dataset.

The goal of clustering is to uncover inherent structures or relationships in the data without any prior knowledge or labels. It is considered an unsupervised learning technique since it does not rely on predefined classes or categories. Clustering algorithms analyze the input data and automatically partition it into clusters based on the similarity or proximity of the data points.

Real-World Applications of Clustering

Customer Segmentation – Grouping customers for targeted marketing.

Anomaly Detection – Detecting fraudulent transactions.

Genetics – Identifying patterns in DNA sequences.

Search Engines – Grouping similar search results.

Clustering vs Classification

Classification and clustering are both techniques used in machine learning, but they serve different purposes and have distinct characteristics. Here are the main differences between classification and clustering:

Aspect	Classification	Clustering
Labeled Data	Requires labeled data (input-output pairs).	No labeled data; finds patterns based on data similarities.
Output Type	Discrete categories (e.g., Spam or Not Spam).	Groups (clusters) with no predefined labels.
Approach	Learns from examples with known labels.	Identifies structure and groups within the data.
Supervision	Supervised learning (uses training data with labels).	Unsupervised learning (no labels available).

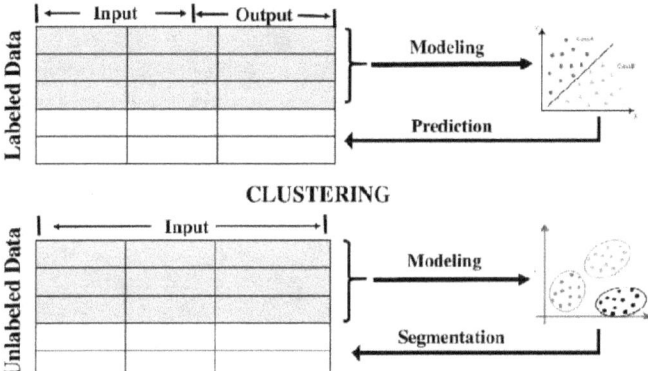

Applications of Clustering

Clustering has various applications in machine learning across different domains. Some of the common applications of clustering are:

1. **Customer Segmentation:** Clustering can be used to group customers based on their similarities in terms of demographics, purchasing behavior, or preferences. This helps in creating targeted marketing strategies, personalized recommendations, and understanding customer segments for better customer relationship management.

2. **Image Segmentation:** Clustering algorithms can be employed to segment images by grouping similar pixels or regions together. It is useful in computer vision tasks, such as object recognition, image compression, and medical image analysis.

3. **Anomaly Detection:** Clustering can help identify unusual patterns or outliers in datasets by considering them as separate clusters. It is valuable in detecting fraud, network intrusions, or any abnormal behavior in various domains like finance, cybersecurity, and healthcare.

4. **Document Clustering:** Clustering methods can organize large collections of text documents into groups based on their semantic similarity. It aids in information retrieval, topic modeling, document organization, and summarization.

5. **Social Network Analysis:** Clustering techniques can be applied to analyze social networks and identify communities or groups of individuals with similar interests or interactions. It is beneficial for understanding social relationships, viral marketing, and recommendation systems.

6. **Gene Expression Analysis:** Clustering can help in grouping genes or samples based on their expression patterns, aiding in gene discovery, understanding disease subtypes, and identifying biomarkers.

7. **Recommender Systems:** Clustering can be used to group users or items based on their preferences, enabling personalized recommendations in e-commerce, movie streaming platforms, and music services.

8. **Image and Video Retrieval:** Clustering algorithms can be utilized to organize and retrieve images or videos based on visual similarities, enabling content-based image retrieval and video indexing.

9. **Market Segmentation:** Clustering can be employed to segment markets based on various factors like demographics, purchasing behavior, or geographical location. It assists businesses in targeted marketing, product positioning, and understanding market trends.

10. **Sensor Data Analysis:** Clustering can group similar patterns in sensor data for various applications, such as anomaly detection in IoT systems, environmental monitoring, and predictive maintenance.

11. **In Identification of Cancer Cells**: The clustering algorithms are widely used for the identification of cancerous cells. It divides the cancerous and non-cancerous data sets into different groups.

12. **In Search Engines:** Search engines also work on the clustering technique. The search result appears based on the closest object to the search query. It does it by grouping similar data objects in one group that is far from the other dissimilar objects. The accurate result of a query depends on the quality of the clustering algorithm used.

13. **In Biology:** It is used in the biology stream to classify different species of plants and animals using the image recognition technique.

14. **In Land Use:** The clustering technique is used in identifying the area of similar lands use in the GIS database. This can be very useful to find that for what purpose the particular land should be used, that means for which purpose it is more suitable.

15. **Retail/Marketing**

16. **Banking**

17. **Insurance**

18. **Publications**

19. **Medicine**

5.1.2.1 Types of Clustering Methods

The clustering methods are broadly divided into Hard clustering (data point belongs to only one group) and Soft Clustering (data points can belong to another group also). But there are also other various approaches of Clustering exist. Below are the main clustering methods used in Machine learning?

    (a) Partitioning Clustering

    (b) Hierarchical Clustering

    (c) Density-Based Clustering

    (d) Distribution Model-Based Clustering

(a) Partitioning Clustering

Partitioning clustering is a type of clustering method that divides a dataset into non-overlapping partitions or clusters. The goal is to group similar data points together within the same cluster while maximizing the dissimilarity between different clusters. Partitioning clustering algorithms typically require the user to specify the number of clusters beforehand. It is also known as the centroid-based method. Centroid-based clustering is the one you probably hear about the most. It's a little sensitive to the initial parameters you give it, but it's fast and efficient.

These types of algorithms separate data points based on multiple centroids in the data. Each data point is assigned to a cluster based on its squared distance from the centroid. This is the most commonly used type of clustering.

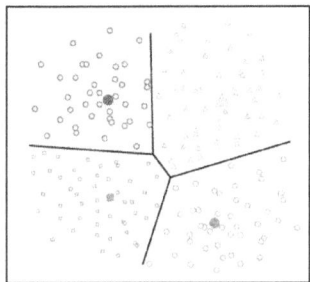

K-means: This algorithm partitions the data into a predefined number of clusters by minimizing the sum of squared distances between data points and the centroid of each cluster.

K-medoids: PAM(K-Medoids), Similar to K-means, but instead of using centroids, it uses representative data points called medoids.

Hierarchical K-means:

Fuzzy C-means: It assigns data points to multiple clusters with varying degrees of membership, allowing data points to belong to multiple clusters simultaneously.

CLARA algorithm: (Clustering Large Applications):

(b) Hierarchical Clustering

Hierarchical clustering is a clustering method in machine learning that aims to build a hierarchy of clusters by iteratively merging or dividing data points or existing clusters. It organizes the data in a tree-like structure called a dendrogram, which provides a visual representation of the clustering process and the relationships between clusters at different levels.

Agglomerative: This method starts with each data point as a separate cluster and iteratively merges the most similar clusters until a termination condition is met. It results in a hierarchy of clusters.

Divisive: It begins with all data points in a single cluster and recursively divides them into smaller clusters until a termination condition is met. It is the reverse of agglomerative clustering.

(c) Density-based Clustering

Density-based clustering is a clustering method in machine learning that groups data points based on their density in the feature space. Unlike other clustering methods that rely on predefined cluster shapes or distances, density-based clustering algorithms are capable of discovering clusters of arbitrary shapes and sizes. The key idea behind density-based clustering is that clusters are regions of high density separated by regions of low density. The density-based clustering method connects the highly-dense areas into clusters, and the arbitrarily shaped distributions are formed as long as the dense region can be connected. This algorithm does it by identifying different clusters in the dataset and connects the areas of high densities into clusters. The dense areas in data space are divided from each other by sparser areas. These algorithms can face difficulty in clustering the data points if the dataset has varying densities and high dimensions.

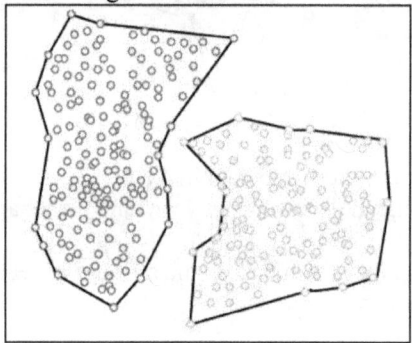

DBSCAN (Density-Based Spatial Clustering of Applications with Noise): It groups data points based on their density and identifies clusters as regions of high density separated by regions of low density. It can discover clusters of arbitrary shape and handle noise and outliers effectively.

OPTICS (Ordering Points To Identify the Clustering Structure): It extends DBSCAN by providing a hierarchical view of the clusters. It creates a reachability plot that orders the data points based on their density reachability.

(d) Model-based Clustering

It is also called as Distribution Model-Based Clustering. Distribution model-based clustering is a clustering method in machine learning that assumes that the data points are generated from specific probability distributions. The goal is to estimate the parameters of these distributions to identify clusters within the data. This approach assumes that the data points within a cluster follow a certain distribution, and the clustering process involves modeling these distributions.

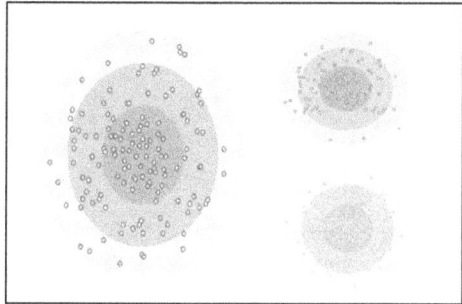

Gaussian Mixture Models (GMM): It assumes that the data is generated from a mixture of Gaussian distributions and estimates the parameters of these distributions to identify clusters. It allows soft assignment of data points to clusters.

Hierarchical Dirichlet Process (HDP): It is a Bayesian nonparametric approach that uses the Dirichlet process to model the distribution of clusters. It allows for automatic determination of the number of clusters.

Spectral Clustering: It treats data points as nodes in a graph and uses techniques from graph theory to partition them into clusters based on the graph's structure. It is effective for clustering data with complex structures and non-linear relationships. Spectral clustering is a clustering method that combines graph theory and dimensionality reduction techniques to group data points based on their similarity. It is particularly effective for clustering data with complex structures or when the traditional clustering methods may not work well. Spectral clustering is a clustering method that utilizes the spectral properties of a similarity matrix or graph to group data points into clusters. It is based on the concept of spectral graph theory and is effective for discovering clusters in datasets with complex structures or non-linear relationships.

5.2 Clustering Algorithms

5.2.1 K-means Clustering

K-means clustering is a popular unsupervised machine learning algorithm used for partitioning a dataset into K distinct clusters. It aims to group similar data points together while maximizing the dissimilarity between different clusters. K-means clustering is an iterative algorithm that assigns data points to clusters based on their proximity to the cluster centroids.

K-Means Clustering is an Unsupervised Learning algorithm, which groups the unlabeled dataset into different clusters. Here K defines the number of pre-defined clusters that need to be created in the process, as if K=2, there will be two clusters, and for K=3, there will be three clusters, and so on.

It is an iterative algorithm that divides the unlabeled dataset into k different clusters in such a way that each dataset belongs only one group that has similar properties.

It is a centroid-based algorithm, where each cluster is associated with a centroid.

the algorithm takes the unlabeled dataset as input, divides the dataset into k-number of clusters, and repeats the process until it does not find the best clusters. The value of k should be predetermined in this algorithm.

The k-means clustering algorithm mainly performs two tasks:

- Determines the best value for K center points or centroids by an iterative process.
- Assigns each data point to its closest k-center. Those data points which are near to the particular k-center, create a cluster.

Hence each cluster has datapoints with some commonalities, and it is away from other clusters.

The below diagram explains the working of the-means Clustering Algorithm:

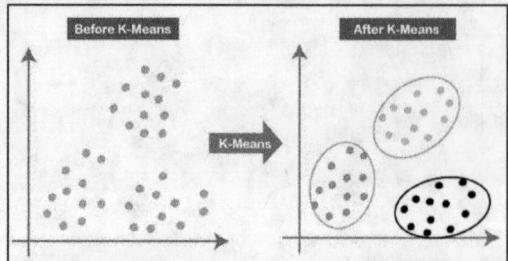

The main aim of this algorithm is to minimize the sum of distances between the data point and their corresponding clusters.

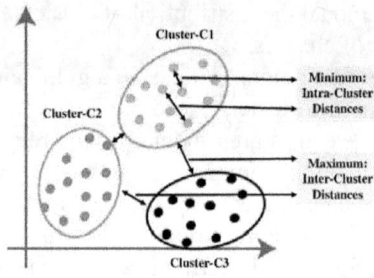

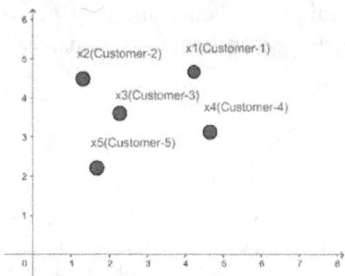

Distance Calculation:

The most commonly used distance metric in k-means is the **Euclidean distance**, but other distance metrics can be used depending on the context. For two points p and q in a multi-dimensional space, the Euclidean distance is calculated using the formula:

$$d(x, y) = \sqrt{\sum_{i=1}^{n} (x_i - y_i)^2}$$

1-Dimentional Distance

Customer No	Data point	Customer Age
1	x1	55
2	x2	50
3	x3	30
4	x4	40
5	x5	50

$$d(x_p, y_q) = \sqrt{\sum_{i=1}^{n} (x_{pi} - y_{qi})^2}$$

$$d(x_1, x_2) = \sqrt{\sum_{i=1}^{n} (x_{1i} - x_{2i})^2}$$

$$d(x_2, x_3) = \sqrt{(50 - 30)^2} = \sqrt{400} = 20$$

$$d(x_3, x_4) = \sqrt{(30 - 40)^2} = \sqrt{100} = 10$$

$$d(x_4, x_5) = \sqrt{(40 - 50)^2} = \sqrt{100} = 10$$

2-Dimentional Distance

Customer No	Data point	Customer Age	Customer Income(1000's)
1	x1	55	20
2	x2	50	22
3	x3	30	30
4	x4	40	40
5	x5	50	25

$$d(x_1, x_2) = \sqrt{(55 - 50)^2 + (20 - 22)^2} = \sqrt{5^2 + 2^2} = \sqrt{7^2} = 7$$

$$d(x_2, x_3) = \sqrt{(50 - 30)^2 + (22 - 30)^2} = \sqrt{20^2 + 2^2} = \sqrt{22^2} = 22$$

3-Dimentional Distance

Customer No	Data point	Customer Age	Customer Income(1000's)	Savings(1000's)
1	x1	55	20	5
2	x2	50	22	6
3	x3	30	30	2
4	x4	40	40	4
5	x5	50	25	6

$$d(x_1, x_2) = \sqrt{(55 - 50)^2 + (20 - 22)^2 + (5 - 6)^2} = \sqrt{5^2 + 2^2 + 1^2} = \sqrt{8^2} = 8$$

$$d(x_2, x_3) = \sqrt{(50 - 30)^2 + (22 - 30)^2 + (6 - 2)^2} = \sqrt{20^2 + 8^2 + 4^2} = \sqrt{32^2} = 32$$

K-means

Initialize the centroids: Choose the number of clusters, k, and randomly initialize the positions of k centroids in the feature space. Each centroid represents the center of a cluster.

Assign data points to the nearest centroid: Calculate the distance between each data point and each centroid. Assign each data point to the nearest centroid based on the distance measure, such as Euclidean distance.

Update the centroids: After assigning all data points to their nearest centroids, compute the new position of each centroid by taking the mean of all the data points assigned to that centroid. This step moves the centroids to the center of their respective clusters.

Repeat steps 2 and 3: Repeat steps 2 and 3 until convergence is reached. Convergence occurs when the centroids no longer move significantly or the maximum number of iterations is reached.

Finalize the clustering: Once convergence is reached, the algorithm outputs the final positions of the centroids. These centroids represent the cluster centers, and each data point is assigned to the cluster corresponding to the nearest centroid.

Evaluate the clustering: Optionally, you can evaluate the quality of the clustering by calculating metrics such as the within-cluster sum of squares (WCSS) or silhouette coefficient.

Let's understand the above steps by considering the visual plots:
Suppose we have two variables M1(age) and M2(income). The x-y axis scatter plot of these two variables is given below:

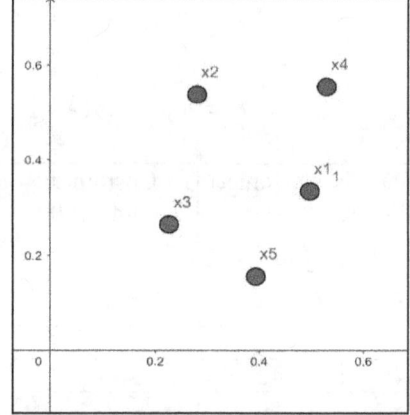

Let's take number k of clusters, i.e., K=2, to identify the dataset and to put them into different clusters. It means here we will try to group these datasets into two different clusters.
We need to choose some random k points or centroid to form the cluster. These points can be either the points from the dataset or any other point. So, here we are selecting the below two points as k points, which are not the part of our dataset. Consider the below image:

Now we will assign each data point of the scatter plot to its closest K-point or centroid. We will compute it by applying some mathematics that we have studied to calculate the distance between two points. So, we will draw a median between both the centroids. Consider the below image:

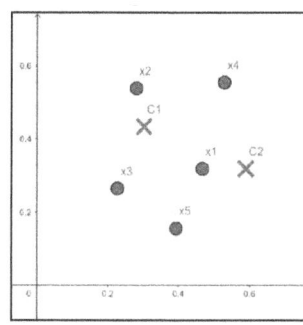

Data point	Distance from Datapoint to Centroid of Cluster C1	Distance from Datapoint to Centroid of Cluster C2
x1	20	10
x2	15	20
x3	10	18
x4	30	20
x5	50	20

Data point	Distance from Datapoint to Centroid of Cluster C1	Distance from Datapoint to Centroid of Cluster C2	Datapoint Belongs Cluster
x1	20	10	C2
x2	15	20	C1
x3	10	18	C1
x4	30	20	C2
x5	50	20	C2

From the above image, it is clear that points left side of the line is near to the K1 or blue centroid, and points to the right of the line are close to the yellow centroid. Let's color them as blue and yellow for clear visualization.

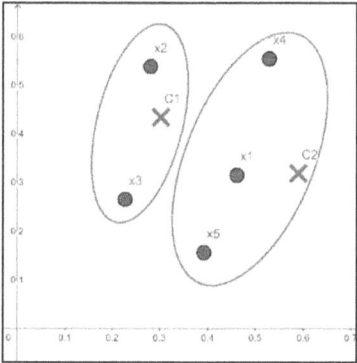

As we need to find the closest cluster, so we will repeat the process by choosing **a new centroid**. To choose the new centroids, we will compute the center of gravity of these centroids, and will find new centroids as below:

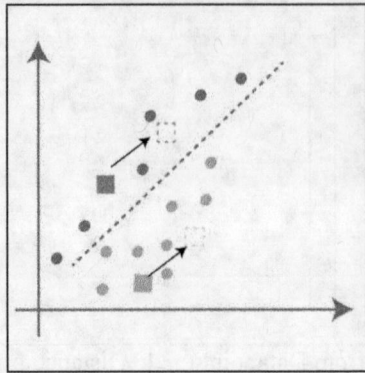

ext, we will reassign each datapoint to the new centroid. For this, we will repeat the same process of finding a median line. The median will be like below image:

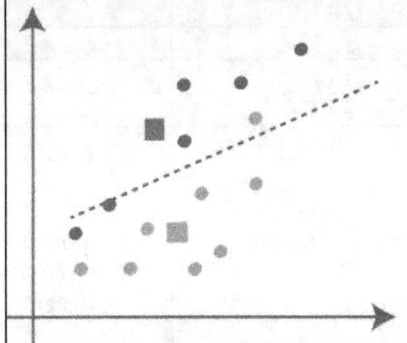

From the above image, we can see, one yellow point is on the left side of the line, and two blue points are right to the line. So, these three points will be assigned to new centroids.

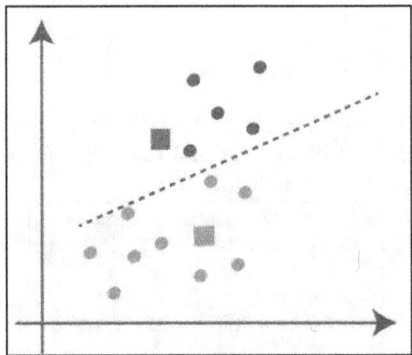

As reassignment has taken place, so we will again go to the step-4, which is finding new centroids or K-points.We will repeat the process by finding the center of gravity of centroids, so the new centroids will be as shown in the below image:

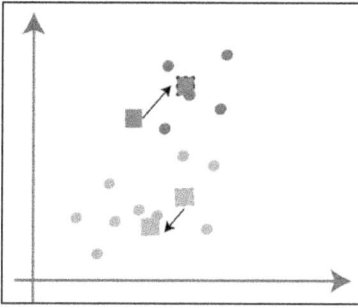

As we got the new centroids so again will draw the median line and reassign the data points. So, the image will be:

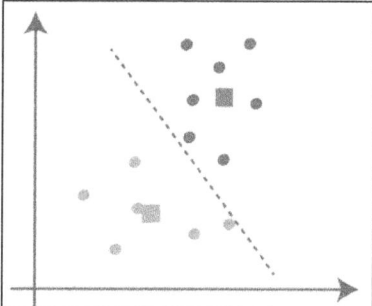

We can see in the above image; there are no dissimilar data points on either side of the line, which means our model is formed. Consider the below image:

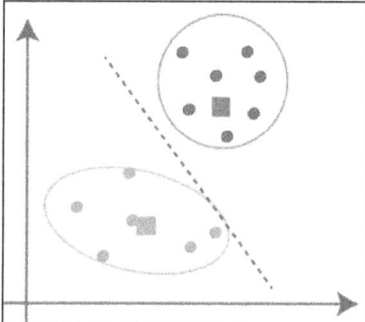

As our model is ready, so we can now remove the assumed centroids, and the two final clusters will be as shown in the below image:

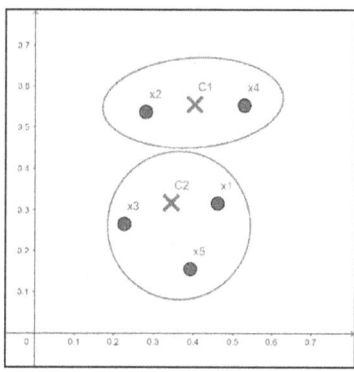

Choosing Right no of Clusters(K value):

Elbow Method: This method involves plotting the within-cluster sum of squares (WCSS) against the number of clusters (k). The WCSS represents the sum of squared distances between each data point and its assigned centroid. The plot resembles an "elbow," and the idea is to identify the value of k at the elbow point, where the WCSS decreases less significantly with further increase in k. The elbow point represents a trade-off between having a low WCSS and not overfitting the data.

$$WCSS = \sum_{x_i \in C_1} d(x_i - c_1) + \sum_{x_i \in C_2} d(x_i - c_2) + ...$$

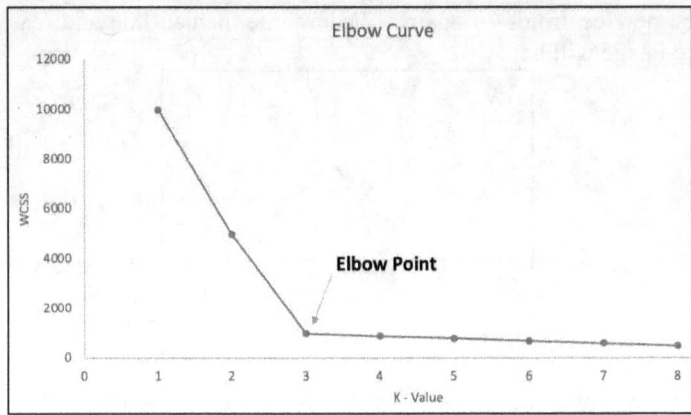

Silhouette Coefficient: The silhouette coefficient measures the compactness of data points within clusters and the separation between different clusters. It considers both the distance between a data point and its own cluster (intra-cluster distance) and the distance between the data point and the nearest neighboring cluster (inter-cluster distance). The silhouette coefficient ranges from -1 to 1, with higher values indicating better-defined and well-separated clusters. The optimal value of k can be determined by selecting the k that maximizes the average silhouette coefficient across all data points.

Gap Statistic: The gap statistic compares the WCSS of the clustering solution with that of randomly generated reference datasets. It measures the relative difference between the observed WCSS and the expected WCSS for each value of k. The optimal value of k corresponds to the k that yields the largest gap statistic, indicating a more significant separation between the clusters in the actual data compared to the random reference datasets.

Incremental Evaluation: Run the k-means algorithm for a range of k values and evaluate the results using domain-specific metrics or visual inspection. Analyze the clustering outputs for different k values and choose the value that best aligns with your expectations and desired outcomes.

Information Criteria: Information criteria, such as the Akaike information criterion (AIC) or Bayesian information criterion (BIC), can be used to assess the goodness of fit of the clustering model. These criteria penalize the complexity of the model (represented by the number of parameters or clusters) to avoid overfitting. The optimal value of k can be selected by choosing the k that minimizes the information criterion.

Domain Knowledge and Interpretability: Consider any prior knowledge or domain expertise you have about the data. If you have specific insights about the problem or the data, it may guide you in selecting an appropriate value for k. For example, if you know there are distinct groups or categories in your data based on prior knowledge, you can choose the corresponding number of clusters.

It's important to note that there is no definitive "best" method to choose the k value, and the selection process is often subjective and context-dependent. It is recommended to try multiple methods and compare the results to make an informed decision about the appropriate number of clusters for your specific dataset and problem.

Python code to implement K-means clustering algorithm
```
#Importing the libraries
import numpy as np
import matplotlib.pyplot as plt
import pandas as pd
#Importing the dataset
dataset = pd.read_csv('Mall_Customers.csv')
X = dataset.iloc[:, [3, 4]].values
#Using the elbow method to find the optimal number of clusters
from sklearn.cluster import KMeans
wcss = []
for i in range(1, 11):
    kmeans = KMeans(n_clusters = i, init = 'k-means++', random_state = 42)
    kmeans.fit(X)
    wcss.append(kmeans.inertia_)
plt.plot(range(1, 11), wcss)
plt.title('The Elbow Method')
plt.xlabel('Number of clusters')
plt.ylabel('WCSS')
plt.show()
```

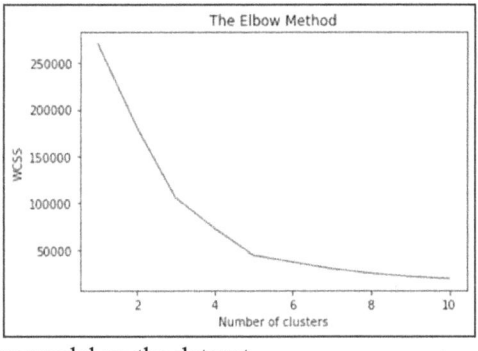

```
# Training the K-Means model on the dataset
kmeans = KMeans(n_clusters = 5, init = 'k-means++', random_state = 42)
y_kmeans = kmeans.fit_predict(X)
#Visualising the clusters
plt.scatter(X[y_kmeans == 0, 0], X[y_kmeans == 0, 1], s = 100, c = 'red', label = 'Cluster 1')
plt.scatter(X[y_kmeans == 1, 0], X[y_kmeans == 1, 1], s = 100, c = 'blue', label = 'Cluster 2')
plt.scatter(X[y_kmeans == 2, 0], X[y_kmeans == 2, 1], s = 100, c = 'green', label = 'Cluster 3')
```

```
plt.scatter(X[y_kmeans == 3, 0], X[y_kmeans == 3, 1], s = 100, c = 'cyan', label =
'Cluster 4')
plt.scatter(X[y_kmeans == 4, 0], X[y_kmeans == 4, 1], s = 100, c = 'magenta', label =
'Cluster 5')
plt.scatter(kmeans.cluster_centers_[:, 0], kmeans.cluster_centers_[:, 1], s = 300, c =
'yellow', label = 'Centroids')
plt.title('Clusters of customers')
plt.xlabel('Annual Income (k$)')
plt.ylabel('Spending Score (1-100)')
plt.legend()
plt.show()
```

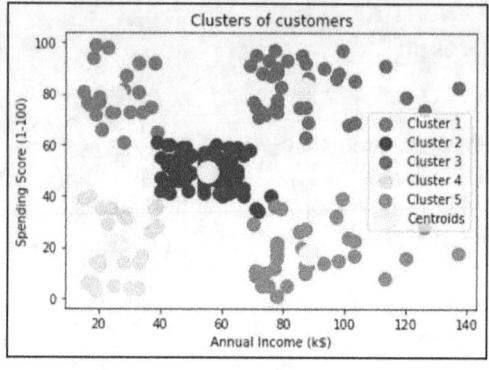

5.2.2 Hierarchical Clustering

Hierarchical Clustering is a type of unsupervised learning algorithm used to group a set of objects into clusters based on their similarities. Unlike flat clustering methods like k-means, hierarchical clustering creates a hierarchy of clusters, allowing for the discovery of data structures at different levels of granularity.

Types of Hierarchical Clustering

1. **Agglomerative Hierarchical Clustering (Bottom-Up):**
    o   **Process:** Starts with each object as its own cluster and progressively merges the closest pairs of clusters until all objects are in a single cluster or until a stopping criterion is met.
    o   **Steps:**
        1. Initialize each data point as a separate cluster.
        2. Compute the distance between all pairs of clusters.
        3. Merge the two closest clusters.
        4. Recalculate distances between the newly formed cluster and all other clusters.
        5. Repeat steps 3-4 until only one cluster remains or the desired number of clusters is achieved.

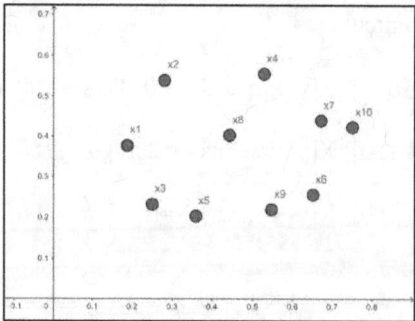

2. **Divisive Hierarchical Clustering (Top-Down):**
    o **Process**: Starts with all objects in a single cluster and recursively splits the clusters into smaller clusters until each object is in its own cluster or until a stopping criterion is met.
    o **Steps**:
        1. Start with one, single cluster containing all data points.
        2. Split the cluster into two sub-clusters.
        3. Continue splitting until each cluster contains a single data point or the desired number of clusters is achieved.

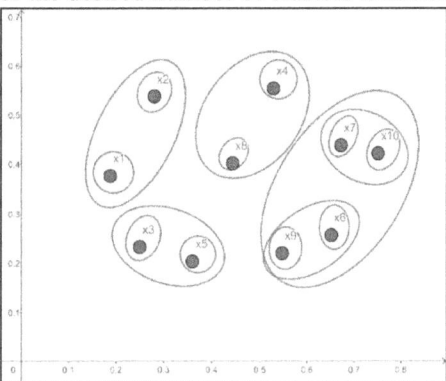

Distance Metrics
The choice of distance metric can significantly influence the clustering result. Common distance metrics include:
- **Euclidean Distance**: Measures the straight-line distance between two points in Euclidean space.
- **Manhattan Distance**: Measures the distance between two points along axes at right angles.
- **Cosine Similarity**: Measures the cosine of the angle between two vectors, used in text data.

Linkage Criteria
Linkage criteria determine how the distance between clusters is computed. Common linkage methods include:
- **Single Linkage (Minimum Linkage)**: The distance between two clusters is defined as the minimum distance between any single pair of points in the two clusters.
- **Complete Linkage (Maximum Linkage)**: The distance between two clusters is defined as the maximum distance between any single pair of points in the two clusters.
- **Average Linkage (Mean Linkage)**: The distance between two clusters is defined as the average distance between all pairs of points in the two clusters.
- **Ward's Linkage**: Minimizes the variance within clusters by merging clusters that result in the smallest increase in total within-cluster variance.

Dendrogram
A **dendrogram** is a tree-like diagram that records the sequences of merges or splits in hierarchical clustering. It visually represents the hierarchy of clusters and can be used to decide the number of clusters by cutting the tree at a desired level.

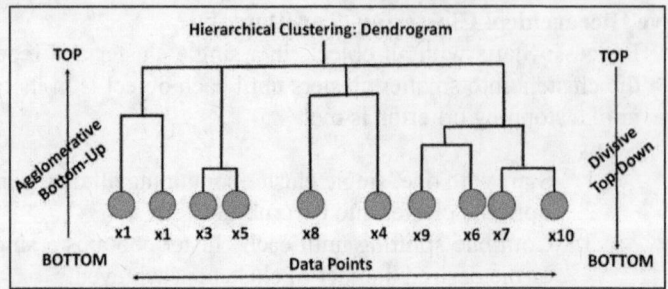

Hierarchical Clustering: Dendrogram

- **Structure**:
  - Leaves of the dendrogram represent individual data points.
  - Branches represent clusters formed by merging or splitting.
  - The height of the branches indicates the distance between clusters when they were merged.

Example of Agglomerative Hierarchical Clustering

Suppose we have a dataset of 5 data points: A, B, C, D, and E, with the following distance matrix:

Suppose we have a dataset of 5 data points: A, B, C, D, and E, with the following distance matrix:

	A	B	C	D	E
A	0	2	6	10	8
B	2	0	5	9	7
C	6	5	0	4	3
D	10	9	4	0	7
E	8	7	3	7	0

Steps:
1. **Initialize Clusters**: Each data point starts as its own cluster: {A}, {B}, {C}, {D}, {E}.
2. **Compute Distances**:
   - Merge the closest clusters: {C} and {E} (distance = 3).
   - Update the distance matrix to reflect the new clusters.
3. **Repeat**:
   - Merge the next closest clusters (e.g., {C, E} with {B}).
   - Continue merging until all data points are in a single cluster or the desired number of clusters is reached.
4. **Dendrogram**:
   - Plot the hierarchical clustering results in a dendrogram to visualize the clustering process.

Advantages of Hierarchical Clustering
1. **No Need for Predefined Number of Clusters**:
   - It does not require specifying the number of clusters in advance.
2. **Hierarchical Structure**:
   - Provides a comprehensive view of the data structure at different levels of granularity.
3. **Flexibility**:
   - Can handle different types of data and distance metrics.

Disadvantages of Hierarchical Clustering
1. **Computational Complexity**:
   - Agglomerative clustering has a time complexity of $O(n^3)$ for large datasets, which can be computationally expensive.

2. **Memory Consumption**:
   o Requires storing distance matrices or cluster memberships, which can be memory-intensive for large datasets.
3. **Sensitivity to Noise and Outliers**:
   o Hierarchical clustering can be sensitive to noise and outliers, affecting the clustering results.

Hierarchical Clustering is a method that builds a hierarchy of clusters either by progressively merging smaller clusters (agglomerative) or by recursively splitting a large cluster (divisive). It is useful for discovering nested structures in data and does not require specifying the number of clusters in advance. Hierarchical clustering can be visualized using a dendrogram, which helps in understanding the relationships between clusters at various levels of granularity. However, it may be computationally intensive and sensitive to noise.

Python code to implement Hierarchical clustering
#Importing the dataset
In [0]:
```
dataset = pd.read_csv('Mall_Customers.csv')
X = dataset.iloc[:, [3, 4]].values
```
Using the dendrogram to find the optimal number of clusters
In [3]:
```
import scipy.cluster.hierarchy as sch
dendrogram = sch.dendrogram(sch.linkage(X, method = 'ward'))
plt.title('Dendrogram')
plt.xlabel('Customers')
plt.ylabel('Euclidean distances')
plt.show()
```

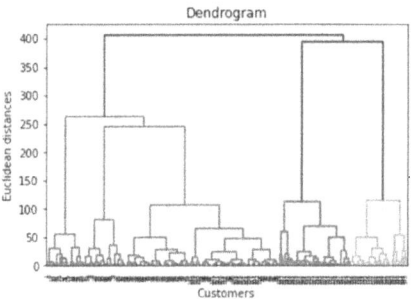

Training the Hierarchical Clustering model on the dataset
In [0]:
```
from sklearn.cluster import AgglomerativeClustering
hc = AgglomerativeClustering(n_clusters = 5, affinity = 'euclidean', linkage = 'ward')
y_hc = hc.fit_predict(X)
```
Visualising the clusters
In [5]:
```
plt.scatter(X[y_hc == 0, 0], X[y_hc == 0, 1], s = 100, c = 'red', label = 'Cluster 1')
plt.scatter(X[y_hc == 1, 0], X[y_hc == 1, 1], s = 100, c = 'blue', label = 'Cluster 2')
plt.scatter(X[y_hc == 2, 0], X[y_hc == 2, 1], s = 100, c = 'green', label = 'Cluster 3')
plt.scatter(X[y_hc == 3, 0], X[y_hc == 3, 1], s = 100, c = 'cyan', label = 'Cluster 4')
plt.scatter(X[y_hc == 4, 0], X[y_hc == 4, 1], s = 100, c = 'magenta', label = 'Cluster 5')
plt.title('Clusters of customers')
plt.xlabel('Annual Income (k$)')
```

146

plt.ylabel('Spending Score (1-100)')
plt.legend()
plt.show()

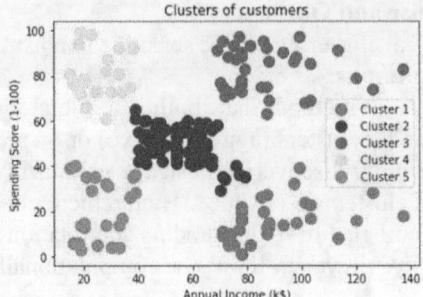

5.2.3 DBSCAN Clustering

The DBSCAN (Density-Based Spatial Clustering of Applications with Noise) algorithm follows a set of steps to cluster data points based on their density. Here are the main steps involved in the DBSCAN algorithm:

Parameter Selection:

Choose the value of epsilon (ε), which defines the radius around each point. Points within this radius are considered neighbors.

Set the minimum number of points (minPts) required to form a dense region or cluster.

1.Initialization:

Select an unvisited data point randomly or sequentially.

2.Neighbor Retrieval:

Retrieve all data points within distance ε from the selected point. These points are considered the neighborhood of the selected point.

3.Core Point Determination:

Check if the number of points in the neighborhood is greater than or equal to minPts.
If yes, mark the selected point as a core point and proceed to form a cluster. Otherwise, mark the point as noise or an outlier.

4.Cluster Expansion:

For each core point, recursively expand the cluster by finding and adding directly reachable points from its neighborhood to the cluster.

Directly reachable points are those that are within distance ε from the core point and also have a sufficient number of neighbors (minPts).

Repeat Steps 3-5:

Continue the process by selecting the next unvisited point and repeating Steps 3-5 until all points have been visited.

Noise Handling:

Any remaining unvisited points are considered noise points or outliers, as they do not belong to any cluster.

The DBSCAN algorithm identifies clusters based on the density of points, where dense regions are separated by regions of lower density. It forms clusters by connecting core points and their directly reachable points. Noise points are points that do not meet the criteria of being a core point or directly reachable from a core point.

It's important to note that the order in which points are visited can affect the clustering result, but the algorithm is not sensitive to the order of the input data within a single run.

By following these steps, the DBSCAN algorithm is able to discover clusters of arbitrary shape and handle datasets with varying densities, making it a valuable tool for unsupervised clustering tasks in machine learning.

we will apply this algorithm to a very small data set to explain it. Some calculations are skipped and the calculated tables are directly presented. It's recommended to verify all such calculations, which will make the concept more vivid to you. Let's take a dataset of 13 points as shown and plotted below:

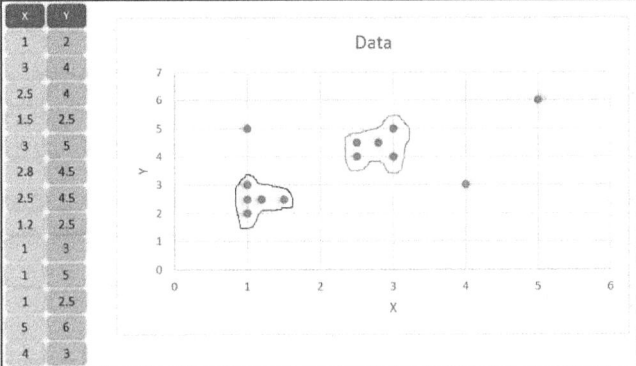

A two-dimensional data is presented for easy visualization and understanding, else DBSCAN can handle multi-dimensional data too. The possible clusters from the data have been marked in the above graph to visualize the clusters that we want. The points (1,5) (4,3) (5,6) in the above graph fall outside the markings and hence should be treated as outliers. The DBSCAN algorithm should actually make clusters and exclude outliers as we did in the graph. Let's first understand the algorithm and various steps involved in it.

Logic and Steps:

The DBSCAN algorithm takes two input parameters. Radius around each point (eps) and the minimum number of data points that should be around that point within that radius (MinPts). For example, consider the point (1.5,2.5), if we take eps = 0.3, then the circle around the point with radius = 0.3, will contain only one other point inside it (1.2,2.5) as shown below:

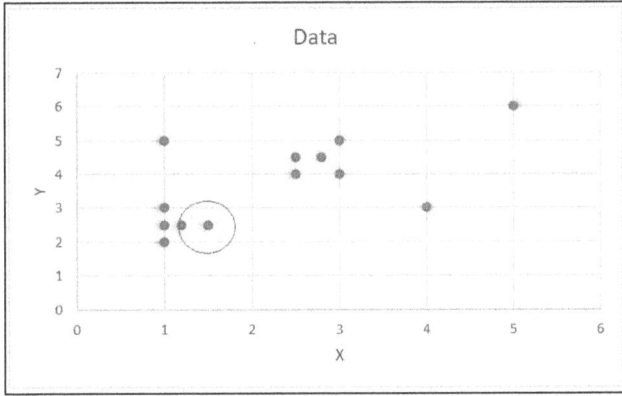

Hence for (1.5, 2.5) when eps = 0.3, the number of neighbourhood point(s) is just one. In DBSCAN each point is checked for these two parameters and the decision about the clustering is made as described through the below steps:

Choose a value for eps and MinPts

For a particular data point (x) calculate its distance from every other datapoint.

Find all the neighbourhood points of x which fall inside the circle of radius (eps) or simply whose distance from x is smaller than or equal to eps.

Treat x as visited and if the number of neighbourhood points around x are greater or equal to MinPts then treat x as a core point and if it is not assigned to any cluster, create a new cluster and assign it to that.

If the number of neighbourhood points around x are less than MinPts and it has a core point in its neighbourhood, treat it as a border point.

Include all the density connected points as a single cluster. (What density connected points mean is described later)

Repeat the above steps for every unvisited point in the data set and find out all core, border and outlier points.

Please note that the above steps constitute a recursive process. After 1st loop of calculations, a point may not be treated as a border point to any core point but it may be treated so in next loop.

If the number of neighbourhood points around x is greater or equal to MinPts then x is treated as a core point, if the neighbourhood points around x are less than MinPts but is close to a core point then x is treated as a border point. If x is neither core nor border point then x is treated as an outlier. The below graph gives an idea about it. We choose eps = 0.6 and MinPts =4, the point tagged as core point has 4 other points (>= MinPts) in its neighbourhood & the one tagged as border point is in the neighbourhood of a core point but has only one point in its neighbourhood (< MinPts). The outlier point is one which is neither border point nor core point.

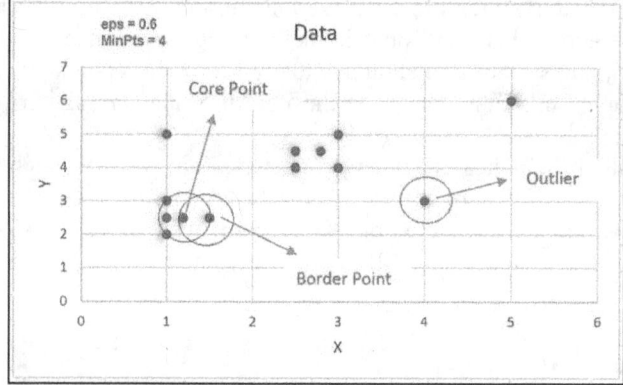

Algorithm in action

Let's now apply the DBSCAN algorithm to the above dataset to find out clusters. We have to choose first the values for eps and MinPts. Let's choose eps = 0.6 and MinPts = 4. Let's consider the first data point in the dataset (1,2) & calculate its distance from every other data point in the data set. The Calculated values are shown below:

X	Y	Distance from (1,2)
1	2	0
3	4	2.8
2.5	4	2.5
1.5	2.5	0.7
3	5	3.6
2.8	4.5	3.08
2.5	4.5	2.9
1.2	2.5	0.53
1	3	1
1	5	3
1	2.5	0.5
5	6	5.6
4	3	3.1

As evident from the above table, the point (1, 2) has only two other points in its neighbourhood (1, 2.5), (1.2, 2.5) for the assumed value of eps, as its less than MinPts, we can't declare it as a core point. Let's repeat the above process for every point in the dataset and find out the neighbourhood of each. The calculations when repeated can be summarized as below:

Point	Neighbourhood Points				
(1,2)	(1.2, 2.5)	(1, 2.5)			
(3, 4)	(2.5, 4)	(2.8, 4.5)			
(2.5, 4)	(3, 4)	(2.8, 4.5)	(2.5, 4.5)		
(1.5, 2.5)	(1.2, 2.5)	(1, 2.5)			
(3, 5)	(2.8, 4.5)				
(2.8, 4.5)	(3, 4)	(2.5, 4)	(3, 5)	(2.5, 4.5)	Cluster 1
(2.5, 4.5)	(2.5, 4)	(2.8, 4.5)			
(1.2, 2.5)	(1, 2)	(1.5, 2.5)	(1, 3)	(1, 2.5)	Cluster 2
(1, 3)	(1.2, 2.5)	(1, 2.5)			
(1, 5)					
(1, 2.5)	(1, 2)	(1.5, 2.5)	(1.2, 2.5)	(1, 3)	Cluster 2
(5, 6)					
(4, 3)					

Observe the above table carefully, the left-most column contains all the points we have in our data set. To the right of them are the data points which are there in their neighbourhood i.e. the points whose distance from them is less or equal to the eps value. There are three points in the data set, (2.8, 4.5) (1.2, 2.5) (1, 2.5) that have 4 neighbourhood points around them, hence they would be called core points and as already mentioned, if the core point is not assigned to any cluster, a new cluster is formed. Hence, (2.8, 4.5) is assigned to a new cluster, Cluster 1 and so is the point (1.2, 2.5), Cluster 2. Also observe that the core points (1.2, 2.5) and (1, 2.5) share at least one common neighbourhood point (1,2) so, they are assigned to the same cluster. The below table shows the categorization of all the data points into core, border and outlier points. Have a look:

Point	Neighbourhood Points				Type	
(1,2)	(1.2, 2.5)		(1, 2.5)		Border Point	
(3, 4)	(2.5, 4)		(2.8, 4.5)		Border Point	
(2.5, 4)	(3, 4)	(2.8, 4.5)	(2.5, 4.5)		Border Point	
(1.5, 2.5)	(1.2, 2.5)		(1, 2.5)		Border Point	
(3, 5)	(2.8, 4.5)				Border Point	
(2.8, 4.5)	(3, 4)	(2.5, 4)	(3, 5)	(2.5, 4.5)	Core Point	Cluster 1
(2.5, 4.5)	(2.5, 4)		(2.8, 4.5)		Border Point	
(1.2, 2.5)	(1, 2)	(1.5, 2.5)	(1, 3)	(1, 2.5)	Core Point	Cluster 2
(1, 3)	(1.2, 2.5)		(1, 2.5)		Border Point	
(1, 5)					Outlier	
(1, 2.5)	(1, 2)	(1.5, 2.5)	(1.2, 2.5)	(1, 3)	Core Point	Cluster 2
(5, 6)					Outlier	
(4, 3)					Outlier	

There are three types of points in the dataset as detected by the DBSCAN algorithm, core, border and outliers. Every core point will be assigned to a new cluster unless some of the core points share neighbourhood points, they will be included in the same cluster. Every border point will be assigned to the cluster-based upon the core point in its neighbourhood e.g. the first point (1, 2) is a border point and has a core point (1.2, 2.5) in its neighbourhood, which is included in Cluster 2, hence, the point (1,2) will be included in the Cluster 2 too. The whole categorization can be summarized as below:

Cluster 1	Cluster 2	Outliers
(3,4)	(1, 2)	(1, 5)
(2.5, 4)	(1.5, 2.5)	(5, 6)
(3,5)	(1.2, 2.5)	(4, 3)
(2.8, 4.5)	(1, 3)	
(2.5, 4.5)	(1, 2.5)	

5.3 Dimensionality Reduction

Dimensionality reduction is a technique used in data analysis and machine learning to reduce the number of features or variables in a dataset while retaining as much of the important information as possible. This process is especially useful when dealing with high-dimensional data, which can be complex and computationally expensive to analyze.

Why Dimensionality Reduction?

1. **Simplification:** Reducing the number of dimensions simplifies the data, making it easier to visualize and understand. This is crucial when working with datasets that have many features.
2. **Noise Reduction:** Dimensionality reduction can help filter out noise and irrelevant features, improving the performance of machine learning models.

3. **Storage and Computational Efficiency:** Fewer dimensions mean less storage space and faster computation times, which can be important for large-scale data.
4. **Avoiding Overfitting:** By reducing the number of features, you decrease the risk of overfitting in models, where the model learns noise rather than the underlying patterns in the data.

Techniques in Dimensionality Reduction

1. **Principal Component Analysis (PCA):**
   o **Concept:** PCA transforms the data into a new coordinate system where the axes (principal components) are ordered by the amount of variance they capture from the data.
   o **Process:** It calculates the eigenvectors and eigenvalues of the covariance matrix of the data. The principal components are the eigenvectors corresponding to the largest eigenvalues. These components are orthogonal (uncorrelated) and capture the most variance.
   o **Use Case:** PCA is widely used for data visualization, noise reduction, and feature extraction.

2. **t-Distributed Stochastic Neighbor Embedding (t-SNE):**
   o **Concept:** t-SNE is a non-linear dimensionality reduction technique that focuses on preserving the local structure of the data. It is particularly effective for visualizing high-dimensional data in 2 or 3 dimensions.
   o **Process:** It converts distances between data points into probabilities and minimizes the divergence between the probability distributions of the original and reduced dimensions.
   o **Use Case:** t-SNE is commonly used for visualizing complex datasets, like in exploratory data analysis.

3. **Linear Discriminant Analysis (LDA):**
   o **Concept:** LDA is both a dimensionality reduction and a classification technique. It finds the directions that maximize the separation between different classes in the data.
   o **Process:** It projects the data onto a lower-dimensional space where the classes are most separated. Unlike PCA, which is unsupervised, LDA takes class labels into account.
   o **Use Case:** LDA is used when you have labeled data and want to reduce dimensions while maintaining class separability.

4. **Autoencoders:**
   o **Concept:** Autoencoders are neural networks designed to learn a compressed representation of the data through an encoder and reconstruct the original data through a decoder.
   o **Process:** The encoder compresses the data into a lower-dimensional latent space, and the decoder attempts to reconstruct the data from this compressed representation.
   o **Use Case:** Autoencoders are used in various applications including anomaly detection and feature learning.

5. **Isomap:**
   o **Concept:** Isomap is a non-linear dimensionality reduction technique that extends classical MDS (Multidimensional Scaling) by incorporating geodesic distances on a manifold.
   o **Process:** It constructs a neighborhood graph of the data and computes the shortest paths between points, preserving the manifold structure.
   o **Use Case:** Isomap is used to uncover the underlying geometric structure of the data.

6. **Locally Linear Embedding (LLE):**
   o **Concept:** LLE is another non-linear dimensionality reduction technique that focuses on preserving local relationships between data points.
   o **Process:** It reconstructs data points based on their neighbors and then reduces dimensions while maintaining these local relationships.
   o **Use Case:** LLE is used to discover the underlying structure of the data and is often applied in image processing and pattern recognition.

Dimensionality reduction is a powerful tool in data science and machine learning. By reducing the number of features, you simplify the data, making it more manageable and revealing patterns and structures that might be obscured in high-dimensional space. The choice of technique depends on the nature of the data and the specific goals of the analysis.

5.4 Principal Component Analysis

Principal Component Analysis (PCA) is a **dimensionality reduction technique** used in machine learning and data science. It transforms **high-dimensional data** into a lower-dimensional form while retaining the most important information.

PCA is primarily used to:

Reduce the number of features in a dataset (**dimensionality reduction**).

Identify patterns and relationships in data.

Remove noise and redundancy from data.

Improve the efficiency of machine learning models.

How PCA Works (Step-by-Step Explanation)

Step 1: Standardize the Data

Before applying PCA, the data should be standardized (normalized) to ensure all features have the same scale. This is done by converting the data into a **zero-mean and unit-variance form**.

Step 2: Compute the Covariance Matrix

The covariance matrix helps understand the relationships between features. It shows how changes in one feature relate to changes in another feature.

Step 3: Calculate Eigenvalues and Eigenvectors

- **Eigenvalues** represent the **amount of variance** captured by each principal component.
- **Eigenvectors** define the **directions** (principal components) in which the data has the most variance.

Step 4: Select the Principal Components

- The principal components (PCs) are ranked based on their eigenvalues.
- The **top k** components (those with the highest eigenvalues) are selected to retain most of the information.

Step 5: Transform the Data

The original data is projected onto the selected principal components, reducing the number of dimensions while preserving as much variance as possible.

Key Properties of PCA

Unsupervised: PCA does not use labeled data.

Feature Extraction: Instead of selecting existing features, PCA creates new features (principal components).

Variance Maximization: PCA tries to capture the **maximum variance** in the data with the fewest components.

Example: PCA in Action

Scenario:

Imagine you have a dataset with **100 features**.

- PCA helps **reduce it to 2 or 3 features** while keeping most of the important information.
- This makes visualization easier and improves machine learning model performance.

Applications of PCA

1. Image Compression
- Reduces storage space while preserving important image details.
- Used in **face recognition** (Eigenfaces).

2. Data Visualization
- PCA reduces high-dimensional data to **2D or 3D** for better visualization.
- Used in **clustering and exploratory data analysis**.

3. Feature Selection in Machine Learning
- Helps remove **irrelevant or redundant features**, improving model performance.

4. Genomics & Bioinformatics
- PCA is used to analyze **gene expression data**, identifying patterns in large datasets.

5. Anomaly Detection
- PCA helps identify outliers in **fraud detection and cybersecurity**.

Limitations of PCA

Loses Interpretability: The transformed features (principal components) don't have direct real-world meaning.

Assumes Linearity: PCA works best when the relationships between variables are linear.

Sensitive to Scaling: Requires proper feature scaling for accurate results.

Principal Components in PCA

As described above, the transformed new features or the output of PCA are the Principal Components. The number of these PCs are either equal to or less than the original features present in the dataset. Some properties of these principal components are given below:

- The principal component must be the linear combination of the original features.
- These components are orthogonal, i.e., the correlation between a pair of variables is zero.
- The importance of each component decreases when going to 1 to n, it means the 1 PC has the most importance, and n PC will have the least importance.

Steps for PCA algorithm

1. **Getting the dataset**
   Firstly, we need to take the input dataset and divide it into two subparts X and Y, where X is the training set, and Y is the validation set.

2. **Representing data into a structure**
   Now we will represent our dataset into a structure. Such as we will represent the two-dimensional matrix of independent variable X. Here each row corresponds to the data items, and the column corresponds to the Features. The number of columns is the dimensions of the dataset.

3. **Standardizing the data**
   In this step, we will standardize our dataset. Such as in a particular column, the features with high variance are more important compared to the features with lower variance.
   If the importance of features is independent of the variance of the feature, then

we will divide each data item in a column with the standard deviation of the column. Here we will name the matrix as Z.

4. **Calculating the Covariance of Z**
   To calculate the covariance of Z, we will take the matrix Z, and will transpose it. After transpose, we will multiply it by Z. The output matrix will be the Covariance matrix of Z.

5. **Calculating the Eigen Values and Eigen Vectors**
   Now we need to calculate the eigenvalues and eigenvectors for the resultant covariance matrix Z. Eigenvectors or the covariance matrix are the directions of the axes with high information. And the coefficients of these eigenvectors are defined as the eigenvalues.

6. **Sorting the Eigen Vectors**
   In this step, we will take all the eigenvalues and will sort them in decreasing order, which means from largest to smallest. And simultaneously sort the eigenvectors accordingly in matrix P of eigenvalues. The resultant matrix will be named as P*.

7. **Calculating the new features Or Principal Components**
   Here we will calculate the new features. To do this, we will multiply the P* matrix to the Z. In the resultant matrix Z*, each observation is the linear combination of original features. Each column of the Z* matrix is independent of each other.

8. **Remove less or unimportant features from the new dataset.**
   The new feature set has occurred, so we will decide here what to keep and what to remove. It means, we will only keep the relevant or important features in the new dataset, and unimportant features will be removed out.

Applications of Principal Component Analysis
   o PCA is mainly used as the dimensionality reduction technique in various AI applications such **as computer vision, image compression, etc.**
   o It can also be used for finding hidden patterns if data has high dimensions. Some fields where PCA is used are Finance, data mining, Psychology, etc.

Benefits of PCA in Machine Learning
By transforming complex datasets into simpler, more manageable forms, PCA not only aids in data visualisation but also enhances the performance of various Machine Learning algorithms. Here's why PCA is a valuable tool for beginners venturing into Data Analysis:
   • **Simplifies complex data:** PCA reduces clutter by identifying the most significant features, making data visualisation and interpretation more manageable.
   • **Improves Machine Learning Performance:** Many Machine Learning algorithms struggle with high-dimensional data. PCA reduces dimensionality, leading to faster training times and potentially improving model accuracy by avoiding overfitting.
   • **Reduces noise and redundancy:** Hidden patterns and trends become clearer as PCA eliminates irrelevant information and noise present in the data.
   • **Reduces overfitting:** High-dimensional data can lead to overfitting in Machine Learning models. By reducing the number of dimensions, PCA helps to simplify the data and prevent the model from memorising irrelevant noise.
   • **Improves training Speed:** Training Machine Learning models on high-dimensional data can be computationally expensive. PCA reduces the number of features, leading to faster training times.

- **Better algorithm performance:** Many <u>Machine Learning algorithms</u> perform better with lower-dimensional data. PCA can improve the performance of these algorithms by reducing the dimensionality of the data.
- **Feature selection:** PCA can help identify the most essential features in a dataset. This can be useful for selecting features for a Machine Learning model.

Python code to implement PCA for logistic regression algorithm

```
#Importing the libraries
import numpy as np
import matplotlib.pyplot as plt
import pandas as pd
Importing the dataset
dataset = pd.read_csv('Wine.csv')
X = dataset.iloc[:, :-1].values
y = dataset.iloc[:, -1].values
#Feature Scaling
from sklearn.preprocessing import StandardScaler
sc = StandardScaler()
X = sc.fit_transform(X)
#Splitting the dataset into the Training set and Test set
from sklearn.model_selection import train_test_split
X_train, X_test, y_train, y_test = train_test_split(X, y, test_size = 0.2, random_state = 0)
Applying PCA
from sklearn.decomposition import PCA
pca = PCA(n_components = 2)
X_train = pca.fit_transform(X_train)
X_test = pca.transform(X_test)
explained_variance = pca.explained_variance_ratio_
#Training the Logistic Regression model on the Training set
from sklearn.linear_model import LogisticRegression
classifier = LogisticRegression(random_state = 0)
classifier.fit(X_train, y_train)
LogisticRegression(C=1.0, class_weight=None, dual=False, fit_intercept=True,
          intercept_scaling=1, l1_ratio=None, max_iter=100,
          multi_class='auto', n_jobs=None, penalty='l2',
          random_state=0, solver='lbfgs', tol=0.0001, verbose=0,
          warm_start=False)
#Predicting the Test set results
y_pred = classifier.predict(X_test)
#Making the Confusion Matrix
from sklearn.metrics import confusion_matrix
cm = confusion_matrix(y_test, y_pred)
print(cm)
        [[14  0  0]
         [ 1 15  0]
         [ 0  0  6]]
#Visualising the Training set results
from matplotlib.colors import ListedColormap
X_set, y_set = X_train, y_train
X1, X2 = np.meshgrid(np.arange(start = X_set[:, 0].min() - 1, stop = X_set[:, 0].max() +
1, step = 0.01),
```

```
                    np.arange(start = X_set[:, 1].min() - 1, stop = X_set[:, 1].max() + 1, step =
0.01))
plt.contourf(X1, X2, classifier.predict(np.array([X1.ravel(),
X2.ravel()]).T).reshape(X1.shape),
            alpha = 0.75, cmap = ListedColormap(('red', 'green', 'blue')))
plt.xlim(X1.min(), X1.max())
plt.ylim(X2.min(), X2.max())
for i, j in enumerate(np.unique(y_set)):
    plt.scatter(X_set[y_set == j, 0], X_set[y_set == j, 1],
            c = ListedColormap(('red', 'green', 'blue'))(i), label = j)
plt.title('Logistic Regression (Training set)')
plt.xlabel('PC1')
plt.ylabel('PC2')
plt.legend()
plt.show()
```

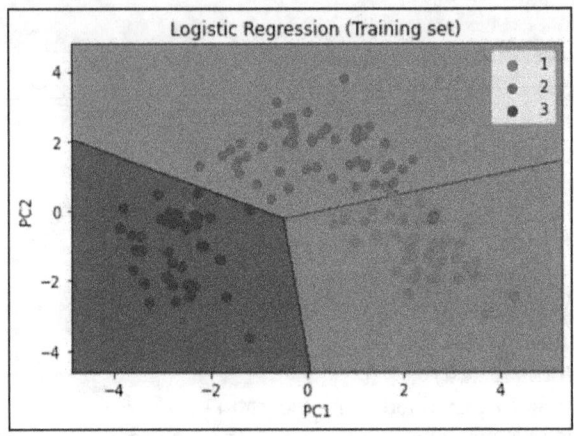

```
#Visualising the Test set results
from matplotlib.colors import ListedColormap
X_set, y_set = X_test, y_test
X1, X2 = np.meshgrid(np.arange(start = X_set[:, 0].min() - 1, stop = X_set[:, 0].max() +
1, step = 0.01),
                    np.arange(start = X_set[:, 1].min() - 1, stop = X_set[:, 1].max() + 1, step =
0.01))
plt.contourf(X1, X2, classifier.predict(np.array([X1.ravel(),
X2.ravel()]).T).reshape(X1.shape),
            alpha = 0.75, cmap = ListedColormap(('red', 'green', 'blue')))
plt.xlim(X1.min(), X1.max())
plt.ylim(X2.min(), X2.max())
for i, j in enumerate(np.unique(y_set)):
    plt.scatter(X_set[y_set == j, 0], X_set[y_set == j, 1],
            c = ListedColormap(('red', 'green', 'blue'))(i), label = j)
plt.title('Logistic Regression (Test set)')
plt.xlabel('PC1')
plt.ylabel('PC2')
plt.legend()
plt.show()
```

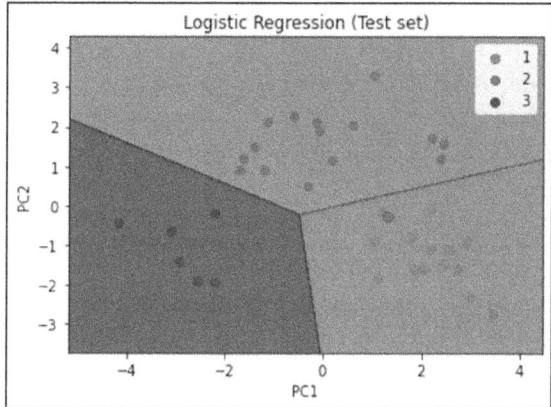

5.5 Linear Discriminant Analysis

Linear Discriminant Analysis (LDA) is a **supervised machine learning technique** used for **dimensionality reduction** and **classification**. It finds a linear combination of features that best separates different classes in the dataset.

LDA is similar to **Principal Component Analysis (PCA)** but with a key difference:
- **PCA** maximizes **variance** without considering class labels (unsupervised).
- **LDA** maximizes **class separation** while reducing dimensionality (supervised).

How LDA Works
Step 1: Compute the Mean Vectors
For each class in the dataset, compute the mean of each feature.
Step 2: Compute Scatter Matrices
- Within-Class Scatter Matrix (Sw): Measures the variance within each class.
- Between-Class Scatter Matrix (Sb): Measures the variance between different classes.
Step 3: Compute the Eigenvalues and Eigenvectors
- Solve the eigenvalue problem for $Sw^{-1}Sb$.
- Eigenvectors define the discriminant axes that best separate the classes.
Step 4: Select the Top k Discriminant Axes
- Sort eigenvalues in descending order.
- Choose the top k eigenvectors to form the new feature space.
Step 5: Transform the Data
- Project the original data onto the new LDA space with fewer dimensions.

Applications of LDA
1. Face Recognition
- LDA is used in Eigenfaces and Fisherfaces for better face classification.
2. Medical Diagnosis
- Helps classify patients into diseased vs. healthy based on medical test data.
3. Fraud Detection
- Identifies fraudulent transactions by separating them from normal transactions.
4. Text Classification
- Used for sentiment analysis, spam filtering, and document categorization.
5. Image Recognition
- LDA helps classify objects in images (e.g., car vs. bicycle vs. pedestrian).

Limitations of LDA
Assumes Normality: Works best if data is normally distributed.
Struggles with Non-Linearity: Fails if classes are not linearly separable.
Overfitting: Can overfit if too many discriminant components are used.

Example
Imagine you have a dataset with two classes (e.g., cats and dogs) and several features (e.g., weight, height, fur length). LDA would:
1. Compute the mean feature vectors for each class.
2. Calculate the scatter matrices to understand how features vary within and between classes.
3. Find the linear combinations of features that maximize the separation between the class means.
4. Project the data onto this lower-dimensional space, where the classes are better separated.

In summary, Linear Discriminant Analysis is a powerful technique for both dimensionality reduction and classification, particularly when class separability is a key objective. Its ability to improve class separation while reducing dimensionality makes it valuable in various applications, from pattern recognition to preprocessing for other machine learning models.

Difference Between LDA and PCA

Feature	LDA (Linear Discriminant Analysis)	PCA (Principal Component Analysis)
Type	Supervised	Unsupervised
Goal	Maximizes class separation	Maximizes variance
Considers Labels?	Yes	No
Best for	Classification	Feature reduction
Application	Face recognition, medical diagnosis, fraud detection	Image compression, exploratory data analysis

Python code to implement LDA
```
#Importing the libraries
import numpy as np
import matplotlib.pyplot as plt
import pandas as pd
#Importing the dataset
dataset = pd.read_csv('Wine.csv')
X = dataset.iloc[:, :-1].values
y = dataset.iloc[:, -1].values
#Feature Scaling
from sklearn.preprocessing import StandardScaler
sc = StandardScaler()
X = sc.fit_transform(X)
#Splitting the dataset into the Training set and Test set
from sklearn.model_selection import train_test_split
X_train, X_test, y_train, y_test = train_test_split(X, y, test_size = 0.2, random_state = 0)
```

```
#Applying LDA
from sklearn.discriminant_analysis import LinearDiscriminantAnalysis as LDA
lda = LDA(n_components = 2)
X_train = lda.fit_transform(X_train, y_train)
X_test = lda.transform(X_test)
#Training the Logistic Regression model on the Training set
from sklearn.linear_model import LogisticRegression
classifier = LogisticRegression(random_state = 0)
classifier.fit(X_train, y_train)
LogisticRegression(C=1.0, class_weight=None, dual=False, fit_intercept=True,
            intercept_scaling=1, l1_ratio=None, max_iter=100,
            multi_class='auto', n_jobs=None, penalty='l2',
            random_state=0, solver='lbfgs', tol=0.0001, verbose=0,
            warm_start=False)
#Predicting the Test set results
y_pred = classifier.predict(X_test)
#Making the Confusion Matrix
from sklearn.metrics import confusion_matrix
cm = confusion_matrix(y_test, y_pred)
print(cm)
        [[14  0  0]
         [ 0 16  0]
         [ 0  0  6]]
#Visualising the Training set results
from matplotlib.colors import ListedColormap
X_set, y_set = X_train, y_train
X1, X2 = np.meshgrid(np.arange(start = X_set[:, 0].min() - 1, stop = X_set[:, 0].max() +
1, step = 0.01),
            np.arange(start = X_set[:, 1].min() - 1, stop = X_set[:, 1].max() + 1, step =
0.01))
plt.contourf(X1, X2, classifier.predict(np.array([X1.ravel(),
X2.ravel()]).T).reshape(X1.shape),
        alpha = 0.75, cmap = ListedColormap(('red', 'green', 'blue')))
plt.xlim(X1.min(), X1.max())
plt.ylim(X2.min(), X2.max())
for i, j in enumerate(np.unique(y_set)):
    plt.scatter(X_set[y_set == j, 0], X_set[y_set == j, 1],
            c = ListedColormap(('red', 'green', 'blue'))(i), label = j)
plt.title('Logistic Regression (Training set)')
plt.xlabel('LD1')
plt.ylabel('LD2')
plt.legend()
plt.show()
```

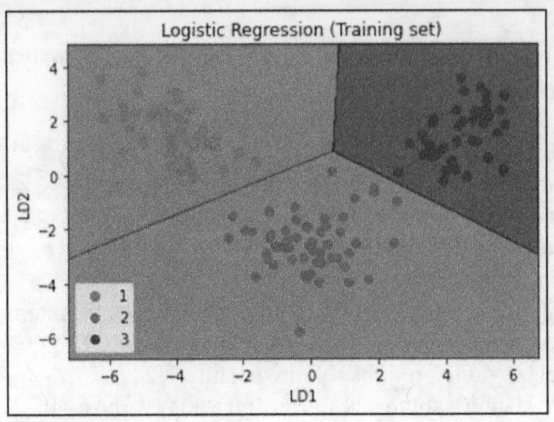

```
#Visualising the Test set results
from matplotlib.colors import ListedColormap
X_set, y_set = X_test, y_test
X1, X2 = np.meshgrid(np.arange(start = X_set[:, 0].min() - 1, stop = X_set[:, 0].max() +
1, step = 0.01),
              np.arange(start = X_set[:, 1].min() - 1, stop = X_set[:, 1].max() + 1, step =
0.01))
plt.contourf(X1, X2, classifier.predict(np.array([X1.ravel(),
X2.ravel()]).T).reshape(X1.shape),
        alpha = 0.75, cmap = ListedColormap(('red', 'green', 'blue')))
plt.xlim(X1.min(), X1.max())
plt.ylim(X2.min(), X2.max())
for i, j in enumerate(np.unique(y_set)):
   plt.scatter(X_set[y_set == j, 0], X_set[y_set == j, 1],
          c = ListedColormap(('red', 'green', 'blue'))(i), label = j)
plt.title('Logistic Regression (Test set)')
plt.xlabel('LD1')
plt.ylabel('LD2')
plt.legend()
plt.show()
```

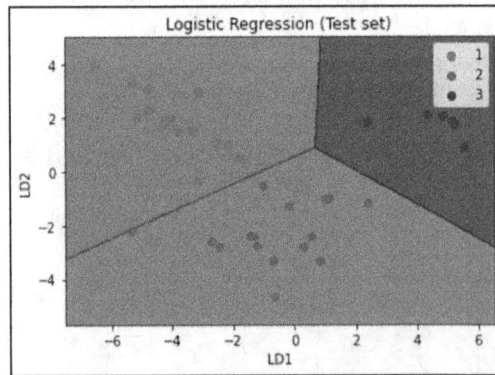

5.6 Anomaly Detection

Anomaly detection is a process of finding those rare items, data points, events, or observations that make suspicions by being different from the rest data points or observations. Anomaly detection is also known as outlier detection.

Anomaly Detection is a technique used to identify data points, events, or observations that deviate significantly from the majority of the data. These deviations, often referred to as anomalies, outliers, or novelties, can indicate important or interesting phenomena, such as errors, fraud, defects, or significant changes in a system.

Key Concepts of Anomaly Detection

1. **Anomaly Definition:**
   - Anomalies are data points that differ markedly from the rest of the data. They can be due to various reasons such as errors, fraud, rare events, or novel patterns.

2. **Types of Anomalies:**
   - **Point Anomalies:** Single data points that are significantly different from the majority of the data.
   - **Contextual Anomalies:** Data points that are unusual in a specific context but not necessarily in the overall dataset. For example, a high temperature might be normal in summer but anomalous in winter.
   - **Collective Anomalies:** A group of data points that are anomalous when considered together but might not be individually anomalous. For instance, a sudden burst of traffic to a website might be anomalous if it typically experiences steady traffic.

Methods of Anomaly Detection

1. **Statistical Methods:**
   - **Z-Score Method:** Measures how many standard deviations a data point is from the mean. Points with a Z-score beyond a certain threshold are considered anomalies.
   - **Probability Distribution Models:** Fit a probability distribution to the data and identify points that have a very low probability of occurrence.

2. **Machine Learning Methods:**
   - **Supervised Anomaly Detection:** Requires labeled data where anomalies are marked. Common algorithms include:
     - **Support Vector Machine (SVM) for Anomaly Detection:** Finds a hyperplane that separates normal data from anomalies.
     - **Decision Trees and Random Forests:** Used to classify data points and identify anomalies based on decision rules.
   - **Unsupervised Anomaly Detection:** Does not require labeled data. Common algorithms include:
     - **K-Means Clustering:** Identifies anomalies based on how far data points are from their cluster centroids.
     - **Isolation Forest:** Randomly isolates data points and identifies anomalies based on the number of isolations required.
     - **Autoencoders:** Neural networks trained to reconstruct input data; anomalies are identified by large reconstruction errors.

3. **Distance-Based Methods:**
   - **k-Nearest Neighbors (k-NN):** Measures the distance to the k nearest neighbors. Data points that have a significantly higher distance compared to their neighbors are considered anomalies.

4. **Density-Based Methods:**
   - **DBSCAN (Density-Based Spatial Clustering of Applications with Noise):** Groups points based on density and identifies points that lie in low-density regions as anomalies.

Applications of Anomaly Detection

1. **Fraud Detection:**

- o **Financial Transactions:** Identifying unusual patterns in transactions that might indicate fraudulent activities, such as credit card fraud or financial theft.
2. **Network Security:**
   - o **Intrusion Detection Systems:** Detecting unusual patterns or behaviors in network traffic that could indicate security breaches or cyberattacks.
3. **Industrial Monitoring:**
   - o **Equipment Failure:** Identifying abnormal patterns in sensor data that could signal potential equipment failures or malfunctions.
4. **Healthcare:**
   - o **Medical Diagnostics:** Detecting rare diseases or unusual patient symptoms that deviate from typical patterns.
5. **Quality Control:**
   - o **Manufacturing:** Identifying defects or anomalies in products based on production data or sensor measurements.
6. **Data Cleaning:**
   - o **Outlier Detection:** Identifying and handling outliers in datasets to improve the quality of data used in analysis and modeling.

Anomaly detection is a crucial technique in data analysis and machine learning for identifying rare and significant deviations from normal patterns. Its applications span various domains, including finance, security, healthcare, and manufacturing. By effectively identifying anomalies, organizations can uncover important insights, prevent potential issues, and improve decision-making processes.

Python code to implement Anomaly Detection

```
import numpy as np
import matplotlib.pyplot as plt
from sklearn.ensemble import IsolationForest
from sklearn.preprocessing import StandardScaler

# Generate synthetic data
np.random.seed(42)
X_train = np.random.randn(100, 2)
X_test = np.vstack([np.random.randn(10, 2) + 5, np.random.randn(10, 2) - 5])

# Standardize the data
scaler = StandardScaler()
X_train_scaled = scaler.fit_transform(X_train)
X_test_scaled = scaler.transform(X_test)

# Train the Isolation Forest model
model = IsolationForest(contamination=0.2, random_state=42)
model.fit(X_train_scaled)

# Predict anomalies
y_test_pred = model.predict(X_test_scaled)
anomalies = y_test_pred == -1

# Plot the results
plt.figure(figsize=(10, 6))
```

plt.scatter(X_test_scaled[:, 0], X_test_scaled[:, 1], c=anomalies, cmap='coolwarm', edgecolor='k')
plt.title('Anomaly Detection using Isolation Forest')
plt.xlabel('Feature 1')
plt.ylabel('Feature 2')
plt.show()

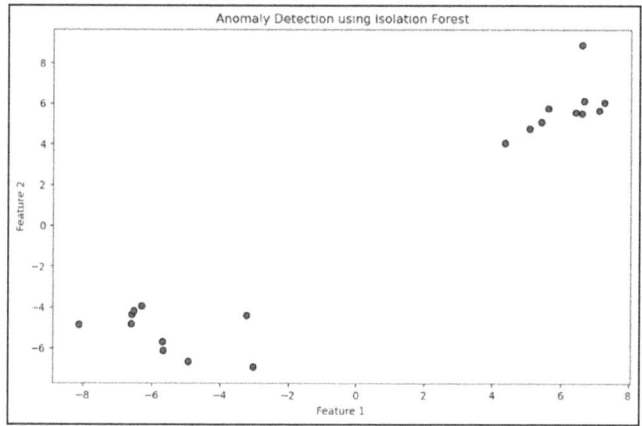

5.7 Association rule learning

Association rule learning is a type of unsupervised learning technique that checks for the dependency of one data item on another data item and maps accordingly so that it can be more profitable. It tries to find some interesting relations or associations among the variables of dataset. It is based on different rules to discover the interesting relations between variables in the database. Association rule learning is a fundamental technique in data mining and machine learning used to discover interesting relationships or patterns among items in large datasets. It is particularly useful in market basket analysis, where the goal is to understand the purchasing behavior of customers by finding associations between items bought together.

The association rule learning is one of the very important concepts of machine learning, and it is employed in Market Basket analysis, Web usage mining, continuous production, etc. Here market basket analysis is a technique used by the various big retailer to discover the associations between items. We can understand it by taking an example of a supermarket, as in a supermarket, all products that are purchased together are put together. For example, if a customer buys bread, he most likely can also buy butter, eggs, or milk, so these products are stored within a shelf or mostly nearby. Consider the below diagram

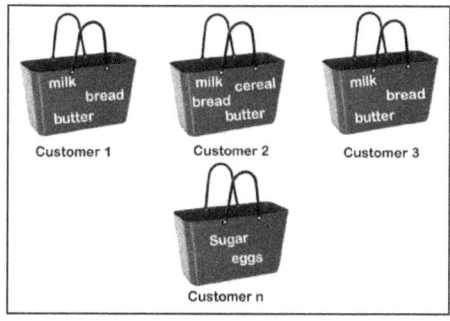

Applications of Association Rule Learning
- *Market Basket Analysis:* Discover which products are frequently bought together.
- *Recommendation Systems:* Suggest products based on previous purchases.
- *Fraud Detection:* Identify unusual patterns that may indicate fraudulent behavior.
- *Medical Diagnosis:* Find relationships between symptoms and diseases.

Association rule learning helps in uncovering patterns that are not immediately obvious, allowing businesses and researchers to make data-driven decisions based on discovered associations.

How does Association Rule Learning work?

Association rule learning works on the concept of If and Else Statement, such as if A then B.

Here the If element is called antecedent, and then statement is called as Consequent. These types of relationships where we can find out some association or relation between two items is known *as single cardinality*. It is all about creating rules, and if the number of items increases, then cardinality also increases accordingly. So, to measure the associations between thousands of data items, there are several metrics. These metrics are given below:
- **Support**
- **Confidence**
- **Lift**

Let's understand each of them:

Support: Support is the frequency of A or how frequently an item appears in the dataset. It is defined as the fraction of the transaction T that contains the itemset X. If there are X datasets, then for transactions T, it can be written as:

$$\text{Supp}(X) = \frac{Freq(X)}{T}$$

Confidence: Confidence indicates how often the rule has been found to be true. Or how often the items X and Y occur together in the dataset when the occurrence of X is already given. It is the ratio of the transaction that contains X and Y to the number of records that contain X.

$$\text{Confidence} = \frac{Freq(X,Y)}{Freq(X)}$$

Lift: It is the strength of any rule, which can be defined as below formula:

$$\text{Lift} = \frac{Supp(X,Y)}{Supp(X) \times Supp(Y)}$$

it is the ratio of the observed support measure and expected support if X and Y are independent of each other. It has three possible values:
- *If Lift= 1:* The probability of occurrence of antecedent and consequent is independent of each other.
- *Lift>1:* It determines the degree to which the two itemsets are dependent to each other.

o ***Lift<1:*** It tells us that one item is a substitute for other items, which means one item has a negative effect on another.

Algorithms for Association Rule Learning
Association rule learning can be divided into three types of algorithms:
Apriori
Eclat
F-P Growth Algorithm
1. **Apriori Algorithm**:
   o **Description**: The Apriori algorithm is one of the most well-known algorithms for mining association rules. It works by identifying frequent itemsets (sets of items that appear together frequently) and then generating association rules from these itemsets.
   o **Approach**: Uses a breadth-first search strategy and prunes the search space by eliminating itemsets that do not meet the minimum support threshold.
2. **Eclat Algorithm**:
   o **Description**: Eclat (Equivalence Class Transformation) is an alternative to Apriori. It uses a depth-first search strategy and relies on a vertical data format, where each item is associated with a list of transactions containing it.
   o **Approach**: More efficient than Apriori in some cases because it reduces the number of candidate itemsets by focusing on itemsets that occur together in the same transactions.
3. **FP-Growth Algorithm**:
   o **Description**: The FP-Growth (Frequent Pattern Growth) algorithm builds a compact tree structure (FP-tree) to represent frequent itemsets and avoids generating candidate itemsets explicitly.
   o **Approach**: Uses a divide-and-conquer strategy to recursively mine the FP-tree, which can be more efficient than Apriori for large datasets.

Python code to implement association rules
```
import pandas as pd
from mlxtend.frequent_patterns import apriori, association_rules

# Sample transactional data
data = {
   'Transaction': ['T1', 'T2', 'T3', 'T4', 'T5'],
   'Item': [['Milk', 'Bread'],
      ['Bread', 'Diaper', 'Beer'],
      ['Milk', 'Diaper', 'Beer', 'Eggs'],
      ['Bread', 'Milk', 'Diaper', 'Beer'],
      ['Bread', 'Milk']]
}

# Convert to one-hot encoded DataFrame
df = pd.DataFrame(data['Item'])
df = df.stack().str.get_dummies().groupby(level=0).sum()

# Apply Apriori algorithm
frequent_itemsets = apriori(df, min_support=0.6, use_colnames=True)
```

```
# Generate association rules
rules = association_rules(frequent_itemsets, metric="confidence", min_threshold=0.7)

# Display rules
print(rules)
     antecedents consequents  antecedent support  consequent support  support  \
0        (Beer)    (Diaper)                 0.6                 0.6      0.6
1      (Diaper)      (Beer)                 0.6                 0.6      0.6
2        (Milk)     (Bread)                 0.8                 0.8      0.6
3       (Bread)      (Milk)                 0.8                 0.8      0.6

   confidence      lift  leverage  conviction  zhangs_metric
0        1.00  1.666667      0.24         inf           1.00
1        1.00  1.666667      0.24         inf           1.00
2        0.75  0.937500     -0.04         0.8          -0.25
3        0.75  0.937500     -0.04         0.8          -0.25
```

Chapter 6: Reinforcement Learning

6.1 Reinforcement learning

Reinforcement Learning (RL) is a type of **machine learning** where an **agent** learns to make decisions by interacting with an **environment** to maximize a **reward**. It is inspired by how humans and animals learn from experiences.

Unlike **supervised learning**, RL does **not rely on labeled data**. Instead, the agent learns by **trial and error**, receiving **rewards** for good actions and **penalties** for bad actions

- o Reinforcement Learning is a feedback-based Machine learning technique in which an agent learns to behave in an environment by performing the actions and seeing the results of actions. For each good action, the agent gets positive feedback, and for each bad action, the agent gets negative feedback or penalty.
- o In Reinforcement Learning, the agent learns automatically using feedbacks without any labeled data, unlike supervised learning.
- o Since there is no labeled data, so the agent is bound to learn by its experience only.
- o RL solves a specific type of problem where decision making is sequential, and the goal is long-term, such as game-playing, robotics, etc.
- o The agent interacts with the environment and explores it by itself. The primary goal of an agent in reinforcement learning is to improve the performance by getting the maximum positive rewards.
- o The agent learns with the process of hit and trial, and based on the experience, it learns to perform the task in a better way. Hence, we can say that "Reinforcement learning is a type of machine learning method where an intelligent agent (computer program) interacts with the environment and learns to act within that." How a Robotic dog learns the movement of his arms is an example of Reinforcement learning.
- o It is a core part of Artificial intelligence, and all AI agent works on the concept of reinforcement learning. Here we do not need to pre-program the agent, as it learns from its own experience without any human intervention.
- o Example: Suppose there is an AI agent present within a maze environment, and his goal is to find the diamond. The agent interacts with the environment by performing some actions, and based on those actions, the state of the agent gets changed, and it also receives a reward or penalty as feedback.
- o The agent continues doing these three things (take action, change state/remain in the same state, and get feedback), and by doing these actions, he learns and explores the environment.
- o The agent learns that what actions lead to positive feedback or rewards and what actions lead to negative feedback penalty. As a positive reward, the agent gets a positive point, and as a penalty, it gets a negative point.

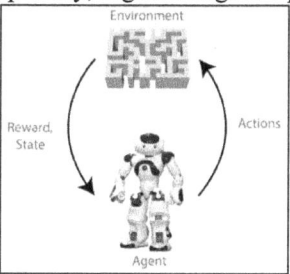

Terms used in Reinforcement Learning

1. Agent – The decision-maker (e.g., a robot, an AI player in a game).
2. Environment – The world in which the agent operates (e.g., a chessboard, a traffic system).
3. State (S) – The current situation of the agent (e.g., the position of a chess piece).
4. Action (A) – The possible moves the agent can take (e.g., move left, right, or stay).
5. Reward (R) – The feedback received after taking an action (e.g., +1 for winning, -1 for losing).
6. Policy (π) – The strategy that the agent follows to choose actions.
7. Value Function (V) – Measures how good a state is in terms of future rewards.
8. Q-Function (Q) – Measures how good a specific action is in a given state.

Key Features of Reinforcement Learning

o   In RL, the agent is not instructed about the environment and what actions need to be taken.
o   It is based on the hit and trial process.
o   The agent takes the next action and changes states according to the feedback of the previous action.
o   The agent may get a delayed reward.
o   The environment is stochastic, and the agent needs to explore it to reach to get the maximum positive rewards.

Approaches to implement Reinforcement Learning

There are mainly three ways to implement reinforcement-learning in ML, which are:

1. *Value-based:*
   The value-based approach is about to find the optimal value function, which is the maximum value at a state under any policy. Therefore, the agent expects the long-term return at any state(s) under policy π.

2. *Policy-based:*
   Policy-based approach is to find the optimal policy for the maximum future rewards without using the value function. In this approach, the agent tries to apply such a policy that the action performed in each step helps to maximize the future reward.

   The policy-based approach has mainly two types of policy:
      o   *Deterministic:* The same action is produced by the policy (π) at any state.
      o   *Stochastic:* In this policy, probability determines the produced action.

3. *Model-based:* In the model-based approach, a virtual model is created for the environment, and the agent explores that environment to learn it. There is no particular solution or algorithm for this approach because the model representation is different for each environment.

Elements of Reinforcement Learning

There are four main elements of Reinforcement Learning, which are given below:

1. Policy
2. Reward Signal
3. Value Function
4. Model of the environment

1) Policy: A policy can be defined as a way how an agent behaves at a given time. It maps the perceived states of the environment to the actions taken on those states. A policy is the core element of the RL as it alone can define the behavior of the agent. In some cases, it may be a simple function or a lookup table, whereas, for other cases, it may involve general computation as a search process. It could be deterministic or a stochastic policy:

For deterministic policy: $a = \pi(s)$

For stochastic policy: $\pi(a \mid s) = P[At = a \mid St = s]$

2) Reward Signal: The goal of reinforcement learning is defined by the reward signal. At each state, the environment sends an immediate signal to the learning agent, and this signal is known as a reward signal. These rewards are given according to the good and bad actions taken by the agent. The agent's main objective is to maximize the total number of rewards for good actions. The reward signal can change the policy, such as if an action selected by the agent leads to low reward, then the policy may change to select other actions in the future.

3) Value Function: The value function gives information about how good the situation and action are and how much reward an agent can expect. A reward indicates the immediate signal for each good and bad action, whereas a value function specifies the good state and action for the future. The value function depends on the reward as, without reward, there could be no value. The goal of estimating values is to achieve more rewards.

4) Model: The last element of reinforcement learning is the model, which mimics the behavior of the environment. With the help of the model, one can make inferences about how the environment will behave. Such as, if a state and an action are given, then a model can predict the next state and reward.

The model is used for planning, which means it provides a way to take a course of action by considering all future situations before actually experiencing those situations. The approaches for solving the RL problems with the help of the model are termed as the model-based approach. Comparatively, an approach without using a model is called a model-free approach.

How does Reinforcement Learning Work?

1. Initialization:
- The agent starts in an **initial state** in the environment.

2. Take an Action:
- The agent selects an **action (A)** based on its **policy (π)**.

3. Receive Reward & Update State:
- The agent receives a **reward (R)** and moves to a **new state (S')**.

4. Learn from Experience:
- The agent updates its **strategy (policy)** based on rewards received.

5. Repeat:
- The agent continues exploring different actions, refining its strategy over time

To understand the working process of the RL, we need to consider two main things:
- ○ *Environment:* It can be anything such as a room, maze, football ground, etc.
- ○ *Agent:* An intelligent agent such as AI robot.

Let's take an example of a maze environment that the agent needs to explore. Consider the below image:

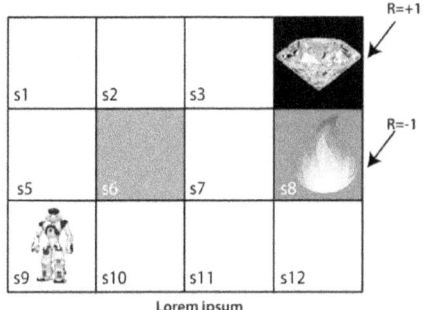

Lorem ipsum

In the above image, the agent is at the very first block of the maze. The maze is consisting of an S_6 block, which is a wall, S_8 a fire pit, and S_4 a diamond block.

The agent cannot cross the S_6 block, as it is a solid wall. If the agent reaches the S_4 block, then get the +1 reward; if it reaches the fire pit, then gets -1 reward point. It can take four actions: move up, move down, move left, and move right.

The agent can take any path to reach to the final point, but he needs to make it in possible fewer steps. Suppose the agent considers the path S9-S5-S1-S2-S3, so he will get the +1-reward point.

The agent will try to remember the preceding steps that it has taken to reach the final step. To memorize the steps, it assigns 1 value to each previous step. Consider the below step:

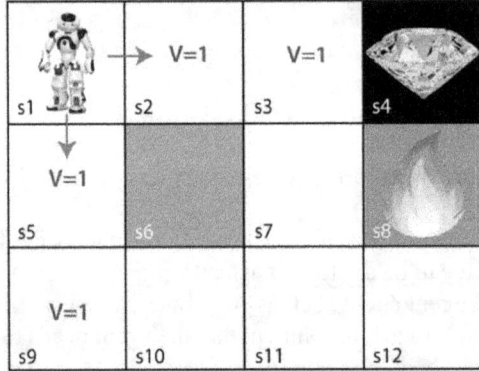

Now, the agent has successfully stored the previous steps assigning the 1 value to each previous block. But what will the agent do if he starts moving from the block, which has 1 value block on both sides? Consider the below diagram:

It will be a difficult condition for the agent whether he should go up or down as each block has the same value. So, the above approach is not suitable for the agent to reach the destination. Hence to solve the problem, we will use the **Bellman equation**, which is the main concept behind reinforcement learning.

Types of Reinforcement Learning

1. Model-Based RL
- The agent builds a model of the environment and plans its actions accordingly.
- Example: Chess-playing AI that predicts opponent moves.

2. Model-Free RL
- The agent learns without understanding the environment's internal rules.
- Example: A robot learns to walk by trial and error.

The Bellman Equation

The Bellman equation was introduced by the Mathematician **Richard Ernest Bellman in the year 1953**, and hence it is called as a Bellman equation. It is associated with dynamic programming and used to calculate the values of a decision problem at a certain point by including the values of previous states.

It is a way of calculating the value functions in dynamic programming or environment that leads to modern reinforcement learning.

The key-elements used in Bellman equations are:

- o Action performed by the agent is referred to as "a"
- o State occurred by performing the action is "s."
- o The reward/feedback obtained for each good and bad action is "R."
- o A discount factor is Gamma "γ."

The Bellman equation can be written as:

$$V(s) = \max [R(s,a) + \gamma V(s`)]$$

Where,

V(s)= value calculated at a particular point.

R(s,a) = Reward at a particular state s by performing an action.

γ = Discount factor

V(s`) = The value at the previous state.

In the above equation, we are taking the max of the complete values because the agent tries to find the optimal solution always.

So now, using the Bellman equation, we will find value at each state of the given environment. We will start from the block, which is next to the target block.

For 1st block:

V(s3) = max [R(s,a) + γV(s`)], here V(s')= 0 because there is no further state to move.

V(s3)= max[R(s,a)]=> V(s3)= max[1]=> **V(s3)= 1.**

For 2nd block:

V(s2) = max [R(s,a) + γV(s`)], here γ= 0.9(lets), V(s')= 1, and R(s, a)= 0, because there is no reward at this state.

V(s2)= max[0.9(1)]=> V(s)= max[0.9]=> **V(s2) =0.9**

For 3rd block:

V(s1) = max [R(s,a) + γV(s`)], here γ= 0.9(lets), V(s')= 0.9, and R(s, a)= 0, because there is no reward at this state also.

V(s1)= max[0.9(0.9)]=> V(s3)= max[0.81]=> **V(s1) =0.81**

For 4th block:

V(s5) = max [R(s,a) + γV(s`)], here γ= 0.9(lets), V(s')= 0.81, and R(s, a)= 0, because there is no reward at this state also.

V(s5)= max[0.9(0.81)]=> V(s5)= max[0.81]=> **V(s5) =0.73**

For 5th block:

V(s9) = max [R(s,a) + γV(s`)], here γ= 0.9(lets), V(s')= 0.73, and R(s, a)= 0, because there is no reward at this state also.

V(s9)= max[0.9(0.73)]=> V(s4)= max[0.81]=> **V(s4) =0.66**

Consider the below image:

V=0.81	V=0.9	V=1	
s1	s2	s3	s4
V=0.73			
s5	s6	s7	s8
↘ V=0.66			
s9	s10	s11	s12

Now, we will move further to the 6th block, and here agent may change the route because it always tries to find the optimal path. So now, let's consider from the block next to the fire pit.

V=0.81	V=0.9	V=1	
s1	s2	s3	s4
V=0.73			
s5	s6	s7	s8
V=0.66			
s9	s10	s11	s12

Now, the agent has three options to move; if he moves to the blue box, then he will feel a bump if he moves to the fire pit, then he will get the -1 reward. But here we are taking only positive rewards, so for this, he will move to upwards only. The complete block values will be calculated using this formula. Consider the below image:

V=0.81	V=0.9	V=1	
s1	s2	s3	s4
V=0.73		V=0.9	
s5	s6	s7	s8
V=0.66	V=0.73	V=0.81	V=0.73
s9	s10	s11	s12

173

6.1.1 Reinforcement Learning Applications

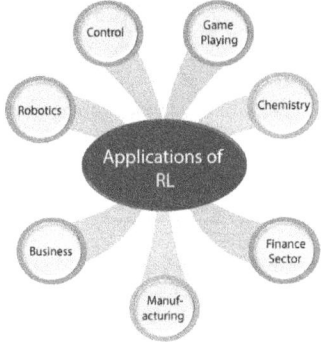

Robotics:
RL is used in Robot navigation, Robo-soccer, walking, juggling, etc.
Control:
RL can be used for adaptive control such as Factory processes, admission control in telecommunication, and Helicopter pilot is an example of reinforcement learning.
Game Playing:
RL can be used in Game playing such as tic-tac-toe, chess, etc.
Chemistry:
RL can be used for optimizing the chemical reactions.
Business:
RL is now used for business strategy planning.
Manufacturing:
In various automobile manufacturing companies, the robots use deep reinforcement learning to pick goods and put them in some containers.
Finance Sector:
The RL is currently used in the finance sector for evaluating trading strategies.

6.1.2 Types of Reinforcement Learning
There are mainly two types of reinforcement learning, which are:
- **Positive Reinforcement**
- **Negative Reinforcement**

Positive Reinforcement:
The positive reinforcement learning means adding something to increase the tendency that expected behavior would occur again. It impacts positively on the behavior of the agent and increases the strength of the behavior.
This type of reinforcement can sustain the changes for a long time, but too much positive reinforcement may lead to an overload of states that can reduce the consequences.
Negative Reinforcement:
The negative reinforcement learning is opposite to the positive reinforcement as it increases the tendency that the specific behavior will occur again by avoiding the negative condition.
It can be more effective than the positive reinforcement depending on situation and behavior, but it provides reinforcement only to meet minimum behavior.
How to represent the agent state?
We can represent the agent state using the Markov State that contains all the required information from the history. The State St is Markov state if it follows the given condition:
$P[S_t+1 \mid S_t] = P[S_t+1 \mid S_1,\ldots, S_t]$
The Markov state follows the Markov property, which says that the future is independent of the past and can only be defined with the present. The RL works on fully observable

environments, where the agent can observe the environment and act for the new state. The complete process is known as Markov Decision process, which is explained below:

Markov Decision Process

Markov Decision Process or MDP, is used to formalize the reinforcement learning problems. If the environment is completely observable, then its dynamic can be modeled as a Markov Process. In MDP, the agent constantly interacts with the environment and performs actions; at each action, the environment responds and generates a new state.

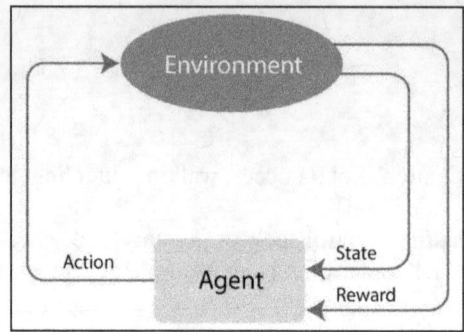

MDP is used to describe the environment for the RL, and almost all the RL problem can be formalized using MDP.

MDP contains a tuple of four elements (S, A, P_a, R_a):

- o   A set of finite States S
- o   A set of finite Actions A
- o   Rewards received after transitioning from state S to state S', due to action a.
- o   Probability P_a.

MDP uses Markov property, and to better understand the MDP, we need to learn about it.

Markov Property:

It says that "If the agent is present in the current state S1, performs an action a1 and move to the state s2, then the state transition from s1 to s2 only depends on the current state and future action and states do not depend on past actions, rewards, or states."

Or, in other words, as per Markov Property, the current state transition does not depend on any past action or state. Hence, MDP is an RL problem that satisfies the Markov property. Such as in a Chess game, the players only focus on the current state and do not need to remember past actions or states.

Finite MDP:

A finite MDP is when there are finite states, finite rewards, and finite actions. In RL, we consider only the finite MDP.

Markov Process:

Markov Process is a memoryless process with a sequence of random states S_1, S_2, ..., S_t that uses the Markov Property. Markov process is also known as Markov chain, which is a tuple (S, P) on state S and transition function P. These two components (S and P) can define the dynamics of the system.

6.2 Reinforcement learning algorithms

Reinforcement learning algorithms are mainly used in AI applications and gaming applications. The main used algorithms are:

> Q-Learning
> Deep Q-Networks (DQN)
> Policy Gradient Methods
> Actor-Critic Method

6.2.1 Q-Learning

Q-Learning is a popular and foundational algorithm in reinforcement learning. It is an off-policy model-free algorithm used to find the optimal policy that maximizes cumulative reward for an agent interacting with an environment. The goal of Q-Learning is to learn the value of action-state pairs, known as Q-values, which help the agent decide the best action to take in any given state.

Key Concepts in Q-Learning

1. **Q-Value (Q(s, a))**: The Q-value of a state-action pair (s,a) represents the expected cumulative reward (or return) of taking action a in state s and then following the optimal policy.
2. **Learning Rate (α\alpha)**: A parameter that controls how much of the new Q-value estimate is incorporated into the old Q-value. It ranges between 0 and 1.
3. **Discount Factor (γ\gamma)**: A parameter that determines the importance of future rewards. It ranges between 0 and 1. A higher value means future rewards are more significant.
4. **Reward (r)**: The immediate feedback received after performing an action a in state s.
5. **Exploration vs. Exploitation**: The balance between trying new actions (exploration) and using known actions that have previously provided high rewards (exploitation).

Q-Learning Algorithm

1. Initialization

Initialize the Q-values arbitrarily for all state-action pairs (s, a). Typically, Q-values are initialized to zero or small random values.

2. Action Selection

At each time step, select an action a in state s based on a policy derived from the Q-values. A common approach is the ϵ-greedy policy:

- With probability ϵ, choose a random action (exploration).

- With probability $1 - \epsilon$, choose the action with the highest Q-value for the current state (exploitation).

3. Update Q-Value

After taking action a in state s and observing the reward r and the next state s', update the Q-value for the state-action pair (s, a) using the Q-learning update rule:

$$Q(s, a) \leftarrow Q(s, a) + \alpha \left[r + \gamma \max_{a'} Q(s', a') - Q(s, a) \right]$$

Where:

- α is the learning rate.
- γ is the discount factor.
- $\max_{a'} Q(s', a')$ is the maximum Q-value for the next state s'.

4. Repeat

Repeat the process for a number of episodes or until convergence, where an episode is a sequence of actions, states, and rewards until reaching a terminal state.

Example calculation

Let's go through an example to illustrate the Q-Learning update:

- Assume an agent is in state s and takes action a.
- The agent receives a reward r and transitions to state s'.
- The Q-value for state s and action a is updated as follows:

Parameters:

- Learning rate $\alpha = 0.1$
- Discount factor $\gamma = 0.9$
- Reward $r = 10$
- Current Q-value $Q(s, a) = 20$
- Maximum Q-value for the next state $\max_{a'} Q(s', a') = 25$

Update Rule:

$$Q(s, a) \leftarrow Q(s, a) + \alpha \left[r + \gamma \max_{a'} Q(s', a') - Q(s, a) \right]$$

Calculation:

$$Q(s, a) \leftarrow 20 + 0.1 \left[10 + 0.9 \times 25 - 20 \right]$$

$$Q(s, a) \leftarrow 20 + 0.1 \left[10 + 22.5 - 20 \right]$$

$$Q(s, a) \leftarrow 20 + 0.1 \times 12.5$$

$$Q(s, a) \leftarrow 20 + 1.25$$

$$Q(s, a) \leftarrow 21.25$$

Q-Learning is a powerful algorithm that helps an agent learn the optimal action-value function through interaction with the environment. It provides a framework to find the best policy for maximizing cumulative rewards without requiring a model of the environment. By iteratively updating Q-values and balancing exploration and exploitation, Q-Learning can efficiently learn effective policies for a wide range of problems.

6.2.2 Deep Q-Networks (DQN)

Deep Q-Networks (DQN) is an advanced extension of Q-Learning that leverages deep learning to handle high-dimensional state spaces, such as those encountered in complex environments like video games. DQN combines the principles of Q-Learning with deep neural networks to approximate the Q-value function, making it suitable for problems where the state space is too large for traditional Q-Learning methods to handle effectively.

Key Concepts of DQN

1. **Q-Value Function Approximation**

   o In traditional Q-Learning, the Q-value function is typically stored in a table, which becomes impractical for large or continuous state spaces. DQN uses a deep neural network to approximate the Q-value function $Q(s,a)$, where the network takes the state s as input and outputs Q-values for all possible actions a.

2. **Experience Replay**

   o **Definition:** A technique to improve training stability and efficiency by storing the agent's experiences (state, action, reward, next state) in a replay buffer and randomly sampling mini-batches from this buffer to train the network.

   o **Advantage:** Breaks the correlation between consecutive experiences and smooths out training, which leads to more stable learning.

3. **Target Network**

   o **Definition:** A separate neural network used to compute the target Q-values during training. The target network is a copy of the main Q-network but is updated less frequently.

   o **Advantage:** Helps to stabilize training by preventing the moving target problem, where the Q-value estimates are constantly changing.

4. **Reward Signal**

   o DQN uses the reward signal to guide the learning process, where the goal is to maximize the cumulative reward over time.

DQN Algorithm

Here's a step-by-step outline of how DQN works:

1. Initialization

- Initialize the main Q-network with random weights.
- Create a target Q-network with the same architecture as the main Q-network.
- Initialize the experience replay buffer to store agent experiences.

2. Interaction with the Environment

- For each episode:

  - Initialize the state s.

  - For each step within the episode:

    - Choose an action a using an ϵ-greedy policy based on the main Q-network:

      - With probability ϵ, select a random action (exploration).

      - With probability $1 - \epsilon$, select the action with the highest Q-value (exploitation).

    - Execute action a, observe reward r and the next state s'.

    - Store the experience (s, a, r, s') in the replay buffer.

    - Sample a mini-batch of experiences from the replay buffer.

    - Compute the target Q-value for each experience using the target network:
      $$y = r + \gamma \max_{a'} Q_{\text{target}}(s', a')$$

- Update the main Q-network by minimizing the loss between the predicted Q-values and the target Q-values:
  $$\text{Loss} = \frac{1}{N} \sum_{i=1}^{N} [y_i - Q_{\text{main}}(s_i, a_i)]^2$$

- Every few episodes, update the target network weights to match the main Q-network weights.

3. Training

- Train the main Q-network using the mini-batches sampled from the replay buffer, optimizing the loss function to minimize the difference between the predicted Q-values and the target Q-values.

Example

1. **Network Setup**

   - Suppose our Q-network is a neural network with a few hidden layers. This network approximates $Q(s, a)$ for state s and action a.

2. **Replay Buffer**

   - The agent stores its experiences (e.g., (s, a, r, s')) in the replay buffer.

3. **Training**

   - The agent samples a batch of experiences from the replay buffer.

   - For each experience (s, a, r, s') in the batch:

     - Compute the target Q-value y using the target network:

       $$y = r + \gamma \max_{a'} Q_{\text{target}}(s', a')$$

- Calculate the loss between this target Q-value y and the predicted Q-value $Q_{\mathrm{main}}(s, a)$ from the main network.
- Perform backpropagation to update the weights of the main Q-network to minimize this loss.

4. Updating the Target Network

- After a set number of episodes, update the target network by copying the weights from the main Q-network.

Deep Q-Networks (DQN) is a powerful approach that combines the benefits of Q-Learning with deep neural networks. It enables reinforcement learning to handle complex environments with high-dimensional state spaces by approximating the Q-value function through a neural network. Key innovations in DQN, such as experience replay and target networks, help to stabilize training and improve performance. DQN has been successfully applied to various domains, including video game playing and robotic control, demonstrating its effectiveness in learning complex policies.

6.2.3 Policy Gradient Methods

Policy Gradient Methods are a class of reinforcement learning algorithms that directly optimize the policy of an agent, rather than approximating the Q-value function as in Q-Learning. These methods aim to find the optimal policy by directly adjusting the parameters of the policy function using gradient ascent.

Key Concepts in Policy Gradient Methods

1. Policy:

- The policy, denoted as $\pi_\theta(a|s)$, is a mapping from states s to actions a parameterized by θ. It represents the probability distribution over actions given a state.

2. Objective Function:

- The goal is to maximize the expected cumulative reward (also known as the return) over time. This is done by optimizing a performance measure that evaluates how well the policy performs.

3. Gradient Ascent:

- Policy gradient methods use gradient ascent to adjust the parameters θ of the policy to maximize the expected return. The gradient of the objective function with respect to the policy parameters is computed and used to update the parameters.

Policy Gradient Algorithm

1. Define the Objective Function

The objective is to maximize the expected return $J(\theta)$:

$$J(\theta) = \mathbb{E}[R]$$

where R is the total return or cumulative reward obtained following the policy π_θ.

2. Compute the Policy Gradient

To maximize $J(\theta)$, we need to compute the gradient of $J(\theta)$ with respect to the policy parameters θ:

$$\nabla_\theta J(\theta) = \mathbb{E}\left[\nabla_\theta \log \pi_\theta(a|s) \cdot R\right]$$

where $\log \pi_\theta(a|s)$ is the log probability of taking action a in state s under policy π_θ, and R is the return from state s after taking action a.

3. Update Policy Parameters

Using the computed gradient, the policy parameters are updated using gradient ascent:

$$\theta \leftarrow \theta + \alpha \cdot \nabla_\theta J(\theta)$$

where α is the learning rate.

Example of Policy Gradient Methods

1. Initialize the Policy

- Initialize the policy network with random parameters θ.

2. Collect Experiences

- Interact with the environment to collect a set of episodes, where each episode consists of sequences of states, actions, and rewards.

3. Compute Returns

- For each episode, compute the total return R_t for each time step t in the episode. Typically, R_t is the sum of discounted future rewards from time step t:

$$R_t = \sum_{k=t}^{T} \gamma^{k-t} r_k$$

where γ is the discount factor, and r_k is the reward received at time step k.

4. Compute Gradients

- For each action taken in the episode, compute the policy gradient using:

$$\nabla_\theta J(\theta) = \frac{1}{N} \sum_{i-1}^{N} [\nabla_\theta \log \pi_\theta(a_i|s_i) \cdot R_i]$$

where N is the number of episodes, (s_i, a_i, R_i) are the states, actions, and returns for each action taken.

5. Update Policy

- Update the policy parameters θ using the computed gradient:

$$\theta \leftarrow \theta + \alpha \cdot \nabla_\theta J(\theta)$$

Advantages of Policy Gradient Methods
1. **Direct Optimization of Policy**:
   - Policy gradients optimize the policy directly, which can be more effective in high-dimensional action spaces and continuous action spaces.
2. **Handling Stochastic Policies**:
   - Policy gradient methods can learn stochastic policies, where actions are probabilistically chosen, which can be beneficial in environments with complex exploration requirements.
3. **Improved Performance in High-Dimensional Spaces**:
   - They are well-suited for problems with large or continuous state spaces, where value-based methods like Q-Learning become impractical.

Disadvantages of Policy Gradient Methods
1. **High Variance**:
   - Policy gradient methods can suffer from high variance in gradient estimates, which can make learning slow and unstable.
2. **Sample Inefficiency**:
   - They typically require a large number of samples to learn effective policies, which can be computationally expensive.
3. **Local Optima**:
   - The gradient ascent approach can get stuck in local optima, and additional techniques such as exploration or regularization may be needed to address this.

Policy Gradient Methods are a powerful approach in reinforcement learning for directly optimizing policies by adjusting their parameters to maximize expected cumulative rewards. Techniques like REINFORCE and Actor-Critic are popular implementations of policy gradients. While they offer significant advantages, such as handling complex state and action spaces and learning stochastic policies, they also present challenges like high variance and sample inefficiency.

6.2.4 Actor-Critic
The **Actor-Critic** method is a type of reinforcement learning algorithm that combines both value-based and policy-based approaches. It addresses some of the limitations of each approach by using two separate components: an **actor** and a **critic**. This combination

allows the algorithm to benefit from the strengths of both methods and improve learning efficiency and stability.

Components of Actor-Critic Methods

1. **Actor:**

   - **Role:** The actor is responsible for determining the policy that the agent follows. It outputs a probability distribution over actions given a state, effectively deciding which action to take.

   - **Function:** The policy function $\pi_\theta(a|s)$ is parameterized by θ, which the actor updates based on feedback from the critic.

2. **Critic:**

   - **Role:** The critic evaluates the action taken by the actor by estimating the value function. It provides feedback on the quality of the actions chosen by the actor.

   - **Function:** The value function $V(s)$ or the action-value function $Q(s, a)$ is parameterized by ϕ, which the critic updates based on the observed rewards and state transitions.

How Actor-Critic Methods Work

1. Interaction with the Environment

- The agent interacts with the environment by following the policy provided by the actor.

- At each time step t:

  - The actor selects an action a_t based on the current state s_t using the policy π_θ.

  - The action a_t is executed, and the agent observes the reward r_t and the next state s_{t+1}.

2. Critic Updates

- The critic evaluates the action taken by the actor by computing the value function or the advantage function.

- If using a value function $V(s)$:

  - Compute the temporal difference (TD) error δ_t:

$$\delta_t = r_t + \gamma V(s_{t+1}) - V(s_t)$$

  - Update the value function parameters ϕ to minimize the TD error.

- If using an action-value function $Q(s, a)$:

  - Compute the TD error δ_t:

$$\delta_t = r_t + \gamma Q(s_{t+1}, a_{t+1}) - Q(s_t, a_t)$$

  - Update the action-value function parameters ϕ accordingly.

3. Actor Updates

- The actor uses the TD error from the critic to update the policy parameters θ.
- The policy gradient is typically computed using the TD error:
$$\nabla_\theta J(\theta) = \mathbb{E}\left[\delta_t \nabla_\theta \log \pi_\theta(a_t|s_t)\right]$$
- Update the policy parameters θ using gradient ascent:

$$\theta \leftarrow \theta + \alpha \cdot \nabla_\theta J(\theta)$$

where α is the learning rate.

Example of Actor-Critic Method

Suppose you are training an agent to navigate a maze using an Actor-Critic method:

1. **Initialize** the actor and critic networks with random weights.
2. **Collect Experience:**
   - The actor chooses actions based on its policy.
   - The agent moves through the maze, collecting rewards and transitioning between states.
3. **Update Critic:**
   - For each time step, compute the TD error using the value function $V(s)$:
$$\delta_t = r_t + \gamma V(s_{t+1}) - V(s_t)$$
   - Update the critic's value function parameters to minimize the TD error.
4. **Update Actor:**
   - Use the TD error to compute the policy gradient:
$$\nabla_\theta J(\theta) = \delta_t \nabla_\theta \log \pi_\theta(a_t|s_t)$$
   - Update the actor's policy parameters to increase the probability of actions that lead to higher rewards.

Advantages of Actor-Critic Methods
1. **Stable Learning**:
   - Combining value-based and policy-based methods helps in stabilizing the learning process. The value function provides a stable learning signal for the policy.
2. **Efficient Learning**:
   - Actor-Critic methods can be more sample-efficient compared to methods that only use policy gradients or value functions alone.
3. **Flexibility**:
   - They can handle continuous action spaces and stochastic policies effectively.

Disadvantages of Actor-Critic Methods
1. **Complexity**:
   - The need to maintain and train two separate components (actor and critic) can increase the complexity of implementation and tuning.
2. **Variance**:

- While using a value function reduces variance compared to pure policy gradient methods, the variance in policy gradient estimates can still be significant.
3. **Hyperparameter Tuning**:
   - Requires careful tuning of hyperparameters for both the actor and critic, including learning rates and discount factors.

The Actor-Critic method is a reinforcement learning algorithm that combines the strengths of value-based and policy-based approaches. By having separate actor and critic components, it provides a more stable and efficient way to optimize the policy of an agent. The actor updates the policy based on feedback from the critic, which evaluates the quality of the actions taken. This combination allows for effective learning in complex environments with high-dimensional state and action spaces.

RL Algorithms:

Algorithm	Description	Example Application
Q-Learning	Learns a value function to maximize rewards	Game AI (Atari, Chess)
Deep Q-Network (DQN)	Uses deep learning with Q-learning for complex environments	Self-driving cars
Policy Gradient Methods	Directly learns the best action policy	Robotics control
Actor-Critic Methods	Combines policy gradient and value-based methods	Stock trading AI
Application	Face recognition, medical diagnosis, fraud detection	Image compression, exploratory data analysis

Reinforcement Learning vs. Supervised Learning vs. Unsupervised Learning

Feature	Reinforcement Learning	Supervised Learning	Unsupervised Learning
Learning Type	Trial & Error	Learns from labeled data	Finds patterns in unlabeled data
Feedback	Reward/Penalty	Correct answers given	No explicit feedback
Use Case	Robotics, Games, Self-Driving Cars	Image Recognition, Spam Detection	Clustering, Anomaly Detection

Chapter 7: Artificial Neural Networks

7.1 Introduction of ANN

An **Artificial Neural Network (ANN)** is a computational model inspired by the structure and functioning of the **human brain**. It is a key component of **deep learning** and is widely used in **image recognition, natural language processing (NLP), robotics, and other AI applications**. In simple terms, an ANN is a **network of artificial neurons** that learns from data to make predictions, classify information, and recognize patterns.

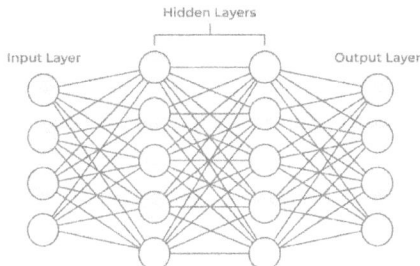

Structure of an Artificial Neural Network

An ANN consists of **three main layers**:

1. Input Layer
- Receives raw data (e.g., pixels in an image, words in a sentence).
- Each neuron in this layer represents a **feature** of the input data.

2. Hidden Layers (1 or more)
- Performs computations and pattern recognition.
- Each neuron processes inputs using **weights, biases, and activation functions**.

3. Output Layer
- Produces the final prediction or classification result.
- Example: In a **spam detection model**, the output could be **"Spam" or "Not Spam"**.

Real-World Applications of ANNs

1. Image Recognition (Computer Vision)
- Used in **facial recognition** (e.g., unlocking your phone).
- Example: **Facebook** uses ANN to identify people in photos.

2. Natural Language Processing (NLP)
- Helps in **language translation, chatbots, and voice assistants**.
- Example: **Google Translate, Siri, Alexa** use deep learning models.

3. Medical Diagnosis
- ANN detects diseases from **X-rays, MRIs, and CT scans**.
- Example: **AI models detect cancerous cells in medical images**.

4. Self-Driving Cars
- ANN processes camera inputs and identifies objects like **pedestrians and road signs**.
- Example: **Tesla Autopilot** uses ANN to make driving decisions.

5. Financial Fraud Detection
- Banks use ANNs to detect **fraudulent transactions** in real-time.
- Example: **Credit card fraud detection systems**.

Advantages of Artificial Neural Networks
- Learns from Data – Improves accuracy as more data is provided.
- Handles Complex Patterns – Can detect hidden relationships in data.
- Self-Improving – Continuously improves through backpropagation.
- Versatile – Used in various fields like healthcare, finance, and security.

Challenges & Limitations of ANNs
- Requires Large Datasets – Needs a lot of data to perform well.Computationally
- Expensive – Training deep neural networks is resource-intensive.
- Black Box Nature – Hard to interpret how ANN makes decisions.
  Overfitting – Can memorize training data instead of generalizing.

7.2 Neural Network Representation

Neural networks are powerful computational models inspired by the human brain's neural structure. These models consist of interconnected neurons (also called nodes) that learn to map inputs to desired outputs through a series of transformations. In this section, we'll break down the various components of a neural network.

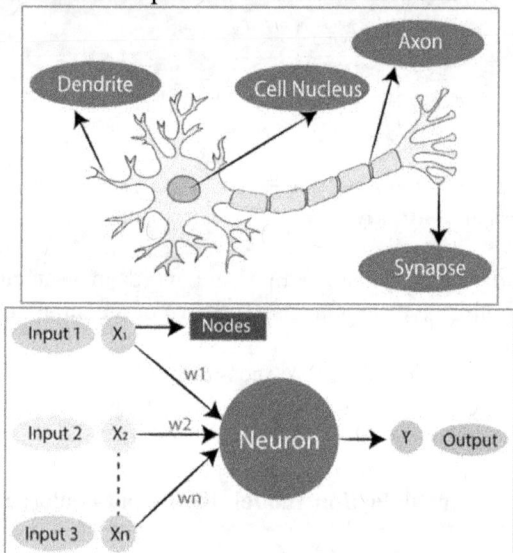

1. Nodes/Neurons:
> Each node in a neural network is analogous to a biological neuron in the human brain. Neurons receive multiple inputs, process these inputs through a weighted sum, and then apply an activation function to produce an output. Nodes are arranged in layers, each performing computations that transform the input data before passing it to the next layer. In visual representations, nodes are depicted as circles, and they play a key role in propagating information forward through the network and receiving feedback during training.

2. Layers:
Neural networks are structured into multiple layers. The simplest neural networks consist of at least three types of layers:
- **Input Layer:** This is the first layer in the network and directly receives the raw input data. The number of neurons in this layer typically corresponds to the number of features in the dataset (e.g., pixel values in an image or attributes in a dataset). Each neuron in this layer represents a distinct feature, and no computations are performed here other than passing the data to the next layer.

- **Hidden Layers:** These layers sit between the input and output layers. They play a crucial role in transforming and learning features from the input data. The neurons in hidden layers are fully connected to those in adjacent layers. The processing in these layers is done by applying weights to connections and passing the weighted sum of inputs through an activation function. A neural network can have multiple hidden layers, and deeper networks (with more hidden layers) are often referred to as "deep neural networks" (DNNs). These layers extract higher-level representations from the data, and their depth allows the network to learn more complex patterns.
- **Output Layer:** This is the final layer in the network, which produces the network's prediction or output. For a classification task, the number of neurons here equals the number of possible classes, and the neuron with the highest activation typically represents the predicted class. For regression tasks, this layer outputs a continuous value. The output layer uses an activation function appropriate for the task, such as the softmax function for classification or a linear activation for regression.

3. Connections/Edges:

The neurons across different layers are connected through weighted edges, depicted by arrows in visual representations. Each connection between two neurons carries a weight that signifies the strength and importance of the connection. The weights are initialized randomly and are learned during the training process to help the network minimize the error in predictions. These connections enable the network to pass data from the input layer through the hidden layers to the output layer.

4. Weights and Biases:

Weights are parameters that control the strength of the connection between two neurons. The network adjusts these weights during the training phase to optimize the accuracy of its predictions. Each neuron also has a bias term, which is an additional parameter added to the weighted sum of inputs before applying the activation function. The bias allows the model to shift the activation function, helping it better fit the data.

Mathematically, for a neuron jjj receiving inputs x1,x2,...,xnx_1, x_2, \dots, x_nx1,x2,...,xn with weights w1,w2,...,wnw_1, w_2, \dots, w_nw1,w2,...,wn, and bias bbb, the output zjz_jzj before the activation function is applied can be written as:

zj=w1x1+w2x2+⋯+wnxn+bz_j = w_1x_1 + w_2x_2 + \dots + w_nx_n + bzj
=w1x1+w2x2+⋯+wnxn+b

This output is then passed through an activation function to determine the final output of the neuron.

5. Activation Function:

An essential component of each neuron is its activation function, which adds non-linearity to the network. Without this non-linearity, the network would essentially become a linear model, unable to capture complex patterns in data.

- **Sigmoid:** Maps the output to a range between 0 and 1, often used in the output layer for binary classification.
- **ReLU (Rectified Linear Unit):** Outputs zero if the input is negative and the input itself if positive, commonly used in hidden layers due to its simplicity and effectiveness in handling large datasets.
- **Tanh (Hyperbolic Tangent):** Maps the output to a range between -1 and 1, often used in networks where negative input values are meaningful.

- **Softmax:** Converts a vector of values into probabilities that sum up to 1, typically used in the output layer of classification networks.

6. Training Process:

The neural network learns through a process called **training**, where it adjusts the weights and biases to minimize the error between its predictions and the actual outcomes. This is achieved through a combination of **forward propagation** and **backpropagation**.

- **Forward Propagation:** In this step, input data is passed through the network, layer by layer, to generate a prediction. The prediction is compared to the true label (for supervised learning) using a **loss function** to calculate the error (or loss).
- **Backpropagation:** After calculating the error, the network adjusts its weights using an optimization algorithm such as **gradient descent**. The gradients of the loss function with respect to the weights are computed, and the weights are updated to reduce the error. This process is repeated over many **epochs** (iterations over the training data) to fine-tune the model.

7. Neural Network Architectures:

Different tasks require different neural network architectures. Some common architectures include:

- **Feedforward Neural Networks (FNN):** The simplest type of neural network where information moves in one direction, from input to output, without loops or cycles.
- **Convolutional Neural Networks (CNN):** Designed for image processing tasks, CNNs use convolutional layers to detect spatial hierarchies in images.
- **Recurrent Neural Networks (RNN):** Suitable for sequential data, such as time series or natural language, RNNs maintain a memory of previous inputs through recurrent connections.

How an Artificial Neural Network Works (Step-by-Step)

Step 1: Input Processing

- Data is fed into the **input layer**.
- Example: A handwritten digit image (28x28 pixels) is flattened into **784 input values**.

Step 2: Weight & Bias Calculation

- Each input neuron is **connected** to neurons in the hidden layers with **weights**.
- A **bias term** is added to adjust learning.

Step 3: Activation Function

- The weighted sum is passed through an **activation function**, which introduces non-linearity.
- Common activation functions:
    - **ReLU (Rectified Linear Unit)** – Used in deep networks.
    - **Sigmoid** – Used in binary classification.
    - **Softmax** – Used in multi-class classification.

Step 4: Forward Propagation

- The input data moves **forward** through the network, layer by layer.
- The output layer generates a prediction.

Step 5: Compute Loss

- The prediction is compared to the actual value using a **loss function** (e.g., Mean Squared Error, Cross-Entropy Loss).

Step 6: Backpropagation & Weight Update

- The network adjusts its **weights** to reduce errors using **gradient descent**.

- The process repeats until the **model converges** (achieves low error).

7.3 Types of ANN

Artificial Neural Networks (ANNs) come in different architectures, each designed for specific tasks. Below are the major types of ANNs and their applications:

1. Feedforward Neural Network (FNN) – The Basic ANN

Description
- The simplest type of ANN, where data flows **in one direction**, from **input → hidden layers → output**.
- No loops or feedback connections.

Applications
Image classificationSpeech recognition
Handwritten digit recognition (e.g., MNIST dataset)

2. Convolutional Neural Network (CNN) – Best for Images

Description
- Designed for **image and spatial data processing**.
- Uses **convolutional layers** to detect patterns like edges, textures, and shapes.
- More efficient than regular FNNs for images.

Applications
Facial recognition (e.g., Face ID)
Object detection (e.g., Self-driving cars)
Medical image analysis (e.g., Cancer detection)
Key Components Convolutional Layers – Extract features from the image.
 Pooling Layers – Reduce dimensionality (e.g., Max Pooling).
Fully Connected Layers – Convert extracted features into final output.

3. Recurrent Neural Network (RNN) – Best for Sequential Data

Description
- Designed for **sequence-based data** (e.g., time-series, text, speech).
- Maintains a **memory** of previous inputs via recurrent connections.
- Uses **loops** to pass information from previous steps to future steps.

Applications
Speech recognition (e.g., Siri, Alexa)
Language modeling (e.g., Chatbots, Machine Translation)Stock price prediction
Key Feature
Hidden State – Stores past information for better sequence prediction.

4. Long Short-Term Memory (LSTM) – Advanced RNN

Description
- A special type of **RNN** that solves the **vanishing gradient problem**.
- Uses **memory cells** to store long-term dependencies.

ApplicationsSentiment analysis (e.g., Positive/Negative movie reviews) Predicting weather patterns
Text generation (e.g., ChatGPT-like models)
Key Feature
Forget, Input, and Output Gates – Helps decide what information to keep or forget.

5. Gated Recurrent Unit (GRU) – Faster than LSTM

Description
- A simplified version of LSTM with fewer gates, making it faster and more efficient.

Applications

Real-time speech recognition
Machine translation
Stock market forecasting
Key Feature
Uses only Reset & Update Gates – Unlike LSTM, which has three gates.

6. Radial Basis Function Neural Network (RBFNN) – Used for Function Approximation
Description
- Uses **radial basis functions** to classify data points based on distance from a center.

Applications
Weather forecasting
Face recognition
Fraud detection
Key Feature
Distance-Based Activation Function – Measures similarity between input and stored data points.

7. Autoencoders – Used for Data Compression & Anomaly Detection
Description
- A special ANN used for **unsupervised learning**.
- Encodes input data into a compressed representation, then reconstructs it.

Applications
Data compression
Anomaly detection (e.g., Fraud detection in banking)Image denoising
Key Feature
Encoder-Decoder Architecture – Learns efficient feature representations.

8. Generative Adversarial Networks (GANs) – Best for Data Generation
Description
- Uses **two competing networks**:
    - **Generator** – Creates fake data.
    - **Discriminator** – Tries to detect if data is real or fake.
- Used for **image and video synthesis**.

Applications
Deepfake videos
AI-generated artwork
Synthetic voice generation (e.g., AI-generated music)
Key Feature
Adversarial Training – Two networks compete to improve data generation.

9. Transformer Networks – Best for NLP & Large-Scale AI Models
Description
- Uses **self-attention mechanisms** instead of recurrence (RNNs).
- Can handle **long text sequences efficiently**.

Applications
Chatbots (e.g., ChatGPT) Machine translation (e.g., Google Translate)
Text summarization
Key Feature
◇ **Self-Attention Mechanism** – Helps process long-range dependencies in text.

Different ANN Types

Type	Description	Example Applications
Feedforward Neural Network (FNN)	Simple ANN where data moves in one direction	Image Classification
Convolutional Neural Network (CNN)	Specialized for processing images & spatial data	Face Recognition, Object Detection
Recurrent Neural Network (RNN)	Uses loops to process sequential data	Speech Recognition, Language Translation
Long Short-Term Memory (LSTM)	Advanced RNN for long-term dependencies	Chatbots, Time-Series Forecasting
Generative Adversarial Network (GAN)	Generates new data by competing neural networks	Deepfake Videos, Image Generation

Comparison of Different ANN Types

ANN Type	Best For	Key Feature
Feedforward Neural Network (FNN)	General classification tasks	Simple forward data flow
Convolutional Neural Network (CNN)	Image processing	Uses convolutional layers
Recurrent Neural Network (RNN)	Sequential data (text, speech)	Uses hidden states for memory
Long Short-Term Memory (LSTM)	Long-term dependencies in sequences	Uses forget, input, and output gates
Gated Recurrent Unit (GRU)	Faster sequence learning	Uses reset and update gates
Radial Basis Function Network (RBFNN)	Function approximation	Distance-based activation function
Autoencoders	Data compression & anomaly detection	Encoder-decoder structure
Generative Adversarial Networks (GANs)	Generating new data (images, videos)	Adversarial training (Generator vs. Discriminator)
Transformer Networks	Large-scale NLP models	Self-attention mechanism

7.3 Appropriate Problems for Neural Network Learning

Neural networks are versatile tools that can be applied to a wide range of problems, particularly those involving large amounts of data and complex patterns. Here are some of the characteristics that make a problem well-suited for neural network learning:

1. **Instances are represented by many attribute-value pairs:**
   Neural networks excel when each instance in a dataset can be represented by a large number of features. For example, in image recognition, each image is represented by the pixel values in a grid. A well-known example is **ALVINN** (Autonomous Land Vehicle in a Neural Network), a system designed to

autonomously drive vehicles by analyzing camera input, where each pixel is an attribute 【Mitchell, p. 84】 . Neural networks can process a vast number of input features, learning from complex relationships between these attributes.

2. **The target function output may be discrete-valued, real-valued, or a vector of several real- or discrete-valued attributes:** Neural networks are highly adaptable. They can be used for classification tasks (where the target output is discrete, such as classifying images of cats and dogs), regression tasks (where the target is continuous, such as predicting house prices), or tasks that require predicting multiple outputs at once (such as multi-label classification). This flexibility makes neural networks suitable for a variety of learning problems.

3. **The training examples may contain errors:** Neural networks are robust to noisy data, meaning that they can still learn effectively even when the training data contains errors or inaccuracies. While perfectly clean data helps improve performance, neural networks can generalize well enough to handle imperfect data, making them useful in real-world applications where data is often noisy or incomplete.

4. **Long training times are acceptable:** Training neural networks, particularly deep networks with many layers, can take significant time due to the complexity of the model and the size of the data. However, in situations where accuracy is more important than training speed, and long training times are acceptable, neural networks can be highly effective. For instance, tasks like image classification, language translation, or speech recognition often involve long training processes.

5. **Fast evaluation of the learned target function may be required:** Once a neural network is trained, its evaluation (i.e., making predictions on new, unseen data) can be very fast. This is crucial in real-time applications like self-driving cars, where quick decisions must be made, or in large-scale search engines, where millions of queries need to be processed rapidly.

6. **The ability for humans to understand the learned target function is not important:** Neural networks are often considered "black-box" models because their internal representations (such as the patterns learned by hidden layers) are difficult for humans to interpret. This is acceptable in situations where the priority is high accuracy over interpretability. For example, in medical diagnosis, as long as the model makes accurate predictions, the need for human understanding of how it works may not be a concern.6

5.4 Perceptron and Multilayer Networks

A **perceptron** is the simplest type of artificial neural network, used as a linear classifier. It is a fundamental building block in neural network theory and serves as the basis for more complex networks like multilayer perceptrons (MLPs). The perceptron is important in the study of machine learning, especially in supervised learning scenarios.

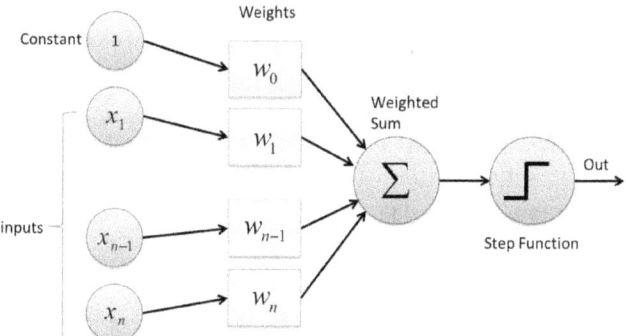

1. Definition:

A **multilayer perceptron (MLP)** is a type of feedforward neural network that includes one or more hidden layers between the input and output layers. This architecture allows the network to model more complex relationships and learn deeper representations of the input data. Here are the main characteristics of multilayer networks:

- **A feedforward structure with hidden layers:**
  An MLP consists of multiple layers, including:
  - An **input layer** made up of neurons that receive input data.
  - At least one **hidden layer**, where neurons transform the input data by applying weights, biases, and activation functions.
  - An **output layer** that produces the network's final prediction.
- **Propagation of signals in a forward direction:**
  In a feedforward network, information flows from the input layer to the output layer without any cycles or loops. The data is processed layer by layer, with the output of one layer serving as the input to the next.
- **Hidden layers are not directly observable:**
  The computations that take place in the hidden layers of a neural network are not visible through the input/output behavior of the network. These layers learn internal representations that are not obvious to human observers, making it difficult to understand how the network arrived at a particular result.
- **No explicit target for hidden layers:**
  Unlike the output layer, where the desired output is clearly defined (e.g., a label in classification or a value in regression), the hidden layers have no explicit targets during training. The desired output for hidden layers is not known beforehand; instead, the hidden layers learn to represent intermediate features that help produce accurate predictions in the output layer.

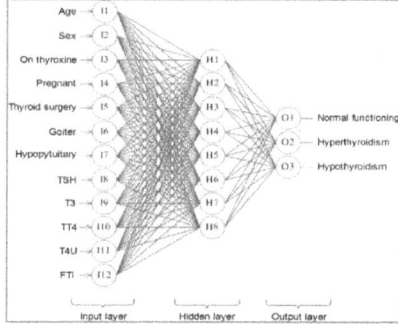

7.5 The back-propagation algorithm

Back propagation works by applying the gradient descent rule to a feed forward network. The algorithm is composed of two parts that get repeated over and over until a pre-set maximal number of epochs, EP max.

Part I, the feed forward pass: the activation values of the hidden and then output units are computed.

Part II, the back propagation pass: the weights of the network are updated starting with the hidden to output weights and followed by the input to hidden weights--with respect to the sum of squares error and through a series of weight update rules called the Delta Rule.

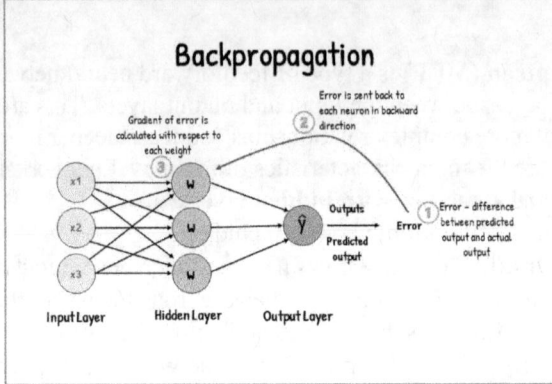

Definition:

The Back propagation algorithm in neural network computes the gradient of the loss function for a single weight by the chain rule. It efficiently computes one layer at a time, unlike a native direct computation. It computes the gradient, but it does not define how the gradient is used. It generalizes the computation in the delta rule. Consider the following Back propagation neural network example diagram to understand:

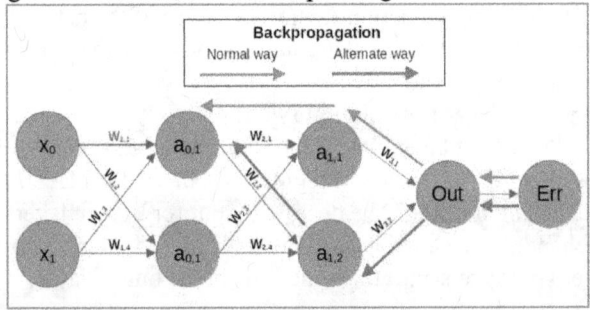

Inputs X, arrive through the preconnected path
• Input is modelled using real weights W. The weights are usually randomly selected.
• Calculate the output for every neuron from the input layer, to the hidden layers, to the output layer.
• Calculate the error in the outputs
ErrorB= Actual Output – Desired Output
• Travel back from the output layer to the hidden layer to adjust the weights such that the error is decreased.
• Keep repeating the process until the desired output is achieved

Why We Need Back propagation?

• Most prominent advantages of Back propagation are:

- Back propagation is fast, simple and easy to program
- It has no parameters to tune apart from the numbers of input
- It is a flexible method as it does not require prior knowledge about the network
- It is a standard method that generally works well
- It does not need any special mention of the features of the function to be learned.

Types of Back propagation Networks

Two Types of Back propagation Networks are:
- Static Back-propagation
- Recurrent Back propagation Static back-propagation:

It is one kind of back propagation network which produces a mapping of a static input for static output. It is useful to solve static classification issues like optical character recognition.

Recurrent Back propagation:

Recurrent Back propagation in data mining is fed forward until a fixed value is achieved. After that, the error is computed and propagated backward.

Disadvantages of using Back propagation
- The actual performance of back propagation on a specific problem is dependent on the input data.
- Back propagation algorithm in data mining can be quite sensitive to noisy data
- You need to use the matrix-based approach for back propagation instead of mini-batch.

Remarks on the Back-Propagation algorithm

Back propagation: The Algorithm

1. Initialize the weights to small random values; create a random pool of all the training patterns; set EP, the number of epochs of training to 0.
2. Pick a training pattern from the remaining pool of patterns and propagate it forward through the network.
3. Compute the deltas, k for the output layer.
4. Compute the deltas, backward. for the hidden layer by propagating the error
   - Update all the connections such that
   - W Newji = wjiold + wji and w Newkj = wkjOld + wkj

If any pattern remains in the pool, then go back to Step 2. If all the training patterns in the pool have been used, then set EP = EP+1, and if EP EPMax, then create a random pool of patterns and go to Step 2. If EP = EPMax, then stop.

Back propagation: The Momentum:
- To this point, Back propagation has the disadvantage of being too slow if is small and it can oscillate too widely if is large.
- To solve this problem, we can add a momentum to give each connection some inertia, forcing it to change in the direction of the downhill "force".
- New Delta Rule: wpq(t+1) = - E/ wpq + wpq(t)
- Where p and q are any input and hidden, or, hidden and output units; t is a time step or epoch; and is the momentum parameter which regulates the amount of inertia of the weights.

Convergence and Local Minima in Backpropagation

Backpropagation, the most commonly used algorithm for training neural networks, calculates the gradient of the loss function with respect to the network's weights. However, while training deep networks, backpropagation can encounter certain challenges, particularly around convergence and local minima.

Evolving Network Weights and Local Minima

As the weights in the network evolve through multiple iterations, particularly during gradient descent optimization, they may encounter regions in the error surface (the plot of loss function with respect to weights) that create challenges, such as local minima. These regions are characterized by certain issues:

1. Local Minima:
   o A local minimum is a point in the error surface where any small change in the weights increases the error, giving the illusion that the model has reached the best solution. However, this local minimum may not be the global minimum, which represents the lowest possible error.
   o The training process can get "stuck" at these local minima because the gradient becomes very small, preventing the weights from moving away to explore better regions of the error surface.

2. Global Minimum:
   o The global minimum is the point on the error surface with the lowest possible error across the entire hypothesis space.
   o Ideally, we want backpropagation to find this point because it would mean optimal training performance, but neural networks may struggle to reach the global minimum due to the complex, non-convex nature of their error surfaces.

Additional Challenges in Backpropagation

1. Saddle Points:
   o A saddle point is a point on the error surface where the slope is zero, but it is neither a maximum nor a minimum. In some directions, the slope of the error function increases, while in others it decreases.
   o Saddle points can be even more problematic than local minima since the gradient at these points is also zero, which means the optimization process can become stagnant even though the error could be reduced if the algorithm could escape this point.

2. Vanishing and Exploding Gradients:
   o During backpropagation, particularly in deep networks, the gradients that are propagated backward may either vanish (become too small) or explode (become too large), leading to slow learning or unstable updates, respectively.
   o This problem exacerbates the challenge of escaping local minima, as vanishing gradients make it even more difficult for the network to update its weights effectively and move away from local minima.

3. Flat Regions (Plateaus):
   o Sometimes, the error surface contains flat regions, where the gradient is near zero over a wide area. In such cases, backpropagation can be slow because it makes very small adjustments to the weights in these regions, slowing down convergence significantly.
   o These flat regions can also lead to the network becoming trapped in a local minimum, as the weights may stop changing, and the network fails to learn further improvements.

7.6 Representation Power of Feedforward Networks

Feedforward neural networks are powerful function approximators. The kinds of functions they can represent depend on the **width** (the number of neurons per layer) and **depth** (the number of layers) of the network. Here's a breakdown of the types of functions that can be represented by feedforward networks:

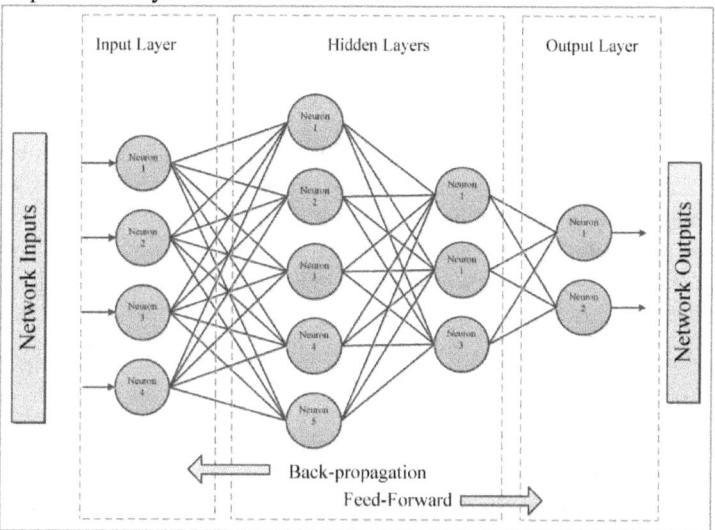

Boolean Functions

- **Every Boolean function can be represented by a two-layer network:**
  A two-layer neural network (one hidden layer and one output layer) can represent any Boolean function. This makes feedforward networks suitable for solving complex logical operations, such as XOR, AND, OR, and more complex logical circuits.

Continuous Functions

- **Approximating continuous functions with two layers:**
  Any bounded continuous function can be approximated with arbitrary accuracy by a network with two layers. This means that, given a large enough hidden layer, a two-layer network can model a continuous function (such as a smooth curve) with an error as small as desired. This approximation ability is what gives neural networks their power in tasks like regression and function approximation.

- **A single hidden layer is sufficient for approximating any continuous function:**
  For inputs within a specified range, a neural network with just one hidden layer is capable of approximating any continuous function. This result, known as the **universal approximation theorem**, highlights the ability of even relatively shallow networks to capture complex relationships in data.

Arbitrary Functions

- **Three layers can approximate any function with arbitrary accuracy:**
  A network with three layers (two hidden layers and one output layer) can approximate any function to arbitrary accuracy, given enough neurons in the hidden layers. This applies to both continuous and discontinuous functions. The key to this representation is the use of different activation functions:
  - **Sigmoid units** in the hidden layers introduce non-linearity, allowing the network to capture complex relationships.

- o **Linear units** in the output layer ensure that the network can approximate a wide range of output values.
- **The number of units required is not known in general:**
  While the theorem guarantees that any function can be approximated, the number of neurons needed in each layer depends on the complexity of the function being approximated. In practice, network design often involves trial and error, as there is no exact formula to determine the ideal number of units for a given task.

Feedforward networks, depending on their architecture, can represent a broad class of functions, from simple Boolean operations to complex continuous and arbitrary functions. This versatility is what makes neural networks so powerful across various fields, from image recognition to financial modeling and beyond.

An illustrative example: face recognition

Introduction: Face recognition is a crucial application of machine learning, extensively used in security, authentication, and human-computer interaction. The goal is to identify or verify individuals from facial images, typically involving feature extraction and classification techniques.

1. Data Collection:
- The first step involves collecting a large dataset of face images, where each image is labeled with the identity of the person.
- Datasets such as LFW (Labeled Faces in the Wild) or custom datasets are often used for training and testing.

2. Preprocessing:
   To ensure consistency in the input data, the following steps are applied:
- **Face Detection:** Algorithms such as **Haar Cascades** or **Multi-Task Cascaded Convolutional Neural Networks (MTCNN)** detect faces within images.
- **Alignment:** Detected faces are aligned based on landmarks (e.g., eyes, nose) to maintain a uniform orientation.
- **Normalization:** Resize images to a fixed size (e.g., 224x224 pixels) and scale pixel values to a consistent range (e.g., 0-1 or -1 to 1).

3. Feature Extraction:
- **Convolutional Neural Networks (CNNs)** are widely used to extract meaningful facial features from images. These features represent unique patterns such as the position of the eyes, shape of the nose, and texture of the skin.
- CNNs output a **feature vector** that represents the face in a high-dimensional space, capturing its unique characteristics.

4. Model Training:
- **Classification Model:** A CNN-based classifier can be trained to recognize individual identities by learning distinctive features from each person's face.
- **Embedding Model (FaceNet):** Alternatively, models like **FaceNet** generate embeddings, where faces of the same person are closer in vector space, and faces of different people are farther apart. This technique is useful for both recognition and verification.

5. Similarity Measurement:
- To recognize a face, the system compares the feature vector of the new face with the stored vectors (embeddings) of known faces.
- **Similarity Metrics** such as **Cosine Similarity** or **Euclidean Distance** are used to measure how closely the new face matches existing faces in the database.

6. Face Matching:

- A threshold value is defined for similarity scores. If the new face's vector falls within the threshold, it is considered a match with a known person.
- If it does not match any known faces, it is labeled as "unknown."

7. Model Evaluation:
- The trained model's performance is evaluated on unseen test data using metrics such as:
  - **Accuracy:** The ratio of correctly identified faces to total faces.
  - **Precision:** The proportion of true positive identifications.
  - **Recall:** The proportion of actual positives identified correctly.
  - **F1-Score:** The harmonic mean of precision and recall.

8. Deployment:
Once trained, the face recognition system can be deployed in various real-world applications:
- **Security Systems** (e.g., surveillance cameras)
- **Smart Devices** (e.g., unlocking phones with facial recognition)
- **Authentication Systems** (e.g., biometric verification)
  Applications of Face Recognition:
- **Access Control**: Unlocking devices, securing data with facial identification.
- **Surveillance**: Tracking individuals in public places for security purposes.
- **Personalization**: Enhancing user experience in smart devices and systems based on recognized identities6.7

7.7 Advanced topics in artificial neural networks
1. Deep Learning Architectures:
- **Deep Neural Networks (DNNs):** Multi-layer networks for complex tasks.
- **Convolutional Neural Networks (CNNs):** Specialized for image processing.
- **Recurrent Neural Networks (RNNs) & LSTMs:** Used for sequential data like time-series and language.
- **Generative Adversarial Networks (GANs):** For data generation, useful in image synthesis.

2. Optimization Techniques:
- **Gradient Descent Variants:** Methods like SGD and Adam improve convergence.
- **Regularization:** Techniques like Dropout, L1/L2 prevent overfitting.
- **Batch Normalization:** Speeds up and stabilizes training.

3. Transfer Learning:
- Using pre-trained models like ResNet and BERT for new tasks with smaller datasets.

4. Autoencoders & VAEs:
- Unsupervised learning models for dimensionality reduction and generative tasks.

5. Reinforcement Learning with Neural Networks:
- Combining neural networks with reward-based learning for tasks like game playing (e.g., DQNs).

6. Attention Mechanisms:
- Focuses on key parts of input data, widely used in NLP models like Transformers.

7. Capsule Networks:

- Enhances CNNs by preserving spatial hierarchies in data.

8. Neural Architecture Search (NAS):
- Automates the design of neural network architectures for efficiency.

9. Explainable AI (XAI):
- Techniques like LIME and SHAP provide transparency and interpretability in complex models.

www.ingramcontent.com/pod-product-compliance
Lightning Source LLC
LaVergne TN
LVHW081525050326
832903LV00025B/1628

The Beginner's Guide to

MCP Server

Practical Skills and Concepts

By Delbert Bloom